Stories OF Faith
AND Courage from
THE CIVIL WAR

B L E S S I N G S

Stories OF **Faith**
AND **Courage from**
THE CIVIL WAR

Battlefields
BLESSINGS

TERRY TULEY

GOD & COUNTRY
PRESS

Battlefields and Blessings: Stories of Faith and Courage from the Civil War
Copyright © 2006 by Terry R. Tuley
Published by God & Country Press, an imprint of AMG Publishers
6815 Shallowford Rd.
Chattanooga, Tennessee 37421

ISBN 978-0-89957-043-3
First printing—September 2006
Third printing—January 2009
Cover designed by Meyer's Design, Houston, Texas
Interior design and typesetting by Reider Publishing Services, West Hollywood, California
Edited and Proofread by Agnes Lawless, Dan Penwell, Sharon Neal, and Rick Steele

Printed in Canada
18 17 16 15 14 13 –M– 9 8 7 6 5

In loving memory of my brother, Jeff Tuley, whose endurance during a long illness was reminiscent of the courageous struggles of the Civil War soldiers in this book.

ACKNOWLEDGMENTS

To my wife, Jill, who has faithfully supported me in ministry and the writing of this Civil War devotional.

To my friend, Jeff Johnson, who gave me computer technical support.

A special thanks to Dan Penwell of AMG Publishers who patiently mentored me through the long process in the writing of *Battlefields and Blessings*. And to the whole AMG staff who have supported me with prayer and the sales of this book.

PREFACE

IN THE ANNALS OF HISTORY, no other war inspires such imagery in the American mind as the Civil War. When the call came for young men to enlist, the average age was twenty-two. The prospect of war presented a lure of adventure, romanticism, and patriotism that could not be satisfied by life on the farm. After these aspiring young soldiers left family and home, adventure soon transformed itself into the harsh realities of a bloody war.

The knife and saw of the army surgeon became familiar tools in battlefield hospital tents while the added threats of starvation, bad weather, and disease brought young soldiers face to face with their own mortality. With such a high death rate, young men and women were motivated to reexamine their personal relationship with God. Many recorded their inner struggles in personal diaries and letters to loved ones. Through these intimate writings one can find faith, hope, and courage for the toughest of times.

It is my prayer that the real-life experiences of the brave men and women of the Civil War will inspire the reader to draw closer to Christ. If that goal is accomplished, the labor of the author will not be in vain.

T. R. Tuley

GENERAL ROBERT E. LEE
The National Archives

The Tenderness and Compassion of General Robert E. Lee

CAPTAIN ROBERT E. LEE, son of General Robert E. Lee wrote about the compassion and tenderness of his father in a letter the general sent to his nephew Fitzhugh's wife after Fitzhugh was wounded near Culpepper, Virginia.

I am so grieved, my dear daughter, to send Fitzhugh to you wounded. But I am so grateful that his wound is of a character to give us full hope of a speedy recovery. With his youth and strength to aid him, and your tender care to nurse him, I trust he will soon be well again. I know that you will unite with me in thanks to Almighty God, who has so often sheltered him in the hour of danger, for his recent deliverance, and lift up your whole heart in praise to Him for sparing a life so dear to us, while enabling him to do his duty in the station in which He had placed him. Ask him to join us in supplication that He may always cover him with the shadow of His almighty arm, and teach him that his only refuge is in Him, the greatness of whose mercy reacheth unto the heavens, and His truth unto the clouds. As some good is always mixed with the evil in this world, you will now have him with you for a time and I shall look to you to cure him soon and send him back to me . . .[1]

> And by his wounds we are healed.
> —ISAIAH 53:5

While we can see the tenderness of Lee through this letter, we also sense his awareness of God's mercy in bringing deliverance to his own nephew. Lee's faith in God was strong. He knew that Fitzhugh would soon be healed, and he expected him to return to the battlefield, believing that the same God who protected and delivered him the first time could do it again.

Lee believed that his nephew's wounds would teach him a greater dependence on God. Christians sometimes get wounded in the Lord's service. We can either let our wounds destroy us or become a means to draw us closer to Christ.

Are you wounded? Try letting the Lord "nurse" your wounds.

The Goodness of God

MARY BETHELL was a godly woman who lived in difficult circumstances spawned by the Civil War, yet she still rejoiced in God's blessings. She reflected on the past two years in her diary saying:

> January 1, 1861. *Ground white with snow. This is new years day, the old year is gone forever with all its sorrows and joys. When I look back to the events of last year, I am led to say that the Lord has been good to me. I had more of joy last year than sorrow, my family was blessed with health, and I had no serious trouble (except when my husband went to Memphis, and Emeline and Dick died last year, and Cinda's twin babies).*

> January 1, 1862. *I am entering upon another new year, I am determined and resolved to live nearer to God, to deny myself, take up my cross and follow the Savior. I hope that I may be built up this year in the most holy faith that I may advance in the divine life.*[2]

Often in our difficulties, we fail to see God's goodness. Like Mary who stood outside the garden tomb weeping, tears blur our vision of a risen Christ. If we will think over the past year we can rejoice like Mary Bethell who found God's blessings in spite of life's unexpected calamities. We are reminded in Psalm 30:5 that "weeping may remain for a night, but rejoicing comes in the morning."

> They asked her, "Woman, why are you crying?" . . . Jesus said to her, "Mary!"
> —JOHN 20:13, 16

When Mary Magdalene stopped weeping and refocused her eyes, she saw the risen Christ right in front of her. Sometimes tears blur our vision. But if we look through the eyes of faith, we will find that Jesus is there all the time.

God's Mercies Are
New Every Morning

DURING 1864 Southern lady Emma LeConte felt hopeless and despairing as she walked through a valley of trials. But she soon realized that "the darkest hour comes before dawn." With the beginning of a new year, Emma was ready to move on and put the past behind her as she wrote in her journal:

> Jan. 1, 1865. *What a bright new year! If only the sunshine be a presage of happier days! Cold but clear and sunny—such a contrast to yesterday's tears. With this bright sun shining on me I can't feel as mournful as I did yesterday. I will try to throw off the sad memories I was brooding over and hope for better things. I will try to forget my struggles and failures and disappointments and begin again with new resolutions.*[3]

For Emma LeConte the previous year had been one of seeming hopelessness. Yet with the dawning of a new day in Christ comes a fresh start and a new hope. The writer of Lamentations was the prophet Jeremiah, who is called by biblical expositors, "the weeping prophet." Jeremiah faced the overwhelming task of preaching to a sinful nation that would not turn back to God. Yet the Holy Spirit reminded the prophet that God's mercies are fresh and new every morning and he will be faithful to his promises.

We can endure problems with the knowledge that our Lord will give new mercies every morning.

I well remember them, and my soul is downcast within me. Yet this I call to mind and therefore I have hope: Because of the Lord's great love we are not consumed, for his compassions never fail. They are new every morning; great is your faithfulness.

—LAMENTATIONS
3:22–24

Life's Unanswered Questions

IN THE SUMMER of 1864, while the Forty-ninth Tennessee Regiment was worshiping in a Georgia woods. Chaplain James McNeilly was leading the meeting when a stray bullet from a battle in another location passed through the head of one of the worshipers and lodged in the chest of another. The soldiers stopped singing when they saw the man die with the bullet in his head. Then they attended to the man who suffered a chest wound.

This incident made the soldiers think about eternity and the mystery of life and death. Why didn't God save the faithful? How did he allow this to happen during a worship service?[4]

Life can be full of unanswered questions concerning God's intervention and providential care for us. Suffering and death are mysteries to us. Until we reach our eternal home, we will never have all the answers to the questions of human suffering. However, we can take comfort in knowing that when we Christians suffer patiently, we are most like our Lord Jesus Christ.

> O the depth of the riches both of the wisdom and knowledge of God! How unsearchable are his judgments, and his ways past finding out!
> —ROMANS 11:33 (KJV)

Many Christians during the Civil War resigned themselves to the providence of God in their affairs. When things happened they could not understand, they knew that the Lord was in control.

Sadly, we do not have the chaplain's words to his men after this incident, but he may have told them that God's ways are higher than our ways and his thoughts than our thoughts. We cannot know why God allows such tragedies to happen, but we know that he never makes a mistake.

The Secret of True Happiness

MARY BETHELL'S faith stands as a testimony of how the Word of God and prayer can have a positive effect on one's outlook. We can view life from either a positive or pessimistic standpoint. Someone said, "Two men looked through prison bars, the one saw mud, the other saw stars." Mary chose to look at life through the divine lens of Scripture. Therefore, her outlook even in undesirable circumstances remained positive. During the Civil War she remained content. As you read the following excerpt from her diary, notice how Mary looked on the bright side of life:

> A New Year and a New Covenant January 1, 1862 New Year's day. *And I live to see another year, I have had some trials last year, my two sons George and Willie left me for the war. They joined the army for twelve months, but the Lord has been with them, and gave them excellent health and every comfort, while many poor soldiers have sickened and died, my sons have been spared to enjoy good health . . . the Lord has been very good to me the past year, I have had good health, and all my children and servants have had good health, and I have enjoyed myself at times, had some refreshing seasons for the Lord. I will praise the Lord for his goodness to me and my family, I will now, on this new years day renew my covenant with God my Saviour. I give myself to him, and pray that I may spend this year to his honor and glory, and that I may live to be useful and happy!!*[5]

True Christian joy does not come from outward circumstances, but from the peace and contentment we have in him. Paul did not allow adverse circumstances to rob him of the joy he had within. He drew his strength from the Lord and found his greatest joy in serving him. Are you unhappy with your circumstances? Maybe you need to look within.

> I have learned to be content whatever the circumstances. I know what it is to be in need, and I know what it is to have plenty. I have learned the secret of being content in any and every situation, whether well fed or hungry, whether living in plenty or in want.
> —PHILIPPIANS 4:11, 12

Cause for Gratitude

NANCY EMERSON of Augusta County, Virginia, wrote detailed accounts in her diaries of the Civil War years. Her entries reveal how many Southern Christians believed in the power of prayer and God's providential care during the War between the States.

> *Jan 1, 1863. When has a year departed so crowded with events, & such events as the last. How many battles have we fought, & how has God blessed our armies with victory. Blessed be the Lord who has not given us up a prey to their battle. As a nation, we have in a measure acknowledged God, & he has appeased for us most wonderfully . . . Our President, [Jefferson Davis] a Christian, as appears, a member of the Episcopal church, has appointed days of special prayer on those occasions, when our cause seems dark, our prospect rather, & in every case, the answer was manifest. After the two victories in one day, a day of thanksgiving was appointed & generally & joyfully observed . . . Robert E. Lee who is said to be a Christian of the same stamp as Davis, Stonewall Jackson, who is an elder in the Presb. church in Lexington, his brother in law, Gen D. H. Hill, & others. Gen. Jackson sent a special request to the churches some time since for their prayers . . .*[6]

> I have not stopped giving thanks for you, remembering you in my prayers.
> —EPHESIANS 1:16

Nancy Emerson wrote of two great victories won by the South, which, in her words, were cause for great thanksgiving. In the Civil War, many people glorified the Lord and gave him credit for victories and providential care. Southern leaders, such as Lee and Jackson, were noted men of prayer and faith.

How long has it been since you have thanked God for his care of your family? By acknowledging his blessings through prayer and thanksgiving, we open the door for him to continue to bless us.

He Died with His Face to the Enemy

A NURSE wrote the following account at a Confederate hospital in Lynchburg, Virginia:

Late one bright spring afternoon when all nature seemed alive, there was brought into us one of the handsomest young boys that I ever saw, certainly not over eighteen. He was the only son of his mother, and she was a widow, and we all knew he had come to die. His clothing was saturated with blood, and soon tender hands had removed the gray jacket and flannel shirt, bathed his body and dressed him in soft clean underclothing But alas! Shot through both lungs every breath caused the bloody water, now a light pink to ooze through the opening and saturate his clothing again. We placed him in a clean bed and waited for the end that was so near.

At last he gaspingly asked if one of the ladies would object to letting him die in her arms. Mrs. Otey volunteered to be the one. A thick folded sheet was laid across her chest to protect her from the constant flowing light stream and he laid back in her motherly arms with a sigh of content. In broken accents, he gave his mother's name and address in South Carolina and asked that she be written to. "Tell her I fell with my face to the enemy." He said, "and that I am proud to die for my country..." [7]

For the Civil War soldier, dying with one's face to the enemy in battle meant to die with courage and honor. Because of Jesus' death, burial, and resurrection, we who receive him can die someday with our faces to the enemy too.

> "Have I not commanded you? Be strong and courageous. Do not be terrified; do not be discouraged, for the LORD your God will be with you wherever you go."
> —JOSHUA 1:9

The Battle Is the Lord's

HANNAH ROPES was a Civil War nurse at the Union hospital in Washington, D.C. In a letter, she wrote of her care for the sick and dying soldiers of the bloody war:

December 14, 1862

Dear Mother,

This is Sabbath morning in good Old New England . . . The bright southern sun lies lovingly across my table onto the paper where my thoughts drip from the pen. Yet there is generally a noise, mingled sound of active purposes, and wailing grief's . . . The old face bending over [The beds of the wounded] *is doubly furrowed now, filled with deep lines. How many eyes she has closed! And, for the sake of, in sorrowing memory of their friends at home, laid a kiss upon their serene brows so cold, but peaceful! Aye! Restful!*

> He said: "Listen, King Jehoshaphat and all who live in Judah and Jerusalem! This is what the LORD says to you: 'Do not be afraid or discouraged because of this vast army. For the battle is not yours, but God's.'"
>
> —2 CHRONICLES 20:15

Often, when the old mother face turns to go away from one dying bed to another, the breaking voice has whispered, "Don't go! It is so good to see a smile somewhere . . . But to these she turns the side whereon the smile of God always shines, and . . . whispers with cheerfulness, "Who should you fear? The angels are here; God is the Friend who never forgets us, you will never be hungry or tired anymore," . . . This is God's war, in spite of uncertain generals . . .[8]

Often our trials and difficulties overshadow God's purposes in our lives because we struggle against them. Hannah Ropes learned to recognize divine appointments when the Lord gives us opportunities to see his smiling face. Sometimes we can see his smiling face only as we minister to others. Hannah did not fully understand why brave young men had to suffer. Yet, as she observed, "This is God's war, in spite of uncertain generals."

A Spy Turns to Christ

T HE FOLLOWING was written by a chaplain of an Ohio regiment on May 18, 1863, near Carthage, Tennessee, after he was asked to pray for a condemned spy:

> *I found Mr. Smith exceedingly anxious to converse upon the subject of his soul's salvation, about which, until the time of his arrest, he had felt no interest . . . He had been a soldier in the rebel army, from whom he deserted some time before his arrest . . . Those who had been acquainted with him represent him to be a very wicked and cruel man . . . His wife and children seemed to absorb his whole attention. "What will become of my poor wife and children?" he exclaimed, while at the same time his whole frame shook with agitation . . . We knelt together, and his cries for mercy and forgiveness, intermingled with earnest solicitations for his wife and children, were truly distressing . . . as he met me in passing from the jail to the ambulance which conveyed him to the place of execution [he said] that he was ready to die; "the Lord has pardoned my sins."*
>
> *I rode with him, seated upon his coffin, to the scaffold, led him, assisted by the executioner, to the platform, and in the presence of 2,000 (at least) soldiers heard him express the same hope . . . The white cap was then placed over the prisoner's face, and in a few moments his spirit was launched into eternity . . .*[9]

> Teach us to number our days aright, that we may gain a heart of wisdom.
>
> —PSALM 90:12

How tragic that a person would wait until his hour of death to repent of his sins and trust Christ. Many who enjoy the pleasures of sin think they will one day give their lives to Christ. Their intentions are good, but good intentions are not enough. Waiting until the hour of one's death is like gambling with eternity.

May we learn to "number our days" so we will be ready to meet the Lord with confidence.

The Little Minie Balls
Spoil the Vine

UNION SOLDIER William Meserve wrote about the realities of war. He especially found minie balls from the Confederate muskets to be menaces as he wrote in his diary:

> [The] *next day as we were leaving this delightful spot a rebel battery wheeled into position at easy range on a hill and opened fire on us. Our battery immediately responded and so for quite a while we witnessed an artillery duel, with an occasional shot thrown into our infantry columns and wagon trains . . . There was no clash of small arms without which an encounter is apt to be very tame. It is the minie bullet that decimates battalions and makes war dreadful.*[10]

Whether one wore a blue or a gray uniform, the sound of a hissing bullet struck fear in a soldier's heart. Because of the caliber and low velocity of heavy lead musket balls or bullets, they literally mangled arms and legs. Such bullets or balls felt like sledgehammers. They would stop whole regiments and make the difference between victory and defeat.

> Catch for us the foxes, the little foxes that ruin the vineyards.
> —SONG OF SOLOMON 2:15

The deceitfulness of sin is much like the menacing minie balls, powerful enough to strike down, mangle, and ruin our characters and moral lives. Yes, it is "the little foxes that spoil the vineyards."

On Fire for the Cause

THE NORTHERN ARMIES appointed an estimated three thousand chaplains to the Union forces. The largest number of chaplains serving at any one time was over 1,079 on active duty. These divided into 930 regimental chaplains, 117 hospital chaplains, and 32 post chaplains.

The Confederate records are incomplete, but an estimated six hundred to one thousand chaplains served and twenty-five known chaplains died in the war. Young Confederate chaplain John J. Hyman was on fire for Christ, and he would do anything for him. He proved this by preaching five or six times a day in a Georgia brigade revival. He worked so hard that he was about ready to break. One day Hyman was in the water baptizing fifty converts when the orders came for him to go to Gettysburg.[11]

> "As long as it is day, we must do the work of him who sent me. Night is coming, when no one can work."
>
> —JOHN 9:4

The Civil War and the prospect of a great loss of life gave chaplains a sense of urgency for the spiritual well-being of the soldiers. Chaplain Hyman was on fire to win the Southern soldiers to Christ. Perhaps the Lord gave Hyman a premonition on the eve of Gettysburg that he must win as many men as he could.

We too should have a divine urgency to win the lost. How many around us are but one-step between this world and eternity? Jesus said that we must work for the night is coming. One day more may be one day too late.

Do you have friends or family members who need to know Christ? Don't delay telling them about him, for "night is coming, when no one can work."

Safe in Battle as in Bed

THE COURAGE of Civil War leader Stonewall Jackson on the battle-field can be a lesson for us believers. Historian Mark Brinsley wrote:

A battlefield is a deadly place, even for generals; and it would be naive to suppose Jackson never felt the animal fear of all beings exposed to wounds and death. But invariably he displayed extraordinary calm under fire, calm too deep and masterful to be mere pretense. His apparent obliviousness to danger attracted notice, and after the first Manassas battle someone asked him how he managed it. "My religious belief teaches me to feel as safe in battle as in bed", Jackson explained. "God [knows the] time for my death. I do not concern myself about that but to be always ready, no matter where it may overtake me." He added, "That is the way all men should live, and then all would be equally brave." [12]

"He who dwells in the shelter of the Most High will rest in the shadow of the Almighty. I will say of the LORD, 'He is my refuge and my fortress, my God, in whom I trust.' . . . He will cover you with his feathers, and under his wings you will find refuge; his faithfulness will be your shield and rampart. You will not fear the terror of night, nor the arrow that flies by day . . . A thousand may fall at your side, ten thousand at your right hand, but it will not come near you."

—PSALM 91:1–7

Psalm 91 reflects the courage, faith, and stamina that Stonewall Jackson possessed. He loved the Bible and read it daily. Surely, this passage was one of his favorites. The secret of bravery in Jackson's opinion was a firm reliance on God's providential care and a readiness to meet him at any moment. Someone has said, "Fear the Lord, and you will have nothing else to fear."

A Longing for Home

MANY YOUNG men marched off to the Civil War, thinking only of the glory and romance of war without considering the hardships they would endure. Soon they longed for the comforts of home:

"Many of the men had not been much from home, and to say that they were homesick is to state the fact very mildly." An Alabama man's letter home spoke the sentiments of vast numbers of soldiers: "I am here and my mind is with you at home." "Shut out from the world," wrote a Virginian to his family, "hid away in a pine thicket, we have nothing to think of but the loved ones at home."

The nostalgia and loneliness of homesickness brought soldiers into the depths of gloom and depression and harmed the armies' morale. "Oh! that I was a boy once more at home in peace and knew nothing of the horrors of war," a Tennessee soldier confided to his journal. . . . One Rebel soldier wrote that he wished a friendly bullet would hit him just severely enough to send him home for 60 to 90 days. "I would gladly welcome such a bullet and consider the Yankee who fired it as a good kind fellow."[13]

"The younger son got together all he had, set off for a distant country and there squandered his wealth in wild living. . . . When he came to his senses, he said, . . . I will set out and go back to my father. But while he was still a long way off, his father saw him and was filled with compassion for him; he ran to his son, threw his arms around him and kissed him."

—LUKE 15:13–20

In hard times we place a higher value on our homes. Distant places are not always what we envisioned them to be, but they can stir within us a longing for family and home. Try spending more quality time with your family at home this week.

Christian Friend, Don't Quit!

MAJOR WILLIAM N. MESERVE was a Union officer in the Thirty-fifth Massachusetts Volunteer Infantry. He was not a big man, but he was strong in character. In spite of personal hardships, inadequate equipment, scant rations, exhausting marches, bouts with jaundice, and the harsh life of the soldier in the field, he survived.

My father had told me when I enlisted that it would be impossible for me to endure the hardships of campaign life; of medium stature and slender form and never inured to a rough life, he seemed to reason well. Yet I saw physical stalwarts fall out every day while I never failed to hold out to the end . . . I wouldn't drop out nor did I in after days; sometimes nearly overcome but never quite.[14]

Like William Meserve, Paul the apostle was not a quitter. He endured trials in the supernatural strength of the Holy Spirit, and his life and words still inspire us. In Western culture success is based on winning, while in Eastern culture success is based on enduring. We will not win every battle in life, but through Christ who strengthens us, we can endure whatever comes.

I have worked much harder, been in prison more frequently, been flogged more severely, and been exposed to death again and again. Five times I received from the Jews the forty lashes minus one. Three times I was beaten with rods, once I was stoned, three times I was shipwrecked, I spent a night and a day in the open sea . . . I have labored and toiled and have often gone without sleep . . . Besides everything else, I face daily the pressure of my concern for all the churches.

—2 CORINTHIANS 11:23–28

Free at Last

GEORGE ROBERTSON wrote a firsthand account of the end of the Civil War in Greenville, Tennessee. As a young boy, his recollection of the events just after the Confederate surrender gives a vivid picture of overwhelming joy by a group of African-American slaves over their newfound freedom.

> *When the Negroes came to the realization of the fact that they were free and could go where and when they pleased, they for some reason pleased to go almost en masse toward Tennessee. Perhaps they went that way because the Yankees had come from that direction and, too, the Yankees themselves were nearer in that direction than they were eastward. So they went to Tennessee . . . The occasion of this spectacle wisely aligned itself with the unforgettable things of life, and this was the one scene of the sort of a lifetime. There were hundreds and hundreds of the freedmen and women and children in almost interminable procession, going by two's even as some of their liberators had gone not many days before . . . Some were on horses which were none too fat for duties . . . One picture especially is before my mind's eye. A rather bony horse on whose back, first, were piled sundry and divers bundles, sacks packed with clothing. On top of this pile sat an elderly Negro woman, her bonnet hanging over her back, held there by its ribbons. She was astride the piled up load, holding the reins in hands that were swinging partly with the motion of riding, and she was shouting to the top of her voice, "Glory, glory! We's free, we's free. Glor, halleluiah!" Others were singing and some were laughing in the ecstasy of their freedom.*[15]

> Let my people go,
> that they may hold
> a feast unto me in
> the wilderness.
> —EXODUS 5:1

For the African-Americans, the end of the Civil War was an exodus to freedom from oppression. It took more than one hundred years before their dream of equal rights under the law could be realized, but nevertheless, it was a joyous occasion to know their slavery had ended.

When Jesus died on the cross he defeated Satan's power. Through Jesus' blood and resurrection, all have the opportunity to obtain spiritual freedom from sin's slavery.

"Lord, Give Me More of You"

RACHEL CORMANY moved to Chambersburg, Virginia, during the Civil War with her husband who was in the Union army. She spent many days alone at home while her husband fought. The following excerpt from her diary in 1863 reveals her sincerity as a genuine Christian.

> June 16, 1863. *Now there are 62 pieces of artillery between us & Harrisburg & between 30,000 & 40,000 men. O it seems dreadful to be thrown into the hands of the rebels & to be thus excluded from all the rest of the world—I feel so very anxious about Mr. Cormany—& who knows when we will hear from any of our friends again. It is no use to try to get away from here now—we must just take our chance with them—trusting in God as our Savior then come life come death if reconciled with God all is well—My God help me—I do wish to be a real true living Christian. Oh for more religion* . . . [16]

Paul knew that whether he lived or died, all would be well. For him, the secret of real living was in serving the Lord Jesus Christ. Paul looked forward to death because of the realization of the glorious inheritance God promised him.

Rachel Cormany's life was filled with uncertainties. She longed for the companionship of her husband and friends, yet she was not alone. Her relationship with Christ was genuine; thus, she prayed for more of God in her life. May our prayer be, "Lord, please give me more of you."

> I eagerly expect and hope that I will in no way be ashamed, but will have sufficient courage so that now as always Christ will be exalted in my body, whether by life or by death. For to me, to live is Christ and to die is gain.
>
> —PHILIPPIANS 1:20, 21

A Soldier of the Cross

CIVIL WAR soldiers found there were lots of days of delay between battles. While many of the men spent their spare time gambling and drinking whiskey, the Christians attended camp revival meetings. William Chambers was a Southern soldier who took his faith in Christ seriously:

October 21st

On Friday 16th we moved to our new camping place. The next day was the monthly preaching service at the Baptist house of worship. When I went in Mr. Rutherford was just closing his "Inquiry meeting." He introduced me to Dr. William Howard, the Baptist pastor. At 11 o'clock the latter preached from II Chronicles XXVI: 5, "As long as he sought the Lord, God caused him to prosper." . . . In the afternoon a large crowd assembled on the left bank of the Chickasahay River, just above the bridge, to witness the ordinance of baptism. There were nine of us to be baptized, and while the people sang "Am I a Soldier of the Cross?" one by one we went down into the water and were baptized in the "name of the Father, Son and Holy Ghost . . .[17]

Isaac Watts wrote:

> Why, you do not even know what will happen tomorrow.
> —JAMES 4:14

"Am I a soldier of the cross,
A follower of the Lamb,
And shall I fear to own His cause,
Or blush to speak His name?
Must I be carried to the skies
On flowery beds of ease, . . .
Sure I must fight if I would reign;
Increase my courage, Lord.
I'll bear the toil, endure the pain,
Supported by Thy Word."[18]

The Lord has called us to be Christian soldiers. He has not called us to "flowery beds of ease." The apostle James reminds us that we do not know what awaits us tomorrow.

The War Is Over

CONFEDERATE SOLDIER Walter Sullivan wrote:

Desertion from the ranks was a major problem for both sides during the war. Fear was only one of the factors that led men to desert. The miserable daily life of the soldier—the lack of food, clothing, shoes, (particularly in the South)—led men to desert the army. The call from the home front might be too great to resist . . . many mothers and wives wrote letters encouraging their men to desert and come home to feed and to protect them. Many soldiers answered the call . . . Two confederate deserters had been caught in Floyd County and placed before a firing squad. As the order to "fire" was about to be given, a rider approached. He bore the message, "The war is over! The war is over!"

The two deserters believed their lives had been spared, but the Confederate officer did not believe the news and gave the command, "Fire." The two deserters died, but for nothing; the war was over indeed.[19]

The word "finished" is *telos* in the Greek meaning "to bring to a sense of completion or end." A war has been waged from eternity past between the forces of heaven and of hell. Satan's foremost plan was to keep Jesus from implementing God's eternal plan. If Satan could erect some type of roadblock, then he would be thwarting the way of salvation for lost people. But when Jesus was dying, his last words were not of gloom and defeat, but words of victory. He won the battle on the cross and sealed it with his resurrection. Unlike the two Confederate soldiers, Jesus' death was not in vain. Therefore, we have no cause to fear death—we can welcome it as a friend.

> When he had received the drink, Jesus said, "It is finished." With that, he bowed his head and gave up his spirit.
> —JOHN 19:30

No Place like Home

ADA BACOT was a Confederate patriot who truly loved the South. In her diary, she wrote with emotion:

Oh, the beautiful sunny South, the home of my birth, my childhood and of my womanhood, could I leave thee, could I claim another home? Ah, no! Thou art dearer to me than all else earthly. As long as I live, let it be on southern soil, and when I die let my remains be covered by her warm and genial sod. Truly, I am a child of the South. I love her as a fond mother. I couldn't survive in a colder, less genial clime.[20]

> By faith Abraham, when called to go to a place he would later receive as his inheritance, obeyed and went, even though he did not know where he was going. . . . For he was looking forward to the city with foundations, whose architect and builder is God.
>
> —HEBREWS 11:8–10

As Christians we should not become too attached to things of this world. The security and familiarity of our homes merit our admiration. Our childhood homes can paint pictures of nostalgic days. Yet, the Lord may want to send us beyond our comfortable borders. If the Lord called you to a distant land to spread the gospel, would you go? Abraham was compelled to go wherever the Lord led him. In fact, Abraham did not even know where he was going. He was more concerned about being in God's will than in the comforts of staying home.

How's your attachment to your earthly home?

While You Were Away

CORNELIA McDONALD was born June 14, 1822, in Alexandria, Virginia, a daughter of a physician whose imprudent financial dealings forced him to move his family to Missouri. She was largely self-educated by reading the books in her father's library. In 1847 she married Angus McDonald, twenty-three years older and a widower with nine children. She returned with him to Virginia where she bore nine children of her own. When McDonald died in December, 1864, like most other Southerners, he had been impoverished by his devotion to the Confederacy. Cornelia kept a diary while her husband lived so he might be acquainted with what happened while he was away fighting.[21]

For many Civil War husbands, leaving family and home was a dear price to pay for loyalty to their cause. Many good fathers felt the weight of fighting a war as they wondered how their families were doing at home. So the dilemma of separation was coupled with the problem of slow mail.

As Jesus was getting ready to leave this earth after his resurrection, he promised that he would not leave us without a comforter. Comforter in the Greek is *paracletos* meaning "one who partners with or goes alongside another." Christians can rejoice that they are not separated from their heavenly Father. Because of Christ's love, we are never alone.

> I will not leave you as orphans; I will come to you. Before long, the world will not see me anymore, but you will see me. Because I live, you also will live. On that day you will realize that I am in my Father, and you are in me, and I am in you.
>
> —JOHN 14:15–20

Wiping Away Tears

W OOD McDONALD, brother of Cornelia McDonald, was called to fight in the Civil War.

After kissing his baby niece, Anne, good-bye in Charlottesville, Wood set off for the war. Three days later, he was killed on the battlefield. Shortly after his death, his sweet one-year-old niece called "Pretty Baby," lay dead in Cornelia's arms. Cornelia mournfully writes:

> *The many voices in the parlour, the laughter and chat of the young people make me remember all I have lost. I miss the sweet blue eyes that sparkled with joy to see me; the outstretched arms and lovely smile. The white baby face hid in the coffin and the smell of those fading roses I can never forget. That odour seems always to linger near. A bitter grief it was to my husband to lose at the same time his young soldier and his pretty baby girl, who, he had said, was to be his old age's darling.*[22]

The following is a poem that became a mournful reminder to Cornelia of the great loss she and her husband had suffered:

> *We parted in silence, we parted by night*
> *On the banks of that lovely river,*
> *Where the fragrant limes their boughs unite*
> *We met, and we parted forever ..."*
>
> —Author Unknown[23]

It is hard to imagine the pain that Cornelia experienced with the loss of a dear brother and a precious baby girl. Yet there are many in our day who have experienced similar losses.

Remember the loving comfort you felt as a child when someone wiped away your tears? A day is coming for us when God himself will wipe away our tears. Take time to think about heaven today and realize that tears in light of eternity are only for a moment.

> He will wipe every tear from their eyes. There will be no more death or mourning or crying or pain.
> — REVELATION 21:4

WASHINGTON, D.C., OFFICERS AT DOOR OF SEMINARY HOSPITAL
(FORMERLY GEORGETOWN FEMALE SEMINARY), 30TH ST. AT N, GEORGETOWN
The Library of Congress

Living Honestly and Uprightly

YOUNG DR. URBAN OWEN, who had just started his first practice in New York City, went home to Owen Hill, Tennessee, to marry sixteen-year-old Laura on September 1, 1859. He never returned to New York after he entered the Army. Owen wrote the following to his wife:

Dear Laura:

I don't know how long we will remain at Camp. Trousdale. We may be ordered from here soon. I may fall in battle in less than two months. If I do I will only be a little ahead of all the rest of mankind on the road we all must travel. I hope to see you once more on earth but if I do not I want you to try to live honest and upright during the time of your widowhood & be ready at all times to die for a better world than this & finally get to heaven where parting is no more. I will write often after this. Please excuse me for not writing sooner. Dear write to me often. No more at present. So I now tell you good-by. May heaven be your portion is the prayer of your unworthy servant.[24]

U.A. Owen
Camp Trousdale, Sumner Co. Tennessee

Dr. Urban Owen did not know what might happen to him as he prepared to go into battle, yet he took nothing for granted. He was ready to meet Christ. A popular country music lyric said, "We ought to live like we are dying." If we lived each day as if it were our last, what could we accomplish for the kingdom of God?

God expects us to be good stewards of our time. Are you living for Christ as if you were dying?

> Why, you do not even know what will happen tomorrow. What is your life? You are a mist that appears for a little while and then vanishes.
>
> —JAMES 4:14

The Effective Power of Prayer

CHAPLAIN A. C. HOPKINS, a former Presbyterian Church pastor in Virginia, served in the Second Virginia Regiment as a soldier on the front lines. Fighting in the Seven Day's Battle near Richmond, Chaplain Hopkins became extremely weary. He had marched all day in the hot sun, had spent a sleepless night in ministering to wounded soldiers, and now his strength was gone. The following day he preached to his men, but fainted from exhaustion. Soldiers carried him to the rear where he remained for ten days. When he finally returned, he found that two dear friends, a colonel and a major, had fallen in battle at Cold Harbor.

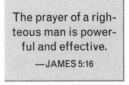

> The prayer of a righteous man is powerful and effective.
> —JAMES 5:16

Hopkins grieved over the loss of his friends so much that he slipped into deep depression. Because of his absence, the spiritual morale of the troops began dropping. Hopkins prayed that the Lord would give him the strength to help his men. Soon he started back to work refreshed and renewed. Hopkins conducted services daily and organized Bible classes.

By the end of February 1863, the spiritual morale of the regiment increased. Group discussions and prayer followed the Bible studies; many soldiers accepted Christ as Savior and were baptized. Christians provided religious literature for the soldiers to read. This revival so affected the general that he made a profession of faith. After confiding in Hopkins that he had a premonition of death, he was killed a few days later while leading his first attack as a brigade commander.[25]

Civil War chaplains carried a tremendous burden for their men. The realities of war often raised questions about God that soldiers expected a chaplain to answer. Hopkins learned to seek renewed strength and wisdom through the Holy Spirit.

Take time to write notes to your pastor and spiritual leaders and encourage them today.

For the Sake of the Call

WHEN PRESIDENT LINCOLN decided to take up arms against the South, he was uncertain of how the general public would respond. Lincoln's fears were soon relieved as told in the following story:

> *President Lincoln thereupon issued a call for seventy-five thousand men to uphold and vindicate the authority of the Government, and to prove, if possible, that secession was not only heresy in doctrine, but impracticability in the American Republic. The response to this call was much more general that the most sanguine had any reason to look for. The enthusiasm of the people was quite unbounded. Individuals encouraged individuals; families aroused families; communities vied with communities and States strove with States. Who could be first and do the most, was the noble contention which everywhere prevailed . . . So vast was the number that presented themselves for their country's defense, that the original call was soon more than filled . . .*[26]

When Lincoln called for volunteers in the Union army, he had an overwhelming response because the North saw the war as important to the future of the nation. People perceived their call as greater than their personal comforts. In a similar way, Christians must see the cause of Christ as being of utmost importance. In New Testament times, disciples left their families and livelihoods to follow Jesus. This cause demanded self-denial and even death. What price are you willing to pay for the sake of God's call?

> Then he called the crowd to him along with his disciples and said: "If anyone would come after me, he must deny himself and take up his cross and follow me."
>
> —MARK 8:34

The Duty of a Chaplain

CIVIL WAR chaplains were vital parts of the morale and spiritual guidance of both the Blue and Gray forces. While some officers viewed them as a menace, many generals such as Stonewall Jackson, Robert E. Lee, and Joshua Chamberlain appreciated their presence.

It is interesting that two-thirds of the 600 Confederate chaplains were under 30 And the average age was 28, while several were only 21 Only a small handful were under 50 The oldest Confederate chaplain was Airstides Smith, who was 53 years of age. The philosophy of one young chaplain named J. M. Campbell (which characterized the attitude of many) in his own words was, "It is my duty to wield the sword of the flesh as well as the sword of the Spirit."[27]

Most Civil War chaplains did not fear wielding their swords against the enemy. Many of them fought valiantly and ministered to the spiritual needs of the soldiers.

Chaplain J. M. Campbell believed it was his duty to wield "the sword of the Spirit." Paul reminds us that in this spiritual battle, we are not wrestling against "flesh and blood." Human efforts will fail us, but the power of the Holy Spirit will never fail. Our weapon is the Bible, the word of the living God. Jesus wielded the powerful sword of the Spirit against Satan on the Mount of Temptation. He said, "Man does not live on bread alone, but on every word that comes from the mouth of God" (Matt. 4:4). The sword of the Spirit can still defeat the power of the enemy, if we are willing to use it.

> Put on the full armor of God so that you can take your stand against the devil's schemes. For our struggle is not against flesh and blood, but against the rulers, against the authorities, against the powers of this dark world and against the spiritual forces of evil in the heavenly realms. . . . Take the helmet of salvation and the sword of the Spirit, which is the word of God.
> —EPHESIANS 6:10–16

God's Judgment?

S OME CHRISTIANS believed that the Civil War was God's judgment on the nation. Even Lincoln felt the same way because the nation had tolerated slavery for so many years. Judgment, or no judgment, God used the Civil War to end slavery and bring unity to our nation.

The following quote from a Southern Soldier stated his belief that the war was God's judgment:

> *We are having some cold and disagreeable weather now, the ground was white with snow last Friday. There was a bloody battle in Kentucky on the 19th of this month, the North got the victory, the South lost 500 killed and wounded, so the paper states. I pity the wounded soldiers, and the wives, Mothers and Sisters that lost dear ones in the battle. Surely God is judging his people, everyone ought to humble themselves in sackcloth and ashes, and fast, and pray to God to spare us, and save us from war and bloodshed.*[28]

In the prophet Jeremiah's time the Hebrew people had turned from God to idolatry, adultery, and general corruption. Sin spread through the nation like an infection. Jeremiah said, "From the prophet even unto the Priest, every one was dealing falsely." The Lord used a northern nation to judge his people in order to correct and discipline them. The Bible says, "The Lord disciplines those he loves" (Heb. 12:6). Notice that Jeremiah said the people were suffering from their own wickedness. He reminded them of how bitter it is to forsake the Lord and live lives out of fellowship with him.

> Your wickedness will punish you; your backsliding will rebuke you. Consider then and realize how evil and bitter it is for you when you forsake the LORD your God and have no awe of me, declares the Lord, the LORD Almighty.
> —JEREMIAH 2:19

No Regrets

THE DEDICATION and courage of Christian soldiers in the Civil War should inspire us to service and dedication in our day. George Squier, a soldier in the Forty-fourth Indiana Regiment, wrote to his wife from camp near Calhoun, Kentucky, on January 12, 1862:

My own Dear Ellen,

I am not sorry I enlisted in the service of my country and most assuredly I am not sorry I enlisted in the service of my God. I find Great comfort and consolation therein. May Heaven's blessings rest on the Dear "folks at Home."

Once more good by.
G. W. Squier[29]

With all the hardships and difficulties, Paul never regretted that he had surrendered his life to Christ to preach the gospel. After his calling on the Damascus road, Paul said, "Lord, what will you have me to do?" He then immediately began serving the Lord.

> I am not ashamed of the gospel, because it is the power of God for the salvation of everyone who believes: first for the Jew, then for the Gentile.
> —ROMANS 1:16

Union soldier George Squier was proud to serve his country, and he delighted he was not ashamed to serve the Lord. We cannot know the painful experiences ahead of us; nevertheless, when we submit our will to God, he blesses us. Someday we will receive our rewards from the Lord and be able to say with Civil War soldier G. W. Squier, "I am not sorry I enlisted in the service of my God."

Preserved and Singing

CONFEDERATE SOLDIER Samuel Agnew rejoiced that his life had been spared for another year:

> *In 2 hours and 25 minutes, this year will have expired. On many accounts it will [be] noted in the history of this country. During its course many new names have been added to the list of battlefields, as Chickamauga, Missionary Ridge, Vicksburg, Gettysburg, Chancellorsville, . . . We have been exposed to Yankee's raids, but amid many dangers we are still preserved and can sing of mercy and not of judgment. At the end of the year I can look back with thankfulness for our many mercies. To God be all the praise who has preserved me to the close of another year.*[30]

Samuel Agnew reminds us that we can look back with gratefulness at the end of a year and be thankful for God's mercy. Life during the Civil War was so fragile that Christians could be thankful the Lord had preserved their lives. So often we evaluate God's blessings through the lenses of materialism. We calculate how many cars are parked in our driveways and how many rooms we have in our houses in order to evaluate whether we have God's blessings on our lives. We don't consider the wonder it is just to draw another breath of life. The Christian Southern soldiers and their families rejoiced when they made it through another year without dysentery, smallpox, or Yankee bullets. As the old hymn says, we need to "count our many blessings." The psalmist felt so blessed that the Lord was a refuge and fortress for him in times of trouble that he broke into singing! Can you sing of God's blessings in your life?

> But I will sing of your strength, in the morning I will sing of your love for you are my fortress, my refuge in times of trouble.
> —PSALM 59:16

The Same in Victory or Defeat

GENERAL ROBERT E. LEE'S sons greatly admired and respected their father. In a story about his father, one son quoted the vice president of the United States, Alexander Stephens, who said of Lee:

> *What I had seen General Lee to be at first child-like in simplicity, and unselfish in character, he remained unspoiled by praise and success. He was the same in victory or defeat, always calm and contained.*[31]

Jesus told his disciples that the way to great leadership was by being servants. General Lee would not ask his men to do anything that he himself would not do. That servant spirit of humility helped him rise to greatness. He never let praise and success affect his attitude toward God and others. When we submit ourselves to the authority and leadership of the Holy Spirit, he gives us calmness in the way we present ourselves. Lee's calmness allowed him to win many battles. At Appomattox that same calmness convinced his armies to lay down their arms in surrender. He carried himself with dignity whether in victory or defeat. The way up for Christians is the way down. We are to humble ourselves in the presence of Almighty God, and he will exalt us in due time.

> He has showed you, O man, what is good. And what does the LORD require of you? To act justly and to love mercy and to walk humbly with your God.
> —MICAH 6:8

One Good Samaritan

A SPECIAL war correspondent of the *National Tribune*, Junius Henri Browne, was sent to St. Louis, Missouri, to cover the activities of the Civil War and wrote:

Having little to occupy me, I was a great observer . . . One saw just then much of "the pomp and circumstance of glorious war." While cavalry companies were constantly dashing through the streets, regiments marching to the inspiring strains of martial music, officers hurrying to and fro on prancing steeds, artillery rumbling along, bugle-notes and drum-rolls rising from the adjacent camps, a funeral cortege passed my window.

> But a Samaritan, as he traveled, came where the man was; and when he saw him, he took pity on him.
> —LUKE 10:33

A rude car contained a coffin, enveloped in the American colors; a squad of soldiers followed, with reversed arms; a bugle played a mournful dirge; but no one noticed the sad procession. All had too much of life to care for the dead. No one paused to think of the poor fellow in the coffin, who sickened and died afar from home and friends, in a military hospital.

No kind sister had spoken comfort to him; no mother's hand had smoothed his pillow; no nearer and dearer friend—kindred only in heart—had bathed his brow or moistened his fevered lips, or received his last word, or sigh, or kiss. He had not even had the consolation of dying in battle, poor fellow! His troubles were over. He had suffered, and was at rest . . . No one noticed the funeral cortege; I have said, yes, there was one. A young man stood on the sidewalk, with head uncovered, his face beautiful with sympathy, and his eye moist with pity and with love. Men who pitied and who felt, what'er his creed or station must have been, was in the largest sense, a Christian and a gentleman.[32]

We don't know whether Junius Browne was a believer, but seeing the pity and mercy in one kind man caused Browne to observe that only a true Christian gentleman would act this way. Today, not many show pity, mercy, and compassion toward others. May we seek to follow the example of the Good Samaritan.

Deaton of East Tennessee

AMONG THE MEN of the Civil War who displayed remarkable courage was Captain Deaton of East Tennessee. War correspondent Junius Browne wrote:

> While they were stoning him, Stephen prayed, "Lord Jesus, receive my spirit."
> —ACTS 7:59

Of the many military murders committed in the South since the inception of the War, none have been more cruel and revolting than the hanging of Captain Deaton, of East Tennessee, in the prison-yard of Castle Thunder, Richmond, Virginia, during the winter of 1864. Deaton was a strong Union man. . . . he was compelled to leave his home-in Knox County . . . soon [he] raised a company of loyal Tennesseans, whom he was chosen to command . . . The Rebels hated him [and he] was fired upon again and again; his clothes pierced with bullets; and yet he was unharmed.[33]

The Rebels laid a trap for Deaton and put him in a dungeon for four or five months. Browne said,

> *"His health gave way; his constitution was broken; his nervous system was shattered, and he became a wreck of himself"* . . . [Transferred to Richmond, he met] *"the meanest, and vilest, and most tyrannical of the insurgents can be ever found."* . . . *The fatal Friday came on which poor Deaton was to be executed . . . The scaffold was erected . . . and into the enclosure the unfortunate victim was taken about the hour of noon."[34]*

He was taken to the scaffold, and the captain in charge cursed him and shook him. As Deaton was held up to them, he smiled with a sweet expression. Courage came back to Deaton in that moment.

> *"The drop beneath Deaton fell and the loyal Tennessean was swaying in the air, struggling with death, and struggling hard . . . For nearly ten minutes, the victim writhed and twisted and turned."[35]*

At last the struggles ceased, and the sufferings of Deaton subsided. East Tennessee had lost a hero and great man of courage.

Deaton's courage reminds us of Stephen in the Bible who showed great courage in martyrdom. How strong is your character when persecution threatens? Evangelist Bob Jones Sr. said, "The true test of a man's character is what it takes to stop him."

WASHINGTON, D.C., PATIENTS IN WARD K OF ARMORY SQUARE HOSPITAL, 1862–1865
The Library of Congress

Making a Mark upon Others

FEW CHAPLAINS in the Civil War had the kind of influence of Confederate Chaplain McNeilly. The following excerpt from the book, *Rebel Religion*, shares why McNeilly had the success and influence that modeled an exemplary chaplaincy:

> *Why was McNeilly so successful as a chaplain? "McNeilly was successful because he visited. He visited on the battlefields, in hospitals, in prisons, and sought out his men at their mess tents. He distributed literature, offered prayer, gave counsel, and stood before God with the condemned. He knew that those who went very little among the privates secured only slight hold on their confidence and made no mark upon them."*[36]

The writer of Hebrews reveals that our high priest, Jesus Christ, could identify with all our human frailties and weaknesses. Even though he was God, he also was fully human, which qualified him to experience the five senses. Therefore, Jesus thirsted, hungered, needed rest, felt compassion and pain, and even shed tears at Lazarus's tomb. He walked among us, visited the sick, the poor, and the needy, and offered prayer and counsel. He stood in behalf of those that society condemned and was condemned himself by Pilate.

Chaplain McNeilly won the confidence of his men because he identified with them. To influence a lost world for Christ we must establish needs-based ministries. When we meet the needs of those around us, we are telling a lost and dying world by our actions that we care.

> For we do not have a high priest who is unable to sympathize with our weaknesses, but we have one who has been tempted in every way, just as we are— yet was without sin.
>
> —HEBREWS 4:15

LINCOLN'S FAMOUS PICTURE FOUND ON THE FIVE DOLLAR BILL
The Library of Congress

The President and Three Kittens

PRESIDENT ABRAHAM LINCOLN's heart was tender toward the soldiers who lost their lives in the Civil War, and his heart of tenderness is revealed in this story:

An excellent example of President Abraham Lincoln's tenderness occurred near the end of the Civil War. Abraham and his family had been invited to visit General Ulysses S. Grant's headquarters at City Point, Virginia. The trip took place in late March of 1865 about three weeks before the assassination. During his visit to City Point, the President happened to be in the telegraph hut on the day that Grant's army began the final advance of the Civil War. In the hut the President came upon three tiny kittens. They appeared to be lost and were wandering around and meowing. Abraham picked up one of the kittens and asked, "Where is your mother?" A person standing nearby said, "The mother is dead." The President continued to pet the little kitten and said, "Then she can't grieve as many a poor mother is grieving for a son lost in battle." Abraham picked up the other two kittens and now had all three in his lap. He stroked their fur and quietly told them, "Kitties, thank God you are cats, and can't understand this terrible strife that is going on." The Chief Executive continued, "Poor little creatures, don't cry; you'll be taken good care of." He looked toward Colonel Bowers of Grant's staff and said, "Colonel, I hope you will see that these poor little motherless waifs are given plenty of milk and treated kindly." Bowers promised that he would tell the cook to take good care of them. Colonel Horace Porter watched the President and recalled, "He would wipe their eyes tenderly with his handkerchief, stroke their smooth coats, and listen to them purring their gratitude to him." Quite a sight it was, thought Porter, "at an army headquarters, upon the eve of a great military crisis in the nation's history, to see the hand which had affixed the signature to the Emancipation . . . tenderly caressing three stray kittens."[37]

Mercy and kindness are rare commodities today. A famous pastor ended his radio program daily with the words, "Be good to everybody, because everybody is having a tough time." Go out of your way to treat someone with mercy and kindness this week.

> Blessed are the merciful, for they will be shown mercy.
> —MATTHEW 5:7

Encouragement for the Home Front

I N THIS LETTER written during the Civil War, Eliza Stouffer described the physical state of those at home and the importance of maintaining religious faith.

> *Dear daughter and friend your letter of Friday evening came to hand on yesterday evening and we were pleased to hear from you, and that you were all well. Lizzie also received a letter from David by the same mail—the trials you have been experiencing this week were not altogether unknown to us . . . When we read the history of Jonah—of Jeremiah—of Moses and many others of Gods messengers, we can easily perceive that . . . the faithful watchman on the walls of Jerusalem had but little glory to expect from the world—but my dear daughter and friend—when we look upon the other Side and view the promises held to those who are faithful here in these Smaller matters—we Should console ourselves—for great Shall be their reward in heaven—that kind Providence who tempers the winds to the Shorn lamb and who provides for the young raven will also truly provide for his people—his chosen flock, if we can but be resigned to his will . . .*[38]

> No temptation has seized you except what is common to man. And God is faithful; he will not let you be tempted beyond what you can bear. But when you are tempted, he will also provide a way out so that you can stand up under it.
> —1 CORINTHIANS 10:13

Christians found the hardships of the Civil War often tempted them to lose faith in the Lord's provision. Eliza Stouffer wrote to remind her daughter and friend they were not alone in their disappointment of humanity. Great men of the Bible, such as Jeremiah, Moses, and others suffered the same frustrations. People will disappoint us. If we place our faith in them, we will surely experience periods of dejection. We must look to God alone who supplies all our needs.

When we trust him, we will never be disappointed.

What Will You Leave Behind?

E LIAS MOORE enlisted into the Union army at age nineteen and served with the 114th Volunteer Regiment of the Ohio Infantry. During their service, the Ohio Volunteers traveled over 10,000 miles in ten years. Moore kept a daily record of his activities. Early in his diary, he recorded the following poem:

> *Thousands of men live, breath and suffer pain,*
> *Pass off of the stage of action and are never heard of again.*
> *Why? Because they did not partake of good in this sphere.*
> *And none were blessed by them and they done no good here.*
> *Not a line they wrote, nor a word they spoke*
> *Could be recalled for to do good, or for a joke.*
> *Their light went out in the darkness, and they were not*
> *Remembered more than men of yesterday in the dim thots [thoughts].*
> *Will you thus live and die, oh man, that will never die?*
> *Leave behind you a memory or a word, not a lie,*
> *Something that can be recalled and remembered.*
> *Elias D. Moore, 1861*[39]

Life's best investment testifies of our contribution long after we are gone. Abel's blood sacrifice pleased God. Abel's testimony still speaks today as a type of Christ's sacrifice on the cross. Jesus was the "firstfruits" from the dead. Abel offered God the "firstfruits" of his flocks. Cain brought of the "fruit of the ground." It seems that Cain gave God the leftovers, while Abel gave his best to the Lord. Abel's offering required the shedding of blood, while Cain's offering cost him little.

Elias Moore wanted to leave something that would speak after he was dead. What kind of legacy are you leaving behind for the kingdom of God?

> By faith Abel offered God a better sacrifice than Cain did. By faith he was commended as a righteous man, when God spoke well of his offerings. And by faith he still speaks, even though he is dead.
>
> —HEBREWS 11:4

Remedy for Loneliness

MARY BETHELL experienced times of loneliness during the Civil War. In her diary on February 5, 1861, she revealed that her only comfort came from God's Word:

> My daughter Mary Virginia Williamson and her little daughter, near three months old, left me this morning for her new home in Arkansas, three days travel from here on the railroad. Mr. Williamson, her husband, is out there now, has been there near 3 months, getting the place ready for my daughter. I feel deserted, it was a trial to give up my child, I do not know that I shall ever see her again . . . I feel stript of one of my pleasures, but I have the comforts of religion. There are many sweet and precious promises in the Bible, to me, they come to me now like ministering angels to comfort me in my distress. The Lord is good to me, he comforts my soul in time of trouble, I look to him, and he hears my prayers, he opens up the way to a happy home in Heaven, where there is no more parting, no more sad farewells. Glory! and honor! to his name.[40]

One of life's difficulties is saying good-bye to those we love. Mary Bethell was close to her children. The prospect of being separated from her daughter brought her great sadness, yet she found peace in reading God's Word. When we have nowhere else to turn in our loneliness, we can find that the Word of God is "sweeter than the honey" and "more precious than gold."

Try reading the psalms daily for comfort and healing.

> The law of the LORD is perfect, reviving the soul . . . The ordinances of the LORD are sure and altogether righteous. They are more precious than gold, than much pure gold; they are sweeter than honey, than honey from the comb.
>
> —PSALM 19:7

Great Calamities for Great Good

GEORGE WASHINGTON BAKER served with Company K of the New York Volunteers. He fought throughout Virginia and marched with General William Sherman on his "march to the sea." The following is a personal letter he sent home to his mother:

My Dear Mother

Events of great importance are constantly passing before us and our fighting days are probably ended, for last night about 12 AM we were aroused by the report that General Johnson had surrendered his Army to Sherman and you can have no idea of the excitement that reigned around the city at the announcement as it is surrounded by our Army. Cheer upon Cheer was heard Guns fired Canteens loaded with powder were fired and every Band & drum Corps were doing their best to swell the din and we were about as happy as could be . . .

We just heard of the death of Lincoln and it seems to cast a gloom over everything it seems as if it was the greatest calamity that could have befel us and is felt by all even his Enemies still it may be for the best as the South may be more willing to come in to the Union under some other man and what is one mans life to the good of the country.

I am one of the kind that think no great calamities come upon us unless for some great good. Still I feel as if we had lost some dear friend . . .

Love to all from your Affectionate Son[41]

> God intended it for good to accomplish what is now being done, the saving of many lives.
> —GENESIS 50:20

Joseph's trials serve as an example of Baker's statement, "No great calamities come upon us unless for some great good." Baker felt that God would use the situation to bring good to the country.

You may be going through a difficult situation right now. Don't be discouraged if you are trusting the Lord, for God will work this difficulty for your good and possibly for the good of many others.

Never Give Up!

AUTHOR H. C. CLARKE cited a narrative from a soldier named Walker. Walker told of the courage of Brigadier General Gladden of South Carolina at the battle of Shiloh:

> *Brigadier General Gladden, of South Carolina, who was in Gen. Bragg's command, had his left arm shattered by a ball on the first day of the fight. Amputation was performed hastily by his staff surgeon on the field; and that instead of being taken to the rear for quiet and nursing; he mounted his horse, against the most earnest remonstrance's of all his staff, and continued to command. On Monday he was again in the saddle, and kept it during the day; on Tuesday he rode on horseback to Corinth, twenty miles from the scene of action, and continued to discharge the duties of an officer. On Wednesday a second amputation near the shoulder was necessary, when Gen. Bragg sent an aid to ask if he would not be relieved of his command, to which he replied: "Give Gen. Bragg my compliments, and say that Gen. Gladden will only give up his command to go into his coffin." Against the remonstrance's of his personal friends, and against the positive injunctions of the surgeons, he persisted in sitting up in his chair, receiving dispatches and giving directions, until Wednesday afternoon, when lockjaw seized him, and he died in a few moments.*[42]

> I have ... been exposed to death again and again.
> —2 CORINTHIANS 11:23

Paul suffered much for the cause of Christ, however, he did not know the word "quit." He was ready to "spend and be spent" for Christ's sake. Paul's cause was much greater than himself and he was willing to die to carry out his mission.

When I attended Bible college years ago, the chancellor told us one day, "I want everyone to go to your dorms, find your Webster's dictionary, take a pair of scissors, and cut out the word 'quit.' I don't want 'quit' in your vocabulary!"

Letters to My Sons

L ETTERS from Charles Lones and his wife Rebecca to their sons, Jacob and Jeremiah, were found carefully kept in Jacob Lones's trunk with this note:

Family legend says that both boys—Jacob, age 19, and Jerry, age 17— left their home at night to join the Union army in Kentucky after a silent farewell to their mother as she slept. Jacob survived the war and returned home in May, 1865. Jerry died of fever at Triune, Tennessee, May 22, 1863. He is buried in Murfreesboro, Tennessee.[43]

A list of admonitions given to Jacob and Jerry by their parents were discovered in a copy of the New Testament with the initials "J. K. L." and "J. J. L." and bearing the date, April 1862:

1 *We want you to place your souls in the hand of the Almighty God.*
2 *Never drink spirituous liquors unless advised by a doctor.*
3 *Never go into gaming with cards or otherwise.*
4 *Never associate with the drunkard or lewd.*
5 *Take care of all you earn and never keep more than 500 on hand.*
6 *Stay together until you return or are separated by death.*
7 *If either of you should die or be killed, I want the body put in a metallic coffin by the other and carefully put away so that it can be removed home at some future day. This is our dying request to you.[44]*

Charles and Rebecca Lones tried to build commonsense principles and spiritual core values in their children. They knew that Jacob and Jerry would have many temptations.

As Christian parents, we have a God-given responsibility to train a child in the way he should go. Not only are we to teach the Word of God to our children daily, we are also to lead them by example.

> Listen, my son, to your father's instruction and do not forsake your mother's teaching. They will be a garland to grace your head and a chain to adorn your neck. My son, if sinners entice you, do not give in to them.
> —PROVERBS 1:8–10

Come On!

CONFEDERATE SOLDIER Captain Dabney Carr Harrison shone as a leader who led by example.

When the sun rose on the morning of that bloody Saturday, it saw him already in the thickest of the battle. Through seven hours of mortal peril, he wrestled with the foe; with dauntless heart, he cheered on his men. They loved him as a father and eagerly followed wherever he led. Their testimony is that he never said "go on," but "come on," while ever before them flashed his waving sword. At length, they saw with fear and pain that his firm step faltered, that his erect form wavered and he was sinking. They sprang forward and bore him from the field to die. He had "warred a good warfare, ever holding faith and a good conscience." . . .

> Therefore, since we have so great a cloud of witnesses surrounding us . . . let us run with endurance the race that is set before us, fixing our eyes on Jesus, the author and perfecter of our faith.
> —HEBREWS 12:1, 2

When he felt that death was just upon him, he gathered up his remaining strength for one more effort. Resting in the arms of one of his men and speaking as if the company, for which he had toiled and suffered and prayed so much, was before him, he exclaimed, "Company K, you have no Captain now; but never give up; never surrender."[45]

When the Scripture admonishes us to run the race, we can be sure that Jesus and a host of others have gone ahead of us. Life would be a hazardous and fearful journey if we had to blaze our own paths. Paul likened the race to the Greek relay. Someone runs ahead, then passes the baton to the next runner who is waiting to continue the race. As captain of our faith, Jesus does not stand along the sidelines of life saying "Go on!" He stands at the finish line saying, "Come on!"

A Lamp to Light Our Way

SOUTHERN LADY Mary Bethell was not satisfied with her spiritual progress. Undoubtedly, the Civil War presented many uncertainties for her and her family, and she struggled with her faith in Christ. She wanted to draw closer to him, as she wrote in her diary:

> *I cannot hear well, I am deaf in one ear, but I read and write a good deal. I find much pleasure in reading my Bible, 'tis a lamp unto my feet, and a light unto my path. "Holy Bible, book divine, Precious treasure thou art mine."*
>
> *I do not see that I make any advancement in the divine life, but I look to the Lord for help and directions in all things. I want to be resigned to his will, and I give myself into his hands, that he may do with me as seemeth good in his sight. I pray to him to make me holy, and carry on his work of grace in my heart. Not every one that sayeth Lord, Lord shall enter the kingdom, but he that doeth the will of my Father which is in Heaven.*[46]

Mary Bethell had a great love for the Bible. The hardships brought on by the Civil War tried the faith of many Southern families like hers. In her trials, Mary went to her precious treasure, the Bible. It was there she found strength to live each day for the Lord. The Scriptures gave light in a world darkened by the bloody Civil War. Mary desired to walk in the light and to submit completely to God.

> Your word is a lamp to my feet and a light for my path.
> —PSALM 119:105

If we are to advance in the Christian life as she did, we must develop a love for the Bible. Then our walk with God will deepen.

The Price of Leadership

GENERAL THOMAS "STONEWALL" JACKSON had a special relationship with wife, Mary Anna. He affectionately called her his little "esposita." Apparently she had written him hoping he would get a furlough. In his reply, Jackson revealed the great character of his leadership:

> August 17. *You want to know whether I can get a furlough. My darling, I cannot be absent from my command, as my attention is necessary in preparing my troops for hard fighting should it be required; and as my officers are not permitted to go and see their wives and families, I ought not to see my "esposita", as it might make the troops feel that they were badly treated, and that I consult my own pleasure and comfort regardless of theirs: So you better stay at Cottage Home for the present, as I do not know how long I shall remain here.*[47]

Many who desire leadership do not count the cost. A true leader shoulders the responsibility of leadership through example. Jackson chose to remain with his men rather than spend time with his wife because he knew the Lord had called him to fulfill a destiny. He paid the price of leadership by not seeking his own comfort at a time when others could not.

Anyone can make commands and give orders, but true leadership that wins a sincere following leads by example. Because Jackson did so, he won a place in the hearts of his men and in the pages of history.

> Encourage the young men to be self-controlled. In everything set them an example by doing what is good.
> —TITUS 2:6

Jackson's Source of Resolve

WITH THE CERTAINTY of war between the North and South, Thomas "Stonewall" Jackson told his wife and friends how much he did not value war. If there was any way to avoid it by the unified prayers of Christians, he would have been delighted to avoid it. Rev. Dr. J. B. Ramsey visited with Jackson and described the general's frame of mind at the impending Civil War:

> *Walking with God in prayer and holy obedience, he reposed upon His promises with a calm and unflinching reliance beyond any man I ever knew. I shall never forget the manner and tone of surprise and child-like confidence with which he once spoke to me on this subject. It was soon after the election in 1860, when the country was beginning to heave with the throes of dissolution. We had just risen from morning prayers in his own house, where I was at that time a guest. Filled with gloom I was lamenting in strong language the conditions and prospect of our beloved country. "Why" said he, "should Christians be disturbed by the dissolution of the Union? It can only come by God's permission, and will only be permitted if for His people's good; for does He not say, 'All things work together for good for them that love God?' I cannot see how we should be distressed about such things whatever be their consequences." That faith nothing could shake, because he dwelt in the secret place of the most high, under the pavilion of the Almighty.*[48]

> He who dwells in the shelter of the Most High will rest in the shadow of the Almighty.
> —PSALM 91:1

If we hide ourselves in the shelter of God's shadow, we will not be distressed. General Jackson had peace because he prayed daily and looked to God for guidance and protection.

Home Sweet Home

A DA CHRISTINE LIGHTSEY shared the account of her father, a veteran of the Civil War, who was from Jasper County, Mississippi. The men who volunteered from Jasper County became known as "the Jasper Grays."

> On the morning of the 11th of December, the Confederate signal guns were sounded to notify us that the Federal army was advancing . . . The ground was covered with snow and we were nearly freezing, but we stood there fully determined to conquer to die. The next morning they moved upon our right hand. There they found Gen. Jackson prepared to receive them . . . It was expected that they would renew the engagement the next day, but they decided to withdraw their forces to the opposite side of the river. That night, they went back to their old quarters and we moved back to ours the next day. A few days after the battle, we were sent out on picket duty, just above Fredericksburg, on the river. While there, late one evening, our band was playing "Dixie" and the Federals were playing "Yankee Doodle". When the bands finished the airs, the Yankees struck up "Home, Sweet Home." Our band too up the strain, and when the bands quit playing, "voice after voice caught up the song, and as far as we could hear on both sides, they were singing "Home, Sweet Home."[49]

> As Jesus and his disciples were on their way, he came to a village where a woman named Martha opened her home to him.
> —LUKE 10:38

An old song written in the 1800s said, "Be it ever so humble, there is no place like home." Even though Jesus did not have a home on this earth, he enjoyed staying in the home of Mary, Martha, and Lazarus. Many young men, as we can discern from the account above, had real longings for the comforts of home where they knew they could receive a good meal and a soft bed. Take some time to appreciate all that your home offers to you.

A Kiss Good-Bye

MARY MORGAN OTEY FORSBERG, after being widowed by the war, worked in the women's corps at a Confederate hospital in Lynchburg, Virginia. She kept a diary entitled, "Hospital Reminiscences," which reveals experiences she had while working there.

Two brothers from Louisiana were inmates at some time recovering from sickness. One, a beardless youth still in his teens, and an older married brother in whose charge the old man gave the boy when he would come to Virginia to fight.

He had been sick in the hospital for some little while and won all hearts by his gentlemanly conduct. He was well enough now, he said, to be at the front and gained his doctor's consent to go. The afternoon before he left. he walked over to Mrs. Speed and gave into her keeping [what] he had kept for his father ever since he left home. After telling her if he was killed to send to his father a curl he asked to be cut from his head, he bade good-bye and started to leave. Reaching the door, he turned and came back to her saying, "would you mind kissing me good-bye? I have no mother and if I should be killed father would be so glad to hear you did it."

> And now these three remain: faith, hope and love. But the greatest of these is love.
>
> —1 CORINTHIANS 13:13

So he gave me a kiss and he asked for a blessing besides. The next day as his train reached its destination, his regiment was just going into action and he joined it. In fifteen minutes he lay a lifeless corpse.[50]

None of us know what a day may bring forth. Nor do we have the promise of another day. Our lives are totally in God's hands. The world is hungry for someone to care. The greatest gift ever given to humankind was the gift of God's love and mercy.

The young Confederate soldier did not know when his life would end, and he wanted someone to love him before he left.

God expects us to offer Christ's love to others while there is still time. Take the opportunity today to love someone.

Leading by Example

BOTH NORTH and South hailed General Robert E. Lee, but he did not see leadership as many of his contemporaries did. He felt that forcing leadership on young men was not right. Instead he believed that a true leader does not rely on force, but on the power of example. Concerning the character of his West Point cadets, Lee said:

> *As a general principle, you should not force young men to do their duty, but let them do it voluntarily and thereby develop their charac- ters . . . Young men must not expect to escape contact with evil but must learn not to be contaminated by it. That virtue is worth but little that requires constant watching and removal from temptation.*[51]

Lee firmly believed that leading by example was the best way to influence others. His example motivated men to follow his command in battle. Even after the surrender at Appomattox, his men were ready to continue the fight if he gave the command. Why did Lee's armies have such a passion to follow his leadership? Because they knew he loved them and had their best interests at heart.

> Join with others in following my exam- ple, brothers, and take note of those who live according to the pattern we gave you.
> —PHILIPPIANS 3:17

A life of power displays discipline, character, and virtue in front of others. Because of his deep devotion in following Jesus' example, Paul could urge others to follow him. When we become aware of the power of self-discipline in our lives, we will influence others. We can make a difference in someone's life. Are we willing to lead by example?

Facing Life's Realities

GENERAL ROBERT E. LEE was a man with deep convictions centered in the Word of God. At the same time, he lived a very practical life and knew how to face up to its realities with a positive attitude. This is exemplified in a letter to his son, Custus, who was a cadet at West Point:

Shake off those gloomy feelings. Drive them away. Fix your mind and pleasures upon what is before you . . . All is bright if you will think it so. All is happy if you will make it so. Do not dream. It is too ideal, too imaginary. Dreaming by day, I mean. Live in the world you inhabit. Look upon things as they are. Take them as you find them. Make the best of them. Turn them to your advantage.[52]

General Lee was commending the same attitude to his son, Custus, that the apostle Paul had. Lee knew that war's harsh realities would face the young man in the near future and that his attitude would make all the difference in the outcome of battles. It would do no good to dream of how ideal things could be; it would be better to face war's realities and make the best of them. Lee felt that learning to make something good out of a bad situation was important to mold his son's character and leadership qualities. And Lee knew that his son's attitude toward the harsh realities of war would make all the difference in the outcome of battle.

> Now I want you to know, brothers, that what has happened to me has really served to advance the gospel.
>
> —PHILIPPIANS 1:12

Next time you face one of life's realities, try accentuating the positive and looking for ways to turn a bad situation into something good for your own spiritual growth.

CIVIL WAR NURSE AND HUMANITARIAN, CLARA BARTON
The Library of Congress

The Intercession of the Spirit

CLARA BARTON, famous Civil War nurse, began her work in April 1861. She pioneered the distribution of supplies to wounded soldiers. Ironically, Barton delivered aid to both the North and South. The following letter to her cousin describes her compassion:

Clara Barton Letter Head Quarters 2nd Div.
9th Army Corps-Army of the Potomac, Camp near Falmouth, Va.
December 12th, 1862— 2 o'clock A.M.

My dear Cousin Vira:

Five minutes time with you; and God only knows what those five minutes might be worth to the many-doomed thousands sleeping around me.
  It is the night before a battle . . . The moon is shining through the soft haze with brightness almost prophetic. For the last half hour I have stood alone in the awful stillness of its glimmering light gazing upon the strange sad scene around me striving to say, "Thy will Oh God be done." . . .
  The acres of little shelter tents are dark and still as death . . . Oh! Sleep and visit in dreams once more the loved ones nestling at home . . . Oh northern mothers . . . would to Heaven that I could bear for you the concentrated woe which is so soon to follow, would that Christ would teach my soul a prayer that would plead to the Father for grace sufficient for you, God pity and strengthen you every one
  . . . the light yet burns brightly in our kind hearted General's tent where he pens what may be a last farewell to his wife and children and thinks sadly of his fated men . . .

> He intercedes for the saints according to the will of God.
> —ROMANS 8:27

Yours in love,
Clara[53]

Barton's letter shows her sense of desperation as she prayed for all the soldiers for comfort and relief from the pain of suffering.

Sometimes we are at a loss for the right words when we pray. When the tears flow but the words will not come, the Holy Spirit intercedes for us before God's throne.

A Soldier and Responsible Dad

WILLIAM BRADBURY, a Union soldier and a devoted husband and father, had a keen interest in the affairs of his family in Illinois. His letters revealed that he was a loving and protective father and desired to remain active in parenting.

Knoxville, Tenn.
February 17, 1864

My Dear Daughter Jane:

> Fathers, do not exasperate your children; instead, bring them up in the training and instruction of the Lord.
> —EPHESIANS 6:4

I received your letter which you sent me last December. I mean the one in which you made the letters of the alphabet. I thought they were very well done for a little girl who had not been learning to write very long . . . Now I want you to try and earn the 5 cents a week by behaving prettily & keeping yourself neat and tidy about the hair and face and dress and shoes and everywhere as a young lady should do. Everybody likes to see neat and graceful little girls. You know what I mean. When I come home next fall, I shall be so pleased to find my daughter Jane not only a good girl and a good scholar (which she is now) but a nice, neat, and graceful girl, and then there is no telling what Father will think of her and do for her.

Now I tell you what you must do besides. You must do just what you know is right and what your mother and teacher tell you and never mind what any of your school-mates or anybody else says . . . kiss . . . all for me & tell Mother that you should all be vaccinated for the smallpox. Don't lose any time.
Your affectionate father[54]

God commands the fathers to lead by example and seek to train and nurture their children in God's instructions. Bradbury did not shirk his fatherly duties even though he was fighting in the Civil War.

Bitter or Better?

COLONEL JOHN C. MOUNGER wrote the following letter to his wife, Lucie, on the death of their son, Terrell, captain of Company "G" of the Fourteenth Georgia Infantry Regiment. Terrell was mortally wounded while charging a Union position during the battle of Chancellorsville.

My Dear Lucie,

I know not how to write you in this hour of affliction. Ask that God, upon whom you are want to lean, to give you grace that you may be able to bear the sad intelligence of the untimely death of our dear, dear son, Terrell, who fell mortally wounded in the late terrible conflict near Chancellorsville while leading his company in a charge against the enemy . . . I found his grave with his name inscribed on the headboard, and with the words, "peace be to thy ashes, thy work is done." . . . I have heard that he died contented and satisfied with his fate. I trust his soul rests with God, who gave it . . . Bear your affliction with Christian patience and fortitude. It is the fate of thousands even the immortal Jackson fell in this great struggle . . . Let me exhort you to be of good cheer. Mourn not over the loss of our dear boy, but humbly bow to the will of a wise and inscrutable God . . .

J.C. Mounger[55]

> In all these things we are more than conquerors through him who loved us.
> —ROMANS 8:37

Life's tragedies often take us by surprise. We are never prepared to deal with the death of our loved ones. Rarely do we expect to hear doctors say that we have malignant cancer. But many of us can testify that God's grace is sufficient to get us through our valley experiences. When tragedies strike, we can either let them make us bitter or better. Evidently, Colonel J. C. Mounger decided to do the latter. His reaction to the death of his dear son made him even more resigned to fight the enemy and do his duty for the cause.

Grant's View on Morality
in the Schools

GENERAL ULYSSES S. GRANT was not open about his feelings toward religion. Yet on a few occasions, he spoke as a man whose wisdom and philosophy comes from Scripture. Grant observed that to make our nation great, we must begin in our public schools.

> *I have had a good opportunity to notice much of the selfishness of the human nature, and the thought occurred to me that the children in our public schools ought to be instructed in the principles of moral philosophy; of course, this instruction should be adapted to their understanding, for there are many children and parents who do not attend church or Sunday school, and some of the former generally grow up without having correct ideas of right and wrong, of duty, service, submission, trade, commerce, etc. While we cannot compel parents and children to attend church and Sunday school (which is one of the glories of our country), yet the State should see to it that the children attending our public schools should receive instruction in the science of morals, so that they may become intelligent citizens, having correct ideas of the laws and rules that govern the relations of parents and children, of citizens and the State, of citizens to each other, etc. This would be one of the strongest form of government and making our nation really great.[56]*

This is what the LORD says: "Stand at the crossroads and look; ask for the ancient paths ask where the good way is, and walk in it, and you will find rest for your souls."
—JEREMIAH 6:16

As a progressive nation, we seek for new ways to do things. Yet, it may be wise to look at what worked in the past. Morality and Christian ethics are timeless. America was built on Judeo-Christian ethics, and we need to recover those lost values that made us great. But the recovering of morality cannot begin with public education—it must begin in our homes.

Encouragement from the Sanctuary

ON A MONDAY morning General Thomas "Stonewall" Jackson wrote to his beloved wife, Mary Anna, speaking of the wonderful Sunday he had the day before. He also told of bad weather conditions that brought great discomfort to the Southern armies.

Monday morning. This is a beautiful and lovely morning—beautiful emblem of the morning of eternity in heaven. I greatly enjoy it after our cold, chilly weather, which has made me feel doubtful of my capacity, humanly speaking, to endure the campaign, should we remain long in tents. But God, our God, does and will do, all things well; and if it is His pleasure that I should remain in the field, He will give me the ability to endure all its fatigues. I hope my little sunshiny face is as bright as this lovely day. Yesterday I heard a good sermon from the chaplain of the Second Regiment, and at night I went over to Colonel Garland's regiment of Longstreet's Brigade, and heard an excellent sermon from the Rev. Mr. Granberry, of the Methodist [church] . . .[57]

All Christians experience weariness in their Christian walk at one time or another. There was no exception for the general. Jackson thanked God for a lovely warm day after enduring much cold, chilly weather. He rejoiced in the beauty and gave praise to the Lord "who will do all things well." Undoubtedly, he had endured long periods while camping in the fields with his armies. The beautiful morning that dawned was to him a glimpse of what heaven may be like. Jackson believed God would help him endure whatever hardships came his way.

> But as for me, my feet came close to stumbling, My steps had almost slipped. For I was envious of the arrogant As I saw the prosperity of the wicked. For there are no pains in their death . . . When I pondered to understand this, It was troublesome in my sight Until I came into the sanctuary of God; Then I perceived their end . . .
> —PSALM 73:2–17

Thank God for Unanswered Prayers

THE FOLLOWING was written by an unknown Confederate soldier who was wounded and severely disabled during a bloody battle. He revealed the priceless spiritual lessons he learned through the disappointments of life.

> *I asked God for strength that I might achieve,*
> *I was made weak that I might learn humbly to obey.*
> *I asked for health that I might do great things,*
> *I was given infirmity that I might do better things,*
> *I asked for riches that I might be happy,*
> *I was given poverty that I might be wise.*
> *I asked for power that I might have the praise of men,*
> *I was given weakness that I might feel the need of God.*
> *I asked for all things that I might enjoy life,*
> *I was given life that I might enjoy all things,*
> *I got nothing that I asked for but everything I had hoped for.*
> *Almost despite myself, my unspoken prayers were answered.*
> *I am, among all men, most richly blessed.*[58]

Growing in the grace and knowledge of Christ does not always come about the way we plan. We often ask the Lord for things that may not be for our best spiritual benefit. Then God steps in and answers our prayers in ways that are the complete opposite of our own human thinking. We do not always see the value in prayers unanswered until we realize what could have happened had the Lord granted our requests.

> But he said to me, "My grace is sufficient for you, for my power is made perfect in weakness." Therefore I will boast all the more gladly about my weaknesses, so that Christ's power may rest on me.
> —2 CORINTHIANS 12:9

Singing in Captivity

FROM A MAKESHIFT Confederate prison in a tobacco warehouse in Richmond, Virginia, a Yankee prisoner wrote of an average Sunday in captivity.

Many around the room are reading the Book of God, recalling a Mother's tender teaching or a father's revered example in a bygone lapse of years. Others are pacing up and down in silent thought; whilst all respect the sacred day and its sacred, solemn duties. As the hours pass on, quiet conversation and warm intercommunion of sympathies and future friendship occupy our little band until the evening meal. At seven o'clock we assemble for divine worship . . . Silently and reverently, we listen to God's holy Word from the lips of our estimable chaplain, Rev. John W. Mines of Bath, Main [who says], "We want you to place your souls in the hand of the Almighty God." . . .

The evening closes quietly; and as the officer of the day commands, "Lights out!" We retire to our straw beds, fully trusting in our God, that he will soon restore us to our beloved ones.[59]

The Hebrew people had been taken captive by the Babylonians. They no longer had a temple and a place of worship. Their hearts were saddened because their beloved Jerusalem had been destroyed. The Babylonians had heard about the songs of Zion, but God's people could not sing because their captivity had stolen their joy and desire to sing.

Difficult circumstances may make us melancholy and sad. Yet, as Christians we should never lose heart. Our God has given us grace to experience his joy. Just as Paul and Silas sang praises at midnight in jail, we too can sing in hard times.

> By the rivers of Babylon we sat and wept when we remembered Zion. There on the poplars we hung our harps, for there our captors asked us for songs, our tormentors demanded songs of joy; they said, "Sing us one of the songs of Zion!" How can we sing the songs of the LORD while in a foreign land?
>
> —PSALM 137:1–4

Supporting Grace

M ARY BETHELL knew what to do in life's emergencies. She wrote the following account in her diary:

Since I last wrote a serious accident happened, last Saturday our carriage horse Mike kicked Willie in his forehead, he fell and was insensible some time . . . Will was behind the horse, he kicked Will down . . . The wound on his forehead looked dreadful, a gash 2 inches long, and half an inch deep. We were fearful the skull was broke . . . Dr. Keen washed the wound and sewed it up, said it was only a flesh wound, the bone was not broken. I felt very much thankful when I found that he would get well, it was a shock to us all, but the Lord did sustain me and comfort me, as soon as I heard it, the children ran in and told me, I said I don't believe it, another came and said the horse had most killed him. I went into my closet, fell on my knees and prayed to God to save him, and help me to bear the trial, my prayer was heard, I felt like God would bless Willie, and so it has turned out. I had grace to support me, I was more composed than any person would be at such an alarming time, and Willie seems to be getting well. Thanks and praise to my kind Saviour, he is good to all and his tender mercies are over all his works.[60]

> And God is able to make all grace abound to you, so that in all things at all times, having all that you need, you will abound in every good work.
> —2 CORINTHIANS 9:8

In life's emergencies we can find God's supporting grace. When Mary Bethell's son was kicked by a horse, she immediately prayed and found the grace to support her. Christians need to have a private place where they can pray during life's unexpected emergencies.

Lead Us Not from the Path of Duty

S. M. POTTER was a Christian soldier in the Sixteenth Philadelphia Cavalry. He prayed daily for his family. To his wife he wrote:

My dear wife:

There are two little boys here about the size of Josey, white headed, they sing, "Rally round the flag boys." & it sounds for all the world like our little fellows at home sing, so you see Josey Lucy & Bell are brought & kept in mind all the time. I think I can hear them singing all the time. What are you doing this Sabbath evening? . . . I would like so well to hear the children singing at worship, no music would sound sweeter . . . Knowing that you & your little ones will join in a psalm in the praise of God I will suppose you to sing the 23rd and at bedtime I will join you. Although we will not hear one another yet he to whose praise we will sing will hear us all & may we not hope unite our songs in Heaven uniting our prayers too. I feel confident that yours & the children are offered to God. May we not hope for his blessing on us all, that we may not be led from the path of Duty, that his blessings may be on our labors, on our lives, on our children, on us in all our relations in life, that we may be good soldiers, good citizens, good Christians & then we will be happy . . .[61]

S. M. Potter

A famous preacher once said, "Happiness is stumbled upon along the pathway of duty." S. M. Potter also believed that the path of Christian duty was the way of blessing from God.

Are you looking for joy? Stick to the pathway of duty; blessing and joy will find you.

> Paul looked straight at the Sanhedrin and said, "My brothers, I have fulfilled my duty to God in all good conscience to this day."
>
> —ACTS 23:1

A Strong Hand to Uphold Us

GEORGE SQUIER, soldier in the Forty-fourth Indiana Regiment, wrote to his wife from a camp near Calhoun, Kentucky, January 12, 1862:

It is Sabbath morning and I write partly for my own comfort and partly thinking you may possibly get it as it seems by your 4th letter rcd. [received] . . . We struck our tents and took up our line of march for Calhoune on Thursday, Jan. 2 . . . [We] march [ed] 6 ? miles, rained [?]. [In the] P.M. [We] pitched tents [and] had plenty straw for beds. And so our march continued day after day through rain and mud, up an down hills, and [we] finally reached this place on Monday last . . . [I] grunted around several days but am now nearly as good as new. But in our trials it is a comfort to know that there is a strong hand to uphold us, a kind Father to care for us, an Almighty power to protect us in time of peril. I feel that I would not give my hope of Heaven for the entire world and all it holds. I know well I do many things which I ought not to—"But I see another law in my members warring against the law of my mind and bringing me into captivity to the law of sin which is in my members".[62]

> "The eternal God is thy refuge, and underneath are the everlasting arms: and he shall thrust out the enemy from before thee; and shall say, 'Destroy them.'"
> —DEUTERONOMY 33:27

Sometimes the very bottom falls out of our security. We may experience financial tragedies, relationship problems, and loss of loved ones among other emergencies. People around us may give good advice, but we find no comfort in human words. During those times we must realize that we can flee to God for support and comfort. Even when we are unaware of his presence, his everlasting arms uphold us.

The Eternal God Is Our Dwelling Place

THROUGHOUT THE CIVIL WAR field hospitals were established along the trail of battles. The nurses who attended to the suffering soldiers became known as "angels of mercy." One such nurse gave a stirring account of a young man who suffered greatly after being wounded in battle, yet showing a remarkable faith in Christ. The wounded soldier asked her to pray, and the nurse wrote the following account:

> *After the prayer was ended, the subject of religion continued to be our theme. He said he was quite resigned to God's will concerning him, and that he was not afraid to die; and while dwelling on the goodness of God, his countenance assumed that serene and beautiful expression, indicative of peace within and joy in the Holy Ghost. Well was it for him that he had strength from on high, and that the everlasting arms of God's love were his support, for in a few hours from the time we conversed together it was found amputation of his arm would be necessary, from which he suffered excruciatingly until death came to his relief. But all the time of his mortal agony his faith remained firm and unshaken, and he pillowed his sinking head on the bosom of Jesus, and "breathed his life out sweetly there," while to all around, witnessing a good confession of Christ's power to save, to the uttermost, all those that put their trust in him.*[63]

None of us know the trials ahead of us. But if we trust in the Lord we will find the strength to bear whatever comes our way.

With the prospect of losing his arm, the young soldier trusted God for strength. Finally, he breathed his last, and the Savior welcomed him home. His courage in the last moments of life testified to God's grace for the dying.

> O LORD, my strength, and my fortress, and my refuge in the day of affliction.
> —JEREMIAH 16:19

A Spiritual Revival at Fredericksburg

MAJOR ROBERT STILES gave one of the most moving speeches of the Civil War at Fredericksburg, Virginia, during a spiritual revival. Stiles said:

> Brethren, I want you to know what a merciful, forgiving being the Lord is, and to do that I've got to tell you what a mean-spirited liar I am. You remember that tight place the brigade got into, down yonder at ____, and you know the life I lived up to that day. Well, as soon as ever the Minies began a-singing and the shell a-bursting around me, I up and told the Lord that I was sorry and ashamed of myself, and if He'd cover my head this time we'd settle the thing as soon as I got out . . .
>
> Well, brethren, He did all I asked of Him, the Lord did; and what did I do? Brethren, I'm ashamed too say it, but I did it again . . . Then, when the bullets begun hissing like rain and the shell was fairly tearing the woods to pieces, my broken promise came back to me . . . and the moment the thing was over . . . I just took out and ran as hard as ever I could into the deep, dark, woods, where God and me was alone together, and I threw my musket down on the ground and I went right down myself, too, on my knees, and cried out, "Thank You, Lord; thank You, Lord! But I'm not going to get up off my knees until everything's settled between us"; and neither I didn't, brethren, The Lord never held it over me at all, and we settled it right there.[64]

> So Jacob was left alone, and a man wrestled with him till daybreak . . . Then the man said, "Let me go, for it is daybreak." But Jacob replied, "I will not let you go unless you bless me."
> —GENESIS 32:24

If you're in a position like Jacob where you wrestle with God for answers and blessing, just keep praying—the answer will come.

Sunk in the Mire

I N THE FIFTY-THIRD Indiana Regiment's march to Corinth, Mississippi, the soldiers suffered many hardships, yet moved steadily forward through the rain, muck, and mire:

> *We were ordered to be ready at 8 o'clock Sunday morning with four days' cooked rations in our haversacks. The time arrived and the Fifty-third was ready in line to march, but we were delayed by other divisions till nearly 11 o'clock, at which time it had commenced to rain. Such another day I never saw. The heavens seemed to have opened and the water descended in torrents. You can imagine what condition the roads in a swampy country would be in after thousands of wagons and horse and heavy artillery had passed over them. We tramped along all day. Sometimes the mud was so deep that my line would mire. I let the men select the best ground they could, but they were mostly in mud from half leg to knee deep.*
>
> *We camped about dark . . . we bivouacked for the night, without tents or anything else, and took the rain. It rained incessantly all night, or more properly speaking, poured down all night. I took it for twenty hours without any covering, not even a gum blanket. I was just as wet as one could be made and continued so until my clothes dried on my back.*[65]

> He lifted me out of the slimy pit, out of the mud and mire; he set my feet on a rock and gave me a firm place to stand.
> —PSALM 40:2

When I was a boy in southern Indiana, I hunted rabbits with my beagle dogs. One mild winter day, as I crossed a cornfield, I found that the further I went the heavier my feet became. The more I walked, the more the mud clung to my boots. This is so indicative of life. Sometimes our burdens pile up, and we become weary. But God is able to take us out of the mud and put us on the solid Rock of Jesus Christ.

Place It in the Hands of God

SOUTHERN CHRISTIAN lady Mary Bethell writes in her diary:

> *I was much gratified last Saturday in receiving letters from Mary Virginia, George and Willie, they were well. I feel thankful to my Heavenly Father for blessing my dear children, my daughter writes that she cannot come and I cannot go to her, as the Yankees are getting the R. Roads, traveling is not as safe as it was. I long to be with my daughter as she expects to be confined this month, it is a great trial to me that I cannot go. I have looked to the Lord for comfort, I have committed her into the hands of God, and I believe he will bless her . . .*[66]

When my daughter Ashley was about five years old, she brought her favorite doll to me—the body in one hand and the head in the other. With sad eyes she said, "Daddy, can you fix my doll? I know you can fix it, because you can fix anything." Whether I thought I could fix the doll became a mute point. I was determined to fix it, and applied a famous Southern ingenuity: duct tape.

Some problems are beyond our abilities to help. God does not intend that Christians fix every situation. Mary Bethell learned to put her inabilities into God's hands. She felt helpless far away from her pregnant daughter and with no way to be with her. So she prayed about it. Our problems become the Lord's opportunities to show us what a powerful and affectionate Father he is.

> Let us then approach the throne of grace with confidence, so that we may receive mercy and find grace to help us in our time of need.
>
> —HEBREWS 4:16

A Hunger for the Word

FIRST LIEUTENANT Albert Goodloe, of the Thirty-fifth, Alabama, was a believer who had a burden to distribute God's Word. He wrote in his diary:

> *While here at Morton we received a good sup-*
> *ply of Bibles, Testaments, hymn books, and*
> *tracts, which had heretofore been ordered. The*
> *need of these we had felt very keenly for some*
> *time in carrying forward our religious under-*
> *takings . . . they came to a multitude of new*
> *converts to the religion of our Lord Jesus Christ,*
> *and to many more who were earnest inquirers*
> *after the truth . . . To be sure there were never many of us who were*
> *never without our pocket Bibles, but there were many others who had*
> *none, having lost theirs or worn them out . . . and especially did we*
> *have an urgent need for a good supply of hymn books. What a mighty*
> *chorus of voices there was raised in songs of praises to our God by the*
> *soldiers when the hymn books were given out in the congregation!*[67]

> Blessed are those who hunger and thirst for righteous-ness, for they will be filled.
> —MATTHEW 5:6

Soldiers in the Civil War were more eager for Bibles than any other time in our history. Goodloe said that many of the soldiers had worn out their Bibles and needed new ones. It is no surprise that revivals broke out in the camps of Northern and Southern soldiers. When there is a hunger for the righteousness of God, the Lord promises to fill it.

Failure Often Proves a Blessing

GENERAL ROBERT E. LEE's attitude toward failure was tested after the war when a sophomore student was called into his office over the matter of his grades.

> *Lee took the student aside and told him that he must apply himself more to his studies, that only hard work would guarantee him success in life. "But General", the sophomore replied, citing Lee's own history, "you failed". Lee neither scowled nor grew sharp with the youngster, but said simply, "I hope that you may be more fortunate than I." Lee knew that, as he wrote a friend, "we failed, but in the good providence of God apparent failure often proves a blessing."*[68]

While attending college many years ago I worked as a correctional officer in the Indiana State Prison. On the archway over the inside door of the prison was a statement that is permanently etched in my memory: *Failure is not the falling down, it is the staying down.*

> For a righteous man falls seven times, and rises again, But the wicked stumble in time of calamity.
> —PROVERBS 24:16

Lee could have become angry with the young student who accused him of failure, but instead he taught the young man a lesson in humility. Lee's faith in God had taught him that failure can often be a blessing.

I once received counsel from Dr. Lee Roberson, former pastor of Highland Park Baptist Church, Chattanooga, Tennessee. Feeling depressed I told Dr. Roberson that I believed I had failed in my last pastorate. He replied, "Alright you failed, that is good. Now examine your failure, learn from it, and move on." He taught me a valuable lesson that day of how failure could actually be a blessing if I would humble myself and learn from the experience.

An Accidental Killing of an African-American Boy

SOUTHERNER SAMUEL AGNEW wrote in his diary:

A melancholy occurrence took place at Aunt Rilla's today between 11 and 12 o'clock. Melly shot a little negro child (Franky) of Abe and Adaline, and the child died in a half hour after. It was accidental. Aunt Rilla sent Melly out with a gun (Mullinix's) to shoot a hawk. The little negroes were in great glee running after him. He wanted them to go back, and to frighten them he pointed the gun at them, when contrary to his expectation it went off, killing Franky. Melly thinks the gun was only half-cocked. The little negro was shot in the head, 5 bullets entering, 2 in the forehead, 1 at the outer corner (below) of the left eye, and 2 near the nostrils [bullets here refer to a number of small grapeshot in one musket shot compared to one shotgun shell in our day]. *It is indeed a sad occurrence. Poor Melly no doubt bitterly regrets the circumstance. What an admonition in reference to the uncertainty of life. "In the midst of life we are in death." Truly as David says, "there is but a step between me and death."*[69]

> Yet as surely as the LORD lives and as you live, there is only a step between me and death.
>
> —1 SAMUEL 20:23

David was on the run from Saul who was trying to take his life. David knew that death, like a hound, was baying closely on his heels. To him there was only one step away from death.

A young man was walking in the fog in his beloved land of Scotland one evening. He was struggling with God and searching for answers. He heard a voice calling to him. He believed it was God. He stopped and fell to his knees in prayer. When he stood to his feet, he realized that one step more, and he would have fallen off a steep cliff to his death. This young man later went on to pastor the New York Avenue Presbyterian Church in Washington, D.C. Eventually, he was called to be the chaplain of the U.S. Senate. His name—Dr. Peter Marshall.

The Power of a
Christian's Influence

A CONFEDERATE SOLDIER named Goodloe made friends with a preacher named Rev. Bluford Faris. The soldier saw Rev. Faris as one of his Christian heroes. Goodloe said of Faris:

He was strikingly modest, humble, and unobtrusive, being altogether unconscious of his own eminent worth. He was well balanced, steady and constant in his religious character and life, full of zeal and the Holy Ghost. He abounded in good works, and had his heart set on maintaining divine worship among the soldiers, and winning his unconverted comrades to Christ. For a long time we were without a chaplain, and very often without a preacher of any kind . . . he would have assemble for religious services, whether in camp or in the trenches. It was an everyday business. He never failed in his high purposes, nor evaded any responsibility whatever. An everyday Christian for everyday work, and for the long pull the world over—such a Christian was my noble friend and yokefellow in the Lord and comrade in arms for our country's cause.[70]

> Therefore, my dear brothers, stand firm. Let nothing move you. Always give yourselves fully to the work of the Lord, because you know that your labor in the Lord is not in vain.
>
> —1 CORINTHIANS 15:58

All of us desire purpose in life. We often wonder if we're making a difference in God's work? It is said that the great missionary Hudson Taylor labored for many years on the mission field before he led his first person to Christ. Taylor's labor was not in vain for in due time he saw the fruit of his work.

If you have grown weary in your work for God, don't give up. According to the apostle Paul, if we continue our work for Christ, we will eventually see positive results.

A Story from Gettysburg

We got to Gettysburg at 1 P.M., 15 miles. We were drawn up in line of battle about one mile south of town, and a little to the left of the Lutheran Seminary . . .

"TAR HEEL"
SOLDIER, L. LEON
*Courtesy University
of North Carolina*

July 3—When under a very heavy fire, we were ordered on Culp's Hill, to the support of Gen. A. Johnson. Here we stayed all day—no, here, I may say, we melted away. We were on the brow of one hill, the enemy on the brow of another. We charged on them several times, but of course, running down our hill, and then to get to them was impossible, and every time we attempted it we came back leaving some of our comrades behind . . . here . . . All of our lieutenants are wounded . . . I know that our company went in the fight with 60 men. When we left Culp's Hill there were 16 of us that answered to the roll call . . . You could see one with his head shot off, others cut in two, then one with his brain oozing out, one with his leg off, others shot through the heart. Then you would hear some poor friend or foe crying for water, or for "God's sake" to kill him.[71]

The price paid in blood at Gettysburg by both North and South was astounding. And the price paid of shed blood at Calvary was astounding also. Because of Jesus' sacrifice, we can experience God's grace and a new freedom in our lives.

> It is for freedom that Christ has set us free. Stand firm, then, and do not let yourselves be burdened again by a yoke of slavery.
>
> —GALATIANS 5:1

The Peace of a Mind Focused on Christ

AS A YOUNG African-American slave girl, Margaret Browne, was taken from her family and sold to an evil slave master. An account in her diary tells of being taken to the whipping post for breaking a china dish in her master's house.

The motion or exertion of being pulled along over the ground, restored me to full consciousness. With a haggard eye, I looked up to the still blue heaven, where the holy stars yet held their silent vigil; and the serene moon moved on in her starry track, never once heeding the dire cruelty, over which her pale beam shed its friendly light. "Oh," thought I, "is there no mercy throned on high? Are there no spirits in earth, air, or sky, to lend me their gracious influence? Does God look down with kindness upon injustice like this?"
. . . These wild, rebellious thoughts only crossed my mind; they did not linger there. No, like the breath-stain upon the polished surface of the mirror, they only soiled for a moment the shining faith which in my soul reflected the perfect goodness of that God who never forgets the humblest of His children, and who makes no distinction of color or race . . . 'Twas faith alone that sustained me. . . .

> You will keep in perfect peace him whose mind is steadfast, because he trusts in you.
> —ISAIAH 26:3

I followed my Master. I saw Him nailed to the cross, spit upon, vilified and abused, with the thorny crown pressed upon His brow . . . I could have shouted, Great is Jesus of Nazareth!! . . . These thoughts had power to cheer; and, fortified by faith and religion, the trial seemed to me easy to bear. . . . In this state of mind, with a moveless eye I looked upon the whipping-post, which loomed up before me like an ogre . . .[72]

A mind focused on Christ brings peace in the most trying circumstances. Take time to reflect on Christ's sufferings and resurrection today.

Doing What We Can

M ARIA CHILD, a sympathizer for the Union cause and an abolition-ist, shared her thoughts concerning the questions that young soldiers had on the battlefield about the purpose of the war.

Alas, thousands of poor, weary soldiers have doubtless gazed on the rivers and hills of Virginia, while they asked themselves, despond-ingly, "What has been accomplished by all our privations, toils, and sufferings?" Thousands of brave young souls have passed away with heroic patience, saying, "My consolation is that I have done what I could."[73]

Those who criticized this woman considered her offering a waste of time and money. "Leave her alone," Jesus said. He knew her heart and memorialized her sacrifice because "she did what she could." She gave her best to him who was preparing to give his all. Some in our day look at war as a waste of time and money, yet many sol-diers are giving their best in a foreign land. We need to be thankful for the men and women in our armed services who are doing what they can to keep our country free.

> Some of those pres-ent were saying indignantly to one another, "Why this waste of perfume? It could have been sold for more than a year's wages and the money given to the poor." And they rebuked her harshly. "Leave her alone," said Jesus. "Why are you bothering her? She has done a beautiful thing to me. The poor you will always have with you, and you can help them any time you want. But you will not always have me. She did what she could. She poured perfume on my body beforehand to pre-pare for my burial."
> —MARK 14:4–7

Losing Ourselves

IN HER DIARY, Mary Bethell told of how she beat the blues:

We are having some pretty weather now. A poor woman came here yesterday, she wanted some things for her husband, as he was going to start to the army on Thursday, he is a soldier. I had the pleasure of giving her something for him. I sent him a Testament to read, sent him word to put his trust in God. I gave her some advice, and exhorted her to seek religion. I feel cheerful and happy today, in trying to help the poor and needy I got blessed and comforted myself, my gloom and fears are all gone. The Lord always blesses me when I try to keep his commandments. I sent two Testaments to the Soldiers this morning to take with them when they go to the army, I have two more that I wish to give away to the Soldiers.[74]

Mary Bethell found that the best way to beat the "blues" was to help others. She said, "In trying to help the poor and needy I got blessed . . ." If we are depressed, we should find others who are dejected and disheartened and try encouraging them. In doing so we, like Mary Bethell, will be cheered. When we forget about ourselves and get involved in the lives of others, we are on our way to Christlikeness. Pastor Jack Hyles said he often prayed, "Lord, help me to cross the path today of someone whom Jesus would help had he been here in my shoes."

> Whoever finds his life will lose it, and whoever loses his life for my sake will find it.
> —MATTHEW 10:39

The Longest Pole Will Knock the Persimmon

A SOLDIER of the Seventh Regiment of Iowa served in St. Louis in 1862. At six feet two, he was eighty years old and blind in one eye, which caused him difficulty in enlisting in the Northern army. Yet, he became one of their most resourceful men. Even more impressive was his ability to quote the Bible.

> *He claims to be able to repeat every word of the Bible from the beginning of Genesis to the end of Revelation, and can neither read nor write—a daughter having read the book to him, his wonderful memory allowing him to retain it after committing it to memory. The daughter commenced her reading to him at five years of age, he being then twenty-six.*

When asked his opinion of the outcome of the war, the old man commented:

> *"Well, I think the longest pole will knock the persimmon. It may take a long time; but the North has got the most men and the most money, and it is bound to come out first best in the end . . . If the young men will do as I intend to do, the rebellion will be put down, for I am in for the war, or as long as I last."*[75]

It was pointed out that "the cheerful and contented disposition of this old man might well be taken for an example by younger soldiers, to say nothing of his strict observance of discipline, or the efficiency and value of such men to the service."[76]

> A happy heart makes the face cheerful, but heartache crushes the spirit.
> —PROVERBS 15:13

We can be cheerful only when we are at peace with God. The old soldier is an example that with Christ and his Word dwelling in our hearts we can look beyond life's conflicts and rest in the complete assurance that all is well with our souls.

Learning to Forgive Ourselves

AN ARTICLE written in a Philadelphia newspaper during the Civil War was disturbing, yet so typical of brother fighting against brother. A cemetery worker had four sons. The eldest two boys who went to work in New Orleans had not been home for five years. The two younger sons, George and Frederick, remained at home to help their father. The older two sons in New Orleans joined the Confederate forces. The younger sons joined the Union army.

When the battle of Fredericksburg took place, George and Frederick were on the front lines. As the rifles of the Confederates fired into the Union lines, the Union forces retreated, but not before the rebel minie balls hit George and Frederick—both dropped dead. The rebel soldiers, clad in rags, robbed the dead Yankees of their money, clothes, and canteens. One rebel reached a dead soldier who lay facedown and turned him over. To his horror, he looked on the face of his youngest brother. A chaplain told the account as follows:

> Therefore, my brothers, I want you to know that through Jesus the forgiveness of sins is proclaimed to you.
> —ACTS 13:38

His brother beheld the corpse . . . his woolen shirt stained with a stream of blood that oozed from the bullet hole above his heart . . . this one [the oldest brother] *made his way into the Union lines and is now in the hospital at Alexandria a hopeless maniac. We learn that in their childhood this youngling of the flock had been the especial charge of the eldest brother. When he left for New Orleans it was in the expectation of entering business to which he could bring up the boy. That boy he lived to shoot down with his own hands. The father died of a broken heart, and was buried last Sunday. This is a simple statement of fact. It is doubtless one of ten thousand never to be written.*[77]

When Christians make mistakes, we seek God's forgiveness. Yet often we find no peace, because we cannot forgive ourselves. Undoubtedly, the brother and father in the above account could not forgive themselves for what happened. Christ died to remove guilt and shame from our lives. We owe it to the Lord to forgive ourselves.

Missed at Home?

AS LIEUTENANT ALBERT GOODLOE left home to engage in the Civil War, he thought about his family.

> *As I rode out of the front lawn gate into the public road I began to hum almost unconsciously a favorite song of ante-bellum days: "Do They Miss Me at Home?" And then I communed with myself and said; "Yes! Yes! Yes! I am missed, I am missed at home." I knew full well, of course, that I was missed at home, but never before that parting afternoon had I been so profoundly and solemnly impressed with the unspeakable value my presence at home was to my family; so much so that their happiness depended on it in a incalculable measure. And also of how much value to me their presence was; so that my life seemed incomplete when they were parted from me, not knowing when we should meet again.*[78]

Everyone needs a place to call home where they can be loved, accepted, and missed. My son, Jonathan, is now in college about an hour away from our home. He lives on campus and travels home on weekends. He and my youngest daughter, Cortney, have a close bond as siblings. While traveling home from church one Sunday night, Cortney started crying, "I miss Jonathan so much!" I'm thrilled that our children love one another so much they can weep over each other's absence.

Lieutenant Goodloe, on leaving to fight in the war, realized the value of home. Someone said, "As goes the home, so goes the church; as goes the church, so goes the nation."

> When Joseph came home, they presented to him the gifts they had brought into the house, and they bowed down before him to the ground.
> —GENESIS 43:26

A Slave Pen, Alexandria, VA
Photographer, Andrew Russell

The Faith of a Slave

AFRICAN-AMERICAN SLAVE Thomas Anderson (affectionately known as "Uncle Tom") was converted at a Baptist church while a slave. The faith of believing, African-American slaves were testimonies of God's sustaining grace in persecution.

My master who owned me at that time having no knowledge of God or godliness, supposed my religion was all a fancy, and said he could and would whip it out of me. He took me up and tie me, and scourged me until feeling of flesh was almost gone . . . And though I was very weak from the beating I got, the Lord make me feel very strong, and this prepare me to answer: "You have whipped out all fear, and I am not afraid of you no more." You can take a gun and shoot me or kill me, as you please, and all for nothing; and that is all you can do: for I know I have a life you cannot touch, and the fear of you will not keep me from doing anything my new Master tells me to do. And if He let you take this poor bruised body of flesh, I feel it ain't worth much; and I feel strength to say something like this: "Thy will, O God! be done, and not mine!" After this my old master was conquered, and never whip me again, and left me in the hands of Jehovah. This gives me confidence to talk to the white or the black folks, and tell what the Lord had done for my poor soul. After this a great many come to me about religion, some good and some bad folks: for it was generally known that a great change had come over Tom.[79]

The story of Thomas Anderson sounds as though it could have come from Roman Emperor Nero's reign of terror during the persecution of the early church. But sadly this story came out of the history of the United States. Tom's faith and courage showed he had Christ dwelling within him. God sustained him through pain, threats, and impending death. He loved his new master (Jesus) and he was not afraid of his old master anymore.

As we draw near to Christ, we lose our fear of what people can do to us.

> So we say with confidence, "The Lord is my helper; I will not be afraid. What can man do to me?"
> —HEBREWS 13:6

Saved by Reading a Tract

A tremendous amount of religious literature was available for distri-
bution among the troops, and hospitalized veterans got their share of
this material. The Southern Baptist Convention in a single year pro-
vided 6,187,000 pages of tracts and 6,000 Bibles. In less than a year,
the Methodists circulated 17,000,000 pages of tracts and 20,000
Bibles. From May, 1863, through March of the following year,
Presbyterians produced more than 6,000,000 pages of religious mate-
rial. In addition, several independent publishers were at work on the
same type of project. A Federal chaplain said in 1863 that Southern
troops had more Bibles than did the soldiers of the North . . . One sol-
dier went to his chaplain with a tract in his hand and tears flowing
down his cheeks. "My parents have prayed for me, and wept over
me," he said, "but it was left for this tract to bring me, a poor con-
victed sinner, to the feet of Jesus."[80]

LET US NOT underestimate the power of a simple gospel tract. During the Civil War church denominations reached multitudes of men with written literature. In between battles, soldiers had time to think about their lives and their relationships with God. Since literature was a precious commodity in the Civil War, Bibles or gospel tracts

> The unfolding of your words gives light; it gives understanding to the simple.
> —PSALM 119:130

did not collect dust. Men read them during the lonesome hours of the day and by candlelight in tents at night. As evidenced by the many handwritten diaries we have today, soldiers were aware of their own mortality. Many times they had premonitions or a kind of "sixth sense" concerning dying in battle.

We do not know what happened to the soldier after he accepted Christ. Like so many others, he may have lost his life in battle within the next few days or months. How powerful to know this soldier is in heaven, all because of a gospel tract.

In the Hands of God

AUGUSTUS ADAMSON, a Confederate soldier from Georgia, was captured by the Union army. He wrote both from the perspective of the battlefield and the Yankee prison in Rock Island, Illinois. It is apparent that his strength to endure came from the Lord:

July 3rd, 1864

This is the Sabbath Day and I am convinced it is better observed by the prisoners here than by the Army of the Confederated States. Oh, how I long to be at home today and have the pleasure of once more going to church in my own neighborhood. Yes, it would indeed be a pleasure to hear my favorite minister preach once more . . . But I will not despair of all hope of again being restored to home and friends . . . but will commit myself to the guardian care of the Great Ruler of the Universe, believing that in the end all things will work out for the best.[81]

When we have done all we can to solve difficult situations, we must place ourselves totally in the hands of God and let him straighten them out. We naturally want to solve our problems ourselves. Yet, the more we do so, the more frustrated we get until we throw up our hands and say, "I give up." This is where the Lord probably wanted us all along. When we give up our struggling, we can then seek God's direction. The obstacles we meet may be part of God's plan to draw us closer to him

God is able to remove life's roadblocks and turn them into stepping-stones. Place your life completely in his hands today.

> Into your hands I commit my spirit; redeem me, O LORD, the God of truth.
> —PSALM 31:5

The Contribution of the Irish

ON THIS Saint Patrick's Day in America, it is good to remember the heroism of the Irish Brigades during the Civil War who fought so bravely. The following are commendations by officers of the Irish Brigades after the battle of Antictam:

> His master replied, "Well done, good and faithful servant! You have been faithful with a few things; I will put you in charge of many things. Come and share your master's happiness!"
>
> —MATTHEW 25:23

> *The officers and men all acted with a coolness and heroism worthy of honorable mention, yet I cannot close this meager report without recommending to your special notice Maj. Richard C. Bentley and Capt. J. O'Neill, whose cool and gallant conduct upon this trying and painful occasion merits the warmest commendation.*
>
> *In conclusion, permit me to congratulate you that your gallant little brigade has once more crowned itself with fresh laurels, and given additional and bloody proofs of its devotion to the Constitution and the flag of our beloved country.*
>
> *Very respectfully,*
> *Henry Fowler, Lieutenant-Colonel Sixty-third Regiment, Irish Brigade.*[82]

Officer Thomas Meagher wrote:

> *For what occurred subsequently to my being carried away from the field I refer you, with proud confidence, not alone to my regimental officers, who remained on the field, but also to many eye-witnesses of superior rank who noticed the opportune action of the Irish Brigade on that day. But I cannot close this communication without specially mentioning the names of Capt. Felix Duffy, of the Sixty-ninth; Captains Clooney and Joyce, of the Eighty-eighth, who, after distinguishing themselves by unremitting assiduity in the discharge of their duties in their commands throughout a very long and very exhausting campaign, fell with their feet to the rebels, with a glow of loyalty and true soldiership upon their dying features.*
>
> *I have the honor to be, captain, yours truly and respectfully,*
> *Thomas Francis Meagher*[83]

As these Irish officers reported the courageous deeds of valor to their commanding officers, we are reminded of the day when we Christians must all stand before God and give accounts. Will you be able to do it with joy?

Building and Battling

SGT. E. N. BOOTS

S ERGEANT EDWARD NICHOLAS BOOTS served in the 101st Regiment of Newberry, North Carolina. His father was a Methodist pastor, and his godly parents had a great influence on him. The following was written from camp in 1863.

Dearest Mother,

You may be sure that yesterday was a gala day with me. The shirt pleases me very much. The Testament is just what I wanted, just the size I wanted . . . You do not know how much I am obliged to you for those nice things. . . . My health has got pretty good. I left the Hospital on last Friday & I am doing duty. I am not very strong, but my appetite is good . . . I still have the testament that I got at Pittsburgh. It is much worn for it has seen hard service. I have carried it in my pocket ever since I started . . . I have found it a precious friend . . . I am still trying to love & serve him who first loved me. Still pray for me Mother dear I kneed your prayers . . . Last Sabbath no one could leave . . . on account of the rebels. Instead of being a day of rest it was a day of excitement & unrest [plus] the sound of the death dealing cannon mingled with the sound of the church bell.

Write to me often,
Your son, with love E N Boots[84]

Boots thought it was strange to hear the church bells ringing along with the blasts of the cannons on Sunday. These sounds should not be strange to us. While the church takes the gospel to the world, the enemy is not far behind. Nehemiah was aware of the conflict between the forces of darkness and the armies of light. But we are not alone in the battle, for the Captain of our faith goes ahead.

> The work is extensive . . . Wherever you hear the sound of the trumpet, join us there. Our God will fight for us!
> —NEHEMIAH 4:19, 20

An Affirmation of Faith

I N THE MIDST of the Civil War, the soldiers's faith was put to the test. The hell of war turned some away, while others affirmed the faith. War was one way to affirm the faith they had been taught at home and in the church. Robertson draws this comparison in his book, *Soldiers, Blue and Gray*:

> *For a majority of soldiers . . . war and its uncertainties led to an affirmation of faith similar in sentiment to Abraham Lincoln's observation: "I have often been driven to my knees by the realization that I had nowhere else to go." Carroll Clark of the 16th Tennessee confessed: "We were cut off from home Communications & had not much hope of ever meeting again the loved ones at home . . . I thought of my earthly home, sweet home & cried . . ."*[85]

Word came to Nehemiah that the wall of Jerusalem had been torn down and its gates burned. God's people had been taken into captivity by the Babylonians and lost both Jerusalem and their identity. Nehemiah was troubled when he heard the news that the city had been destroyed. This prompted him to go to his knees in fasting and prayer.

Lincoln shared similar circumstances with Nehemiah. Lincoln was dealing with a nation that had been torn apart. The immensity of the task of leading such a nation prompted Lincoln to fall on his knees and pray.

One of the characteristics of great men of God is their ability to realize their own limitations and humble themselves before God. Someone has said, "The best theology is 'kneeology.' "

> They said to me, "Those who survived the exile and are back in the province are in great trouble and disgrace. The wall of Jerusalem is broken down, and its gates have been burned with fire." When I heard these things, I sat down and wept. For some days I mourned and fasted and prayed before the God of heaven.
>
> —NEHEMIAH 1:1–5

Encouragement for a
Poor Distressed Soul

IN THIS LETTER to a dear friend named Polly, Eliza Stouffer empha-
sized the importance of maintaining the Christian faith:

Chambersburg, Pa.

February 20th 1863

My dear friend Mary Polly.

*I am rejoiced to hear through your letter, that you have not laid aside
yet this one thing needful, and are desiring to Know the truth, and learn
of Christ, For he says come unto me all ye that labor, and are heavy
laden, and I will give you rest, and learn of me, for I am meek and lowly
in heart, These are very encouraging words for a poor distressed soul,
and much more, he says that he will draw nigh unto them, that draw
nigh unto him . . . he has also promised that he will send us his spirit,
and that shall lead us into all truth, is this not a comfort, that he will
not leave us in the dark, but will teach us the way that he would have
us go . . . and I would advise you dear friend, not to get weary in well
doing . . . do not get discouraged if you are opposed in your views of
the scriptures, but search deep, and pray to God,
for an enlightened spirit. you may be the means
to bring others to more [enlightenment] . . .[86]*

> Evening, morning
> and noon I cry out in
> distress, and he
> hears my voice.
> —PSALM 55:17

When we are distressed, we can call upon the
Lord who is always accessible. Eliza mentioned to
her friend that the Holy Spirit would lead them
into all truth and not leave them in the dark.

The Psalmist said that when walking through
the dark valley of distress we should fear no evil (Ps. 24:4). The key word
here is "through." God tells us we will go through valleys, but not remain
there. Are you walking through a valley at this moment? It will not last forever. Jesus is there and he will bring you through.

Marshaled before the
Reviewing Officer

HERMAN NORTON in his book, *Rebel Religion*, reveals how soldiers believed they could obtain favor with God before battle:

Communion services played an important role in the faith of soldiers in the Civil War who were contemplating death. Communion was viewed by the men as a way to obtain the grace and favor of God before battle. Some of the men of a certain fighting unit made the comment after they had taken communion that they were ready to receive the "great reviewing officer, should they immediately be marshaled before Him."[87]

The soldiers that partook of communion were trying to gain God's grace before going into battle. Although they were sincere, communion could not assure peace with God—peace and acceptance with God comes only through Jesus.

> For we will all stand before God's judgment seat.
> —ROMANS 14:10

In the ancient Greek games, athletes passed before a reviewing stand of dignitaries. Some proudly showed their medals while others passed by in defeat. The apostle Paul reminds us that we are going to stand before the judgment seat of Christ where we will give an account of our deeds, whether good or bad.

Several years ago the United States fought its first war with Iraq. After accomplishing their mission, a great parade was organized in Washington. The victorious armed forces of the United States marched before a presidential reviewing stand in honor of their Commander and Chief. Likewise, there is coming a day when the soldiers of Christ will stand before God. In that day we will hear him say, "Well done."

A Spiritual Drought

THE REV. SAMUEL AGNEW wrote in his diary:

March 27, 1864

There is a lamentable torpor among the people in reference to their souls. They hear and attend the sanctuary but seem unaffected by the preacher's word. It is discouraging, but it is God that is the efficient worker. Ministers can only dispense the word and ordinances faithfully, leaving the issue to God. A large congregation was gathered. McDaniel preached the action sermon from Eph. 5:25–27 Mr. Young fenced the table [or Lord's Supper Table] and served the 1st, McDaniel the 2nd. I returned thanks and dismissed the congregation. Very few communed. More members were absent than ordinarily, and some who were present did not commune. I noticed that Polly Caldwell did not commune. There is a spiritual drought in that community. May God bless my labors . . . (http://docsouth.unc.edu/agnew/agnew.html)

Samuel Agnew, a minister during the Civil War period, suffered many of the same frustrations that ministers suffer today. A declining attendance, little participation in spiritual ministries, and a lack of applying the Bible to daily life. These are signs of a spiritual drought and signal an urgent need for a spiritual revival.

Agnew admitted through his disheartening experience that God was in charge, and all he could do was faithfully preach the Word. As Christians we won't always see fruit from our witness, but we must be faithful in prayer and sowing the seed

> They draw nigh to me with their lips, but their hearts are far from me.
> —ISAIAH 19:13

of the Word of God because the Lord promised, "So is my word that goes out from my mouth: It will not return to me empty, but will accomplish what I desire and achieve the purpose for which I sent it" (Isa. 55:11).

"The Church Seems to Be Occupied by Sick Prisoners"

S AMUEL AGNEW writes:

March 27, 1864,

Holland rode on over to Brice's. See the marks of the battle: but not so apparent as I had supposed. His house and yard are public property now. Sick men occupy the rooms. Some poor fellows are mortally wounded. I felt sorry when I looked on the poor fellows, dieing so far from the dear ones at home. They are lying on pallets. Some Yankees are also there. The Church seems to be occupied by sick prisoners. The principle surgeon was operating on a Yankee while I was there. He was lying on a table insensible being under the influence of Chloroform. His right foot had been amputated and his left hand ½ taken out . . .

In Virginia Grant and Lee are very near each other. The battles of the 4 & 5th of May were not decisive. In some places the lines of the armies are only 50 yds. apart. The decisive battle is yet to be fought . . . The N. Y. Herald of the 8th announces that on the 8th the Republican convention nominated Abraham Lincoln for the Presidency and Andrew Johnson of Tennessee for the Vice Presidency. They are a delicious duo . . .[88]

> On hearing this, Jesus said to them, "It is not the healthy who need a doctor, but the sick. I have not come to call the righteous, but sinners."
>
> —MARK 2:17

Samuel Agnew said, marking the aftermath of a battle, "The church seems to be occupied by sick prisoners." So often, a church seems to be a "country club" for saints rather than a hospital for sinners. Because Jesus came to minister to sinners, the church should be a place where the spiritually sick find recovery.

Try reaching out to others in need and be surprised what the Lord may do through your efforts.

Confederate Prisoners Captured in Shenandoah Valley
Guarded in a Union Camp, May 1862
The National Archives

Finding Strength in
the Midst of Great Sorrow

IN 1862, after the loss of their son, Willie, Mrs. Lincoln said that her hus-band drew closer to the Lord. Lincoln's proclamation for a day of fasting and prayer showed that he depended even more on God during the second half of his presidency. As one author put it regarding his proclamation, "Few ministers of the gospel could have done better."

March 30, 1863,

> *It is the duty of nations as well as of men to own their dependence upon the overruling power of God, and to confess their sins and trans-gressions in humble sorrow, yet with assured hope that genuine repentance will lead to mercy and pardon, and to recognize the sublime truth, announced in Holy Scripture, and proven by all history, that those nations only are blessed whose God is the Lord . . . But we have forgot-ten God. We have forgotten the gracious hand which has preserved us in peace and multiplied and enriched and strengthened us . . . It behooves us, then, to humble ourselves before the offended power, to confess our national sins and to pray for clemency and forgiveness.*[89]

> Blessed is the nation whose God is the LORD, the people he chose for his inheritance.
> —PSALM 33:12

President Lincoln deeply loved his children, so when Willie died at twelve years of age, he surely must have suffered greatly. However, through that experience Lincoln grew closer to the Lord.

We do not understand why the Lord sometimes takes our young chil-dren from us. These are mysteries that will be revealed someday in heaven. As the old gospel song says, "We will understand it better by and by." If we submit to God through our losses as Lincoln did, we will find peace. Remember, God chooses his greatest servants from the fires of affliction.

He Warn't Afraid of Nuthin' or Nobody

J OHN DYER writes an interesting characterization of General Joseph
Wheeler:

"FIGHTING" JOE
WHEELER, 1863
*The Library
of Congress*

*"Tell me about General 'Fightin' Joe' Wheeler. What
was he like?" "I have put that request to scores of people in all walks of life—to old soldiers at reunions, to
politicians, to grizzled farmers on porches of their dog-
run houses in Alabama, to retired army officers putter-
ing about in their gardens. And almost invariably the
reply has been the same, so much the same that one
might suspect collusion. They all express the same esti-
mate as that given by a North Alabama farmer who had
been the General's neighbor for years. 'I'll tell you,' he
said, 'Joe Wheeler was the gamest little banty I ever
seen. He warn't afraid of nuthin' or nobody' . . . They
all smile when they remember Wheeler."*[90]

General J. E. B. Stuart said, "Wheeler was
characterized by General Robert E. Lee as one of
the two outstanding cavalrymen in the War
between the States." The courageous spirit of
"Fighting" Joe Wheeler reminds us of the courage
the Holy Spirit gives to the believer. God does not
want us to go through life with a spirit of fear.
Satan wants us to be spiritually timid, but with
Jesus as the captain of our faith, we can face life
without fear.

> For God did not give
> us a spirit of timidity,
> but a spirit of power,
> of love and of self-
> discipline.
> —2 TIMOTHY 1:7

A Rude Soldier and a Little Angel

FOLLOWING THE BATTLE of Sharpsburg, an unknown soldier told a story of a young girl who became known as the "little angel" of the battlefield:

> *After the battle of Sharpsburg, we passed over a line of railroad in Central Georgia. The disabled soldiers from Gen. Lee's armies were returning to their homes. At every station the wives and daughters of the farmers came on the cars, and distributed food and wines and bandages among the sick and wounded.*
>
> *"We shall never forget how very like an angel was a little girl— how blushingly and modestly she went to a great rude, bearded soldier, who had carved a crutch for a rough plank to replace a lost leg; how this little girl asked him if he was hungry—and how he ate like a famished wolf! She asked if his wound was painful, and in a voice of soft, mellow accents, "Can I do nothing more for you? I am sorry that you are so badly hurt; Have you a little daughter, and wont she cry when she sees you?"*
>
> *The rude soldier's heart was touched, and tears of love and gratitude filled his eyes. He only answered, "I have three little children; God grant they may be such angels as you." With an evident effort he repressed a desire to kiss the fair brow of the pretty little girl. He took her little hand between both his own, and bade her "good-by—God bless you."* (Univ. of Michigan digital library, *The Making of America*, 181)

> And the Syrians had gone out by companies, and had brought away captive out of the land of Israel a little maid; and she waited on Naaman's wife. And she said unto her mistress, would God my lord were with the prophet that is in Samaria! for he would recover him of his leprosy.
>
> —2 KINGS 5:2, 3

God often uses children to touch hearts and inspire faith. The innocence and honesty of the little "angel girl" brought the wounded soldier memories of home and melted his hard heart. Like the little maid who helped Naaman, the "little angel" ministered to a hardened soldier in a great hour of need.

We should never underestimate the power of a child's testimony.

Let the Past Be the Past

GENERAL ROBERT E. LEE said,

The gentleman does not needlessly and unnecessarily remind an offender of a wrong he may have committed against him. He can not only forgive; he can forget; and he strives for that nobleness of self and mildness of character, which imparts sufficient strength to let the past be put in the past.[91]

Dr. Charles Stanley states that unforgiveness is one of the land mines in the way of believers:

An unforgiving spirit is the primary cause of many of our health problems, much of our unanswered prayer, many of the feelings of stress that you and I experience. . . . Unforgiveness is disastrous to the Christian. It affects every single aspect of life. Your body, your mind, your relationships, your work, your goals, your ambitions, your desires in life. It affects your effectiveness in your Christian life, your witness . . . It affects the power of the Holy Spirit in your life.[92]

Jesus died on Calvary's cross for the sins of the world. He was totally innocent, yet he was willing to suffer because he "so loved the world." Through the forgiveness he obtained for us, God will allow our "past to be in the past." In our daily lives we should forgive others when they sin against us.

> Jesus said, "Father, forgive them, for they do not know what they are doing."
> —LUKE 23:34

Walking among the Dead

GOING AMONG THE DEAD after the battle of Manassas and Bull Run, a soldier from the Eighth Georgia Regiment wrote:

I shall never forget the feeling that came over me as I walked among the dead that afternoon. "Surely, surely," I said, "there will never be another battle." It seemed to me barbarous for men to try to settle any dispute or controversy by shooting one another, and now that it had been realized what a battle meant, I felt sure there would never be another. But not so thought those both North and South who had not taken part in this battle. And so there was no trouble in getting volunteers by the thousand from both sections to take the places of those who had been killed.

The day after the battle I walked over the battlefield and stopped a few minutes at a hospital. The surgeons were still busy amputating legs and arms. I saw a squad of soldiers burying the dead, and there were other squads with wagons gathering up guns and cartridge boxes. I went among the saplings in the thicket where we had fought. I saw trees not more than eight inches in diameter that had been struck by at least twenty balls, and I wondered how any of us escaped. As I am not writing a history, but only telling what I saw I will not attempt to give an account of the battle. In fact, I know of my own knowledge very little beyond what occurred right around me.[93]

> An offended brother is more unyielding than a fortified city, and disputes are like the barred gates of a citadel.
> —PROVERBS 18:19

The Civil War is proof of the devastation of unresolved conflict. Brother was often pitted against brother. Many were not aware they were fighting their own relatives until they discovered their lifeless bodies on the battlefield.

When conflict, bitterness, and disputes are allowed to fester and take root, they result in misunderstanding and even violence. As Christians, our real fight is not with each other but with Satan and demonic powers.

Execution in the Civil War

MILITARY LAW was strict during the Civil War. An unknown Civil War soldier shared the following account of two men who were executed for assault on an officer:

> On one occasion I saw two men executed, men who had been tried by a court-martial and sentenced to be shot. It was in the fall or early part of the winter of 1861–1862 . . . We had in the army a battalion of men from Louisiana, known as the "Tiger Rifles." They wore Zouave uniforms, that is, baggy knee breeches, stockings, a jacket, and a turban . . . Two of them had overpowered an officer and was about to kill him, and for this they had been court-martialed and condemned to be shot.
>
> Announcement had been made in an order from General Johnston, commanding the army at that time that the execution would take place on a certain day, and it seemed to be expected that it would be witnessed by the whole army . . . They came in a wagon, which also contained their coffins . . . Their hands were tied behind them and then tied to the posts, and they were blindfolded. Two platoons of twelve soldiers each were marched out in front of them. They were of the same command with the men who were to be shot . . . The officer in charge . . . Without saying a word . . . raised his hands and the men brought their guns to the position of aim. He dropped his hand and they fired . . .[94]

General Johnston's strict and regimented approach would not tolerate insubordination or assaults on officers. The sentence of death for attempted murder would be questionable in our day, but under the guidelines for the Civil War conduct there was little mercy when an officer was assaulted.

Fortunately, God did not give us what we deserved, but showed mercy by allowing his son to take our penalty. If we must make a mistake, then let us err on the side of mercy.

> But because of his great love for us, God, who is rich in mercy, made us alive with Christ even when we were dead in transgressions—it is by grace you have been saved.
> —EPHESIANS 2:4, 5

Selfishness unto Death

A SOLDIER of the Eighth Georgia Regiment recounted a battle story where the selfishness of one soldier cost him his life:

Not more than fifteen feet above me and in an exposed place lay a man who had been wounded. The cannonballs were plowing up the ground around him, and it seemed every moment he would be torn to pieces.

Presently a soldier came running and dropped into the gully between us. The wounded man immediately appealed to him to pull him down where he was, saying he had both legs broken and would be killed. Just then a shell exploded right at him. He exclaimed, "My God, friend, please"—but he never finished the sentence, for at that moment another shell exploded right at his friend, and when the smoke cleared away he was nowhere to be seen. Where he had lain was a hole big enough to bury a mule in. He had probably been blown to pieces. I think of him in connection with the Scripture, "Whosoever will save his life shall lose it." With that shell the firing ceased, for our boys had captured the guns, and there was no longer any danger for me and the man with the broken legs. If the comrade to whom he had so earnestly appealed had gone to his relief, he would have saved his own life; but he was too much concerned for his own safety to help his wounded brother.[95]

> For even the Son of Man did not come to be served, but to serve, and to give his life as a ransom for many.
> —MARK 10:45

When we please our own interests, we become selfish and prideful. When we serve others as Jesus did, we find abundant life. If the soldier would have listened to the cries of his friend, he might have saved his own life. But thinking only of himself, he lost his life.

A Father Finds His Son

A YOUNG unknown Southern soldier told the story how his loving father looked for him after receiving word he had been wounded in battle.

A week after the Second Battle of Manassas, in which I was wounded, Father set out to come to me. In Richmond he learned that most of the wounded from that battle had been sent back . . . He reached the terminus and was informed that it was fifty-three miles by the turnpike to Warrenton . . . and so he set out on foot, with a party of others on the same mission, hunting for their sons that had been wounded in that battle. They made a continuous trip of it, except a rest of one hour at midnight, and walked the fifty-three miles in twenty-three hours. He was at that time sixty-four years old.

When he reached Warrenton, he explained his mission to the first man he met and was told that it was said there were eighteen hundred wounded men in the place; that all the churches, the courthouse, schoolhouse, and railroad warehouse were full, and there were many in private families.

> If a man owns a hundred sheep, and one of them wanders away, will he not leave the ninety-nine on the hills and go to look for the one that wandered off?
>
> —MATTHEW 18:13

Father said he never realized until then what it meant to hunt for one among eighteen hundred. "Are there any in that building yonder?" he inquired, pointing to a nearby church. "Yes, sir, it's full. You see a man's head on the floor in the preacher's door right now." "Then," said father, "I'll begin my search right here, and may the Lord direct me."

He came to the church, to the preacher's door; he came up the steps, and the man whose head was lying in the door was his boy. It, indeed, must be true that the Lord directed him . . .[96]

Who can put a price on an eternal soul? For the determined father who searched for his wounded son, no price was too high to pay and no distance was too far to travel.

Lincoln's Death and God's Providence

GEORGE WASHINGTON BAKER wrote the following letter home:

April 18th

We just heard of the death of Lincoln and it seems to cast a gloom over everything. It seems as if it was the greatest calamity that could have befell us and is felt by all, even his Enemies . . . Still it may be for the best as the South may be more willing to come in to the Union under some other man and what is one mans life to the good of the country? I am one of the kind that think no great calamities come upon us unless for some great good (still I feel as if we had lost some dear friend. Things seem to be undecided here as yet and we do not hear what success Sherman and Johnson have in negotiations but think every thing will be well).

Love to all from your Affectionate Son— George[97]

During the Civil War most Americans in the North and in the South believed in the overruling providence of Almighty God. Lincoln himself ascribed to this theology, which is evident from his many references to providential care in his speeches.

Ironically, Lincoln would agree with George Baker's theology even though a great sense of sadness enveloped the land. George Baker admitted Lincoln's death "may be for the best." The South finally united with the North during a reconstruction period. Today Abraham Lincoln is considered as one of our nation's greatest presidents.

As Christians, we can have confidence that God is actively involved in our lives through great calamities.

> [Joseph said] And now, do not be distressed and do not be angry with yourselves for selling me here, because it was to save lives that God sent me ahead of you.
>
> —GENESIS 45:5

Trusting the Lord in Extremities

SOUTHERN CHRISTIAN lady Mary Bethell wrote:

My little Anna was sick most a week and Willie was kicked by a horse; we all thought he might die. I was very much cast down as my husband was not at home to help bear the burden, but the Lord was with me to comfort and support me in these trying times. I was sorely tempted nearly all last week, my soul was surrounded by darkness, doubts and gloomy fears, it seemed like the Lord had forsaken me.

I wept and prayed to Jesus Christ to remove my burden of fears, and gloom, he heard and answered, last Sunday evening he blessed my soul. These words came forcibly to mind, "The Lord knoweth how to deliver the godly from temptation." Just then light broke into my soul, I could praise my precious Saviour, because he heard and answered me, and gave me peace and comfort. Hallelujah! The Lord God omnipotent reigneth!!! I will trust him in every extremity.[98]

> And if he rescued Lot, a righteous man, who was distressed by the filthy lives of lawless men (for that righteous man, living among them day after day, was tormented in his righteous soul by the lawless deeds he saw and heard)—if this is so, then the Lord knows how to rescue godly men from trials and to hold the unrighteous for the day of judgment.
> —2 PETER 2: 7–9

Mary Bethell faced discouraging situations, but she prayed that God would remove her fears. After recalling a Scripture verse, "light broke" into her life. She rejoiced that God answered her prayers and gave her comfort and peace.

Like Mary, we must be resolved to pray until the "light breaks" into our lives, then we will find comfort and peace.

The Precious Word of God

B INGHAM FINDLEY JUNKIN was a private in the 100th Pennsylvania Volunteers during the Civil War. He was a man who loved the Lord and the Bible. He recorded the following in his diary:

Sunday, April 3, 1862

Slept very little last night, although it continued to rain. Woke about daylight, took up my Bible and read awhile before I got up. I make it a rule to read a portion of scripture every day, although I cannot have any set time; have to be guided by circumstances in a great measure, but always try if possible to read a chapter just before going to sleep. It would be very hard indeed to endure the separation from those that are dear were it not for the consciousness of being in the line of duty, and that God Rules; and that he doeth all things well. Oh how comforting the thought that we have such a God to go to . . .

> Seeing that His divine power has granted to us everything pertaining to life and godliness, through the true knowledge of Him who called us by His own glory and excellence. For by these He has granted to us His precious and magnificent promises, so that by them you may become partakers of the divine nature, having escaped the corruption that is in the world by lust.
> —2 PETER 1:3–5

The Bible contains God's great and "precious promises." These promises kept private Junkin at peace when facing the enemy on the battlefield. Notice that Junkin read his Bible before going to sleep at night and upon rising early in the morning.

God's promises can sustain us on the battlefields of life, giving us comfort and encouragement.

Lincoln's Sympathy for a Bereaved Mother

PRESIDENT LINCOLN understood the price of freedom during the Civil War. He wrote the following letter to a grieving mother over the loss of five sons in battle:

Executive Mansion, Washington, Nov. 21, 1864

Dear Madam,

I have been shown in the files of the War Department a statement of the Adjutant-General of Massachusetts, that you are the mother of five sons who have died gloriously on the field of battle.

> But the king replied to Araunah, "I will not sacrifice to the LORD my God burnt offerings that cost me nothing."
>
> —2 SAMUEL 24:24

I feel how weak and fruitless must be any words of mine which should attempt to beguile you from the grief of a loss so overwhelming. But I cannot refrain from tendering to you the consolation that may be found in the thanks of the Republic they died to save.

I pray that our Heavenly Father may assuage the anguish of your bereavement, and leave you only the cherished memory of the loved and lost, and the solemn pride that must be yours, to have laid so costly a sacrifice upon the altar of Freedom.

Yours, very sincerely and Respectfully,
Abraham Lincoln[100]

Lincoln's letter is a reminder of our modern-day soldiers who have sacrificed their lives upon the altar of freedom. Someone said, "Freedom isn't free."

David understood that serving God would cost him something. Jesus paid the price by dying on the cross. As Christians, we have an obligation to be thankful for his sacrifice. The writer of Hebrews said, "Through Jesus, he would continually offer the sacrifice of praise."

5

We'll Never Say
Good-Bye in Heaven

THE REV. DR. SEHON, one of the Chaplains in General Lee's army, wrote concerning a most touching scene of a soldier and his Bible:

A most interesting incident occurred during the exercises of the evening: A request was made for a Bible for the stand. Several were ready to respond. The book was received from a tall and interesting looking young man. I noticed his large blue eyes and attractive face as he came forward and placed the holy book before them. Instantly his home rose before me. I fancied how father, mother, brothers, sisters, felt when he left, and how they thought of and prayed for him. While lining the hymn I turned to the title page of the Bible and then my eyes were filled with tears. On the blank leaves were written the parting words of love and affection of the dear ones at home, with the kind advice and earnest prayers for the safety and happiness of the owner of the book. I closed the book with feelings of most sacred character, and was far better prepared for the services of the hour.[101]

One of the heartbreaks of life is learning to say good-bye. In John 14, Jesus was saying his final good-byes to men who could not comprehend the meaning of the crucifixion. Even though the disciples would experience sorrow for a few days, in the end their sorrow would be turned to joy when they discovered that Jesus had risen from the grave. The resurrection of Christ means that in heaven we will never have to say good-bye again.

> Do not let your heart be troubled; believe in God, believe also in Me. In My Father's house are many dwelling places; if it were not so, I would have told you; for I go to prepare a place for you. If I go and prepare a place for you, I will come again and receive you to myself, that where I am, there you may be also.
>
> —JOHN 14:1–6 (NASB)

A "Know So" Faith

JAMES P. CROWDER, who was a Confederate soldier in General Longstreet's army, contracted typhoid fever at Petersburg, Virginia, and was hospitalized. A chaplain visited him there and wrote a kind letter to Crowder's mother explaining the situation giving both his physical and spiritual condition.

Petersburg VA, 1863

I write at the request of your son, J.P. Crowder, who is now sick in the hospital at this place . . . I think, therefore, under the kind providence of God you may soon expect to hear from him as again being in good health and better prepared for the duties that await him in life.

As a minister and Army [Chaplain] *I visited his bed this morning and in religious conversation with him found that he was very much in doubt as to the genuineness of his early profession of religion. He fears he has been deceived as to the true condition of his heart, and that he is not really a Christian. I conversed with him freely and read to him a little tract entitled "Christian Invitation" . . .*[102]

> I write these things to you who believe in the name of the Son of God so that you may know that you have eternal life.
> —1 JOHN 5:13

Jesus Christ paid the price on Calvary to secure for us a "know so" salvation. J. P. Crowder was in doubt as to his salvation experience. Either he was so young when he made a profession that he didn't understand he was a sinner who needed to turn completely to God, or else, he never made a true profession of faith.

The Holy Spirit must have awakened Crowder to see his need to settle the matter of his salvation, and he used an army chaplain to talk to him about it. Do you have total confidence that if you died today that you would go to heaven? We have a God who gives us a "know so" salvation.

A Compassionate Notification

CHAPLAIN JOHN M. CARLISLE of the Seventh South Carolina Infantry witnessed the savage slaughter on Snodgrass Hill in Chattanooga. He later notified his friend, Congressman Richard Simpson, of the death of his son. The compassion and love Carlisle had for the family is evident by his kind words:

My Dear Bro. Simpson:

It is my mournful duty to communicate to you and your dear family the fact that your son and my dear young friend, Tally, fell on the bloody field of Sunday last . . . He was shot through the heart by a Minnie ball, his left arm was broken . . . He was doing his duty and met his fate as a brave soldier. He fell with his face to the foe . . . I buried him yesterday, putting him away as carefully as the circumstances allowed . . .

My Bro., you have my prayers and sympathies under this bereavement, for though I know that as much as possible you were prepared for such an event, yet you can but mourn for your first born and noble son. I feel as though I too had lost a child. I have known him since he was a boy, and then him the son of you whom I number among my dearest friends. May God's grace sustain you and the family and enable you to say, "Thy will be done."[103]

Yours in sadness
John M. Carlisle

> The LORD is gracious and compassionate, slow to anger and rich in love.
> —PSALM 145:8

Chaplain Carlisle's compassion for a grieving father reminds us of our Savior's compassion. We cannot even imagine giving one of our children to wicked men to be crucified on a cruel cross. Yet, God loved us so much that he allowed his only son to suffer and die on the cross.

We must be thankful for a compassionate God who went to such extremities to show his love for us.

Jackson's Christian Character

GENERAL JOHN BROWN GORDON, an eyewitness testimony to the Christian character of Stonewall Jackson, said,

> But a truth of more importance than anything I have yet said of Jackson may be compassed, I think, in the observation that he added to a marvelous genius for war a character as man and Christian which was absolutely without blemish. His childlike trust and faith, the simplicity, sincerity, and constancy of his unostentatious piety, did not come with the war, nor was it changed by the trials and dangers of war. If the war affected him at all in this particular, it only intensified his religious devotion, because of the tremendous responsibilities which it imposed; but long before, his religious thought and word and example were leading to the higher life young men entrusted to his care, at the Virginia Military Institute. In the army nothing deterred or diverted him from the discharge of his religious duties, nor deprived him of the solace resulting from his unaffected trust. A deep-rooted belief in God, in His word and His providence, was under him and over him and through him, permeating every fiber of his being, dominating his every thought, controlling his every action. Wherever he went and whatever he did, whether he was dispensing light and joy in the family circle; imparting lessons of lofty thought to his pupils in the schoolroom at Lexington; planning masterful strategy in his tent; praying in the woods for Heaven's guidance; or riding like the incarnate spirit of war through the storm of battle, as his resistless legions swept the field of carnage with the fury of a tornado— Stonewall Jackson was the faithful disciple of his Divine Master. He died as he had lived, with his ever-active and then fevered brain working out the problems to which his duty called him, and, even with the chill of death upon him, his loving heart prompted the message to his weary soldiers, "Let us cross over the river and rest in the shade of the trees." That his own spirit will eternally rest in the shade of the Tree of Life, none who knew him can for one moment doubt.[104]

> For to me, to live is Christ and to die is gain.
> —PHILIPPIANS 1:21

Just as Stonewall Jackson's religious fervor possessed every area of his life, the apostle Paul realized that the life worth living is spent following God's will and destiny. Jackson knew the Lord had given him a special calling, and nothing deterred him from fulfilling it.

Alone with a Depressed
Robert E. Lee

GENERAL JOHN B. GORDON wrote:

During the month of February, 1865 (I cannot now recall the exact date), General Lee sent a messenger, about two o'clock in the morning, to summon me to his headquarters. It was one of the bitterest nights of that trying winter, and it required a ride of several miles to reach the house on the outskirts of Petersburg where the commanding-general made his headquarters. As I entered, General Lee, who was entirely alone, was standing at the fireplace, his arm on the mantel and his head resting on his arm as he gazed into the coal fire burning in the grate. He had evidently been up all the previous part of the night. For the first time in all my intercourse with him, I saw a look of painful depression on his face. Of course he had experienced many hours of depression, but he had concealed from those around him all evidence of discouragement. He had carried the burden in his own soul—wrapping his doubts and apprehensions in an exterior of cheerfulness and apparent confidence. The hour had come, however, when he could no longer carry alone the burden, or entirely conceal his forebodings of impending disaster . . . and I found myself alone with the evidently depressed commander.[105]

Moses is hailed in Hebrew history as one of the great leaders of Israel, yet he grew weary and needed encouragement from others. As a leader, Lee carried the burden of the entire Confederacy on his shoulders. Near the end of the war the weight got too heavy to bear. Like Moses, he needed encouragement. Is there someone in leadership who needs your encouragement today?

> When Moses' hands grew tired, they took a stone and put it under him and he sat on it. Aaron and Hur held his hands up—one on one side, one on the other—so that his hands remained steady till sunset.
> —EXODUS 17:12

A One-Legged Soldier Prays

GENERAL JOHN B. GORDON recalled a Confederate prayer meeting:

From the commander-in-chief to the privates in the ranks, there was a deep and sincere religious feeling in Lee's army. Whenever it was convenient or practicable, these hungry but unyielding men were holding prayer-meetings. Their supplications were fervent and often inspiring, but now and then there were irresistibly amusing touches. At one of these gatherings for prayer was a private who had lost one leg. Unable to kneel, he sat with bowed head, while one of his comrades, whom we shall call Brother Jones, led in prayer. Brother Jones was earnestly praying for more manhood, more strength, and more courage. The brave old one-legged Confederate did not like Brother Jones's prayer. At that period of the war, he felt that it was almost absurd to be asking God to give the Confederates more courage, of which virtue they already had an abundant supply. So he called out from his seat: "Hold on there, Brother Jones. Don't you know you are praying all wrong? Why don't you pray for more provisions? We've got more courage now than we have any use for!"[106]

> When you ask, you do not receive, because you ask with wrong motives, that you may spend what you get on your pleasures.
> —JAMES 4:3

Brother Jones's prayer did not impress the crippled soldier; he felt that Brother Jones was praying all wrong. There may be times when we do not receive answers to our prayers. Possibly we're asking for wrong things or have incorrect motives. It's when we begin to say like Jesus, "Not my will, but yours be done," that we show true Christian maturity.

Offering Mercy to Johnny Reb

GENERAL BENJAMIN BUTTERWORTH of Ohio told General John B. Gordon about the genuine comradeship that often existed between the soldiers of the hostile armies:

On that doleful retreat of Lee's army, it was impossible for us to bury our dead or carry with us the disabled wounded. There was no longer any room in the crowded ambulances which had escaped capture and still accompanied our trains. We could do nothing for the unfortunate sufferers who were too severely wounded to march, except leave them on the roadside with canteens of water. A big-hearted soldier-boy in blue came across a desperately wounded Confederate shot through legs and body, lying in his bloody bed of leaves, groaning with pain and sighing for relief in death. The generous Federal was so moved by the harrowing spectacle that he stopped at the side of the Confederate and asked:

"What can I do for you, Johnny? I want to help you if I can."

"Thank you for your sympathy," the sufferer replied, "but no one can help me now. It will not be long till death relieves me."

The Union soldier bade him good-by, and was in the act of leaving, when the wounded Southerner called to him: "Yes, Yank; there is something you might do for me. You might pray for me before you go."

> But I tell you who hear me: Love your enemies, do good to those who hate you.
> —LUKE 6:24

This Union boy had probably never uttered aloud a word of prayer in all his life. But his emotions were deeply stirred, and through his tears he looked around for some one more accustomed to lead in prayer. Discovering some of his comrades passing, he called to them: "Come here, boys, and come quick. Here is a poor Johnny shot all to pieces, and he's dying. One of you must come and pray for him . . ."[107]

The Civil War pitted American against fellow American. Even though there was a time when the Yanks hated "Johnny Reb," time has a tendency to heal old wounds. In the same sense, Christian love and compassion can win over our worst enemies.

A Touching Scene of Surrender

A T A VETERAN'S RALLY, General Joshua Chamberlain described a touching scene of surrender by General John B. Gordon and his men at the conclusion of the Civil War:

> At the sound of that machine-like snap of arms, General Gordon started, caught in a moment its significance, and instantly assumed the finest attitude of a soldier. He wheeled his horse, facing me, touching him gently with the spur, so that the animal slightly reared, and, as he wheeled, horse and rider made one motion, the horse's head swung down with a graceful bow, and General Gordon dropped his sword-point to his toe in salutation.
>
> By word of mouth the general sent back orders to the rear that his own troops take the same position of the manual in the march past as did our line. That was done, and a truly imposing sight was the mutual salutation and farewell.
>
> Bayonets were affixed to muskets, arms stacked, and cartridge-boxes unslung and hung upon the stacks. Then, slowly and with a reluctance that was appealingly pathetic, the torn and tattered battle-flags were either leaned against the stacks or laid upon the ground. The emotion of the conquered soldiery was really sad to witness. Some of the men who had carried and followed those ragged standards through the four long years of strife rushed, regardless of all discipline, from the ranks, bent about their old flags, and pressed them to their lips.
>
> And it can well be imagined, too, that there was no lack of emotion on our side, but the Union men were held steady in their lines, without the least show of demonstration by word or by motion. . . . Our men felt the import of the occasion, and realized fully how they would have been affected if defeat and surrender had been their lot after such a fearful struggle.[108]

> Carry each other's burdens, and in this way you will fulfill the law of Christ.
> —GALATIANS 6:2

The final surrender of the Confederates after the Civil War invoked emotions in both the blue and gray armies. Jesus wants us to identify with the hurts and needs of others—to carry one another's burdens.

CONFEDERATE DEFENSES IN FRONT OF ATLANTA, GA
Photographer, Andrew Russell

An Alarming State of Things

R EV. THOMAS CREIGH, pastor of the Presbyterian church in Mercersburg, Virginia, kept a personal diary in which he jotted down items of local interest and national happenings.

> Paul looked straight at the Sanhedrin and said, "My brothers, I have fulfilled my duty to God in all good conscience to this day."
> —ACTS 23:1

On Sunday, September 7, the exclamation reads: "An alarming state of things!" This was caused by the information that "the Rebels are crossing the Potomac in large force near Harper's Ferry, and that guerilla companies are being formed in Washington County, Md., to invade this portion of our valley." Notice was given of this to the congregation and all who could bear arms were urged to meet in this place (the church) tomorrow "to concert means to our defense." A meeting was held that very night after the church service, at which W. D. McKinstry was made chairman, and a committee of Safety was appointed. Persons were sent to Clear spring Greencastle and Chambersburg for information which was to be reported at the meeting the next day.

By Thursday the excitement was intense. "Many persons in town . . . Companies training, one of cavalry and two of infantry. The Rebels have taken Hagerstown and are destroying the railroad at that end." This fact elicits the following statement from the minister: "The Lord enables us in quietness to possess our souls. He reigns, who can control all the movements of the enemies. Our best plan is to be in the place and path of duty, and look to God for grace, wisdom, and strength in time of peril."[109]

God's blessings are most often found on the pathway of duty. Are you seeking a blessing from God? Stay faithful in worship, Bible reading, and prayer, and the blessings will come when you least expect them!

A Rekindling of Love

On the evening of April 14, 1865, President Abraham Lincoln and his wife, Mary, were enjoying the British comedy Our American Cousin *at Ford's Theatre. They were sitting in an upper right-hand box. Mary wore a black and white striped silk dress, with black lace veiling on her hair. A young couple, Major Henry Rathbone and Miss Clara Harris, shared the box with the Lincolns. As the play progressed, Mary sat very close to her husband, her hand in his. She whispered to him, "What will Miss Harris think of my hanging on to you so?" The President replied, "She won't think anything about it."*

Those are the last recorded words of Abraham Lincoln. Estimates vary, but it was approximately 10:15 P.M. On stage actor Harry Hawk was saying, "Don't know the manners of good society, eh? Well, I guess I know enough to turn you inside out, old gal—you sockdologizing old mantrap!" John Wilkes Booth opened the door behind where the President was sitting and shot him in the head at near point blank range. Mary, still holding Mr. Lincoln's hand, clutched her husband. His head inclined toward his chest . . .[110]

DEPICTION OF THE
LINCOLN ASSASSINATION

THERE SEEMED to be a special rekindling of love and tenderness between the President and his wife that historic night. Previously, they had problems in their marriage, probably over the stress they were enduring related to the War. The Lincolns were trying to hold hands. Yet, in just a few moments, Lincoln slipped from the bonds of this life to the arms of his Savior. Even though Mary would face the trial of her life, she could remember those last sweet moments when their love had been rekindled.

> Husbands love your wives just as Christ loved the Church.
> —EPHESIANS 5:25

A Canteen of Cold Water
at Fort Sanders

CONFEDERATE GENERAL John Brown Gordon writes:

In the city of Knoxville, Tennessee, there occurred an incident equally honorable to the sentiment and spirit of Confederate and Federal. During a recent visit to that city, a party representing both sides in that engagement accompanied me to the great fort [Sanders] *which General Longstreet's forces assailed but were unable to capture. These representatives of both armies united in giving me the details of the incident. The Southern troops had made a bold assault upon the fort. They succeeded in reaching it through a galling fire . . . Then in the deep ditch surrounding the fortress and at its immediate base, the Confederates took their position. They were, in a measure, protected from the Union fire; but they could neither climb into the fort nor retreat, except at great sacrifice of life. The sun poured its withering rays upon them and they were famishing with thirst. A bold and self-sacrificing young soldier offered to take his life in his hands and canteens on his back and attempt to bring water to his fainting comrades. He made the dash for life and for water, and was unhurt; but the return—how was that to be accomplished? Laden with the filled and heavy canteens, he approached within range of the rifles in the fort and looked anxiously across the intervening space. He was fully alive to the fact that the chances were all against him; but, determined to relieve his suffering comrades or die in the effort, he started on his perilous run for the ditch at the fort. The brave Union soldiers stood upon the parapet with their rifles in hand. As they saw this daring American youth coming, with his life easily at their disposal, they stood silently contemplating him for a moment. Then, realizing the situation, they fired at him a tremendous volley—not of deadly bullets from their guns, but of enthusiastic shouts from their throats. If the annals of war record any incident between hostile armies which embodies a more beautiful and touching tribute by the brave to the brave, I have never seen it.*[111]

> And if anyone gives even a cup of cold water to one of these little ones because he is my disciple, I tell you the truth, he will certainly not lose his reward.
> —MATTHEW 10:42

The Absence of Initiative

M ASTER USED to say that if we didn't suit him he would put us in his pocket quick meaning that he would sell us."—Former slave William Johnson

For the 39 million African American slaves counted in the census of 1860, life was brutal. Each day promised ceaseless toil, threats, or punishment, and the looming, nightmarish possibility of being sold away from beloved family members and friends. Even those slaves who accepted their situation without complaint, who had kind owners, or who were given lighter work duties suffered from the absence of self-determination, the possibility of freely choosing the course of their own lives.[112]

The blight of slavery is a sad chapter in our history, and America has paid for this sin in many ways. Yet the toil, punishment, and separation the slaves experienced can be likened to sin's perils. A friend of mine, Pastor Randy Ray, drew this analogy in his famous quote on the Prodigal Son: "Sin

> So if the Son sets you free, you will be free indeed.
> —JOHN 8:36

will take you farther than you want to go, keep you longer than you want to stay, and cost you more than you will ever want to pay."

Working as a correctional officer in Indiana State Prison, I soon learned that a person can be imprisoned on the outside and be free on the inside if he has Christ dwelling in his heart. On the other hand, people can be free on the outside and enslaved on the inside. According to converted inmates in the Indiana State Prison, imprisonment on the inside is the worst form of imprisonment.

When Jesus sets sinners free, they are free indeed!

The Most Important Victory

THE CIVIL WAR brought a dilemma to the preachers of both North and South. Unlike other wars, this war pitted American against American. Pastors found it difficult to know God's mind in such a terrible time in our nation's history. Pastor Joseph Atkinson spoke to the real heart of the matter in his sermon preached on September 18, 1862.

> *Never were Christians called to more diligence, self-denial, courage, benevolence and industry than at this solemn juncture; and it is, at such a time as this, that God and all good men are most fruitfully active. In a contest like this every man must serve his country according to his several ability and in his appointed sphere. Every man must find the place and the duty suited to him, and to which he is suited. None can be more important than practical prayerful labor for the religious welfare of our heroic soldiers; directly seeking their salvation by preaching to them—by writing and distributing Tracts and Hymns and Bibles—by praying for them—and by tender sympathy with them in the trials and temptations to which they must be inevitably exposed. If God should breathe over these Confederate States the spirit of devotion, of humility, of dependence and of faith, it would be better than any victory in the field, however brilliant—for it would be at once a proof of His favour and a pledge of our prosperity.*[113]

> But Samuel replied: "Does the LORD delight in burnt offerings and sacrifices as much as in obeying the voice of the LORD? To obey is better than sacrifice, and to heed is better than the fat of rams."
> —1 SAMUEL 15:22

Even though the South lost the Civil War, it gained much in the spiritual realm. Confederate men and women learned more of devotion, humility, and dependence on God.

When we go through battles in life, we will not win every time, but we can gain much spiritually if we are willing to learn from our defeat.

A Baby on a Battlefield

DURING A BATTLE at Hatchie while the conflict was at its peak, soldiers found a blue-eyed baby hugging close to the cold ground with tears on his cheek. The following is an eyewitness account:

> Unalarmed 'mid the awful confusion of that fearful battle, with the missiles of death flying thick about it and crowding close upon its young existence, yet unhurt, it seemed a wonderful verification of the Divine declaration: "Out of the mouths of babes and sucklings I will ordain wisdom." That little "child of war," as it lay in its miraculous safety, seemed to say to me these words of profound instruction: "My helplessness and innocence appealed to God, and he preserved me in the midst of this wrecking carnage. If you will make your plaint to heaven, God will preserve your poor bleeding country."[114]

The soldiers adopted this baby as part of their regiment. In the days ahead a panic-stricken mother came looking for her child. The soldiers were thrilled to place this beautiful baby back into the arms of his weeping mother.

This baby on the battlefield illustrates how God's children are resting securely in his arms. Our Lord often used the faith of little children to picture how we must act and react as children of the kingdom. When fiery missiles come from our enemy Satan, we can be certain that the Lord will protect us with his mighty hand and deliver us safely to our home in heaven.

> From the lips of children and infants you have ordained praise because of your enemies, to silence the foe and the avenger.
> —PSALM 8:2

Jackson's Hatred of War

ON APRIL 17, 1860, a few weeks before Virginia seceded from the Union, a peace conference was held in Washington, D.C., to try to avoid war. Stonewall Jackson was heard to say:

> *"If the general government should persist in the measures now threatened, there must be war. It is painful to discover with what unconcern they speak of war, and threaten it. They do not know its horrors. I have seen enough of it to make me look upon it as the sum of all evils."*
> [His wife Mary Anna writes] *(However it may surprise those who knew him only as a soldier, yet it is true that I never heard any man express such utter abhorrence of war. I shall never forget how he once exclaimed to me, with all the intensity of his nature, "Oh, how I do deprecate war!")*

> "So Peter was kept in prison, but the church was earnestly praying to God for him."
> —ACTS 12:5

Jackson went on to say:

> *"Should the step be taken which is now threatened, we shall have no other alternative; we must fight. But do you not think that all the Christian people of the land could be induced to unite in a concert of prayer to avert so great an evil? It seems to me that if they would thus unite in prayer, war might be prevented and peace preserved."* [His wife Mary concluded] . . . *In his public prayers after this, his most fervent petition was that God would preserve the whole land from the evils of war.*[115]

It's interesting that the great warrior, Stonewall Jackson, hated war so much. He took no pleasure in the prospect of war, but he was willing to do his duty if called upon to defend his cherished state of Virginia.

Jackson's faith in the power of prayer was his first answer to war's inevitable horrors. He believed that if all Christians would unite in prayer, war could be avoided. Jackson describes this united effort as "a concert of prayer." There is power in the united effort of praying people.

A Parson with Convictions

R EV. JOHN H. AUGHEY, a Presbyterian pastor and Unionist who lived in the South, was tried for treason and put into prison for his views on slavery. The following is a conversation between Rev. Aughey and his interrogators at his trial:

"Parson Aughey, you have been reported to us as holding abolition sentiments, and as being disloyal to the Confederate States." . . . *"Proceed, then, with the trial, in your own way." "We propose to ask you a few questions, and in your answers you may defend yourself, or admit your guilt. In the first place, did you ever say that you did not believe that God ordained the institution of slavery?" "I believe that God did not ordain the institution of slavery." "Did not God command the Israelites to buy slaves from the Canaanitish nations, and to hold them as their property for ever?" "The Canaanites had filled their cup of iniquity to overflowing, and God commanded the Israelites to exterminate them; this, in violation of God's command, they failed to do. God afterwards permitted the Hebrews to reduce them to a state of servitude . . ."*

"Did you say that you were opposed to the slavery which existed in the time of Christ?" "I did, because the system of slavery prevailing in Christ's day was cruel in the extreme; it conferred the power of life and death upon the master, and was attended with innumerable evils . . . "You have Wesley's writings, and Wesley says that 'Human slavery is the sum of all villainy.'" . . .

"Parson Aughey, are you in favor of the South?" "I am in favor of the South, and have always endeavored to promote the best interests of the South. However, I never deemed it for the best interests of the South to secede. I talked against secession, and voted against secession, because I thought that the best interests of the South would be put in jeopardy by the secession of the Southern States. I was honest in my convictions and acted accordingly. Could the sacrifice of my life have stayed the swelling tide of secession, it would gladly have been made."[116]

> "But none of these things move me, neither count I my life dear unto myself, so that I might finish my course with joy, and the ministry."
> —ACTS 20:24 (KJV)

Lincoln Saw the Dawn

DR. PHINEAS D. GURLEY was pastor of the New York Avenue Presbyterian Church where Abraham Lincoln attended while president. Gurley preached the funeral sermon in the East Room of the White House. This excerpt reveals how he viewed President Lincoln's position in history:

Washington, D.C.
April 19, 1865

He is dead; but the God in whom he trusted lives, and He can guide and strengthen his successor, as He guided and strengthened him. He is dead; but the memory of his virtues, of his wise and patriotic counsels and labors, of his calm and steady faith in God lives, is precious, and will be a power for good in the country quite down to the end of time . . . The light of its brightening prospects flashes cheeringly to-day athwart the gloom occasioned by his death, and the language of God's united providences is telling us that, though the friends of Liberty die, Liberty itself is immortal. There is no assassin strong enough and no weapon deadly enough to quench its inextinguishable life . . . Though our beloved President is slain, our beloved country is saved. And so we sing of mercy as well as of judgment. Tears of gratitude mingle with those of sorrow. While there is darkness, there is also the dawning of a brighter, happier day upon our stricken and weary land. God be praised that our fallen Chief lived long enough to see the day dawn and the daystar of joy and peace arise upon the nation . . .[117]

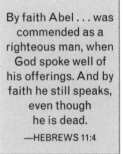

By faith Abel . . . was commended as a righteous man, when God spoke well of his offerings. And by faith he still speaks, even though he is dead.
—HEBREWS 11:4

The life and legacy of Abraham Lincoln still affects us. Over 140 years later, his words shed light on our past and hope for our future. It is amazing what God can do with one solitary life committed to him.

Clasping Our Loved Ones
in a Long Embrace

C. E. MERRILL, a writer for the *Nashville World* newspaper, wrote in 1884:

I look back across the tide of twenty fateful years, recalling the then light heart and thoughtless words of youthful ardor as we moved into the fight. I see now through a mist of unbidden tears the returning brave, who, in the face of that leaden doom, with dauntless tread passed "over the perilous edge of battle to the harvest home of death", swept in the twinkling of an eye from our sight forever into the shoreless gulf.

I wonder now, as I sit here and recall that terrible day, how could we have been so thoughtless and unconcerned. As we formed in line to move upon the foe, youthful eyes flashed fire and downy cheeks glowed with the rapture of the coming fight.

Ah, as we looked upon our loved ones then for the last time, as brave John Weller says, "knowing that death lurked just over the hill, why did we not clasp one another in a long embrace?"[118]

In our busy lives, we seldom take time to love and appreciate one another. When my father came home from the hospital after a diagnosis of terminal cancer, his greatest treasures were his love for Christ and his family. A steady stream of relatives and friends came to say good-bye. Laughter and chatter filled the house as he remembered the "good old days." Thankfully, my father had no regrets when he passed from this life to his eternal home. Knowing that he would soon be meeting the Lord, he wisely illustrated Merrill's philosophy and spent his last days clasping his loved ones in a long embrace.

> Let no debt remain outstanding, except the continuing debt to love one another, for he who loves his fellowman has fulfilled the law.
> —ROMANS 13:8

Life Is but a Vapor

THOMAS "STONEWALL" JACKSON was awakened one Sunday morning with orders to bring his Virginia Military Institute cadets immediately to Richmond, Virginia. While he prepared for such a journey, he asked his pastor, Dr. White, to come and pray with him before his departure. Jackson's wife Anna told what her husband did next:

> *Then, in the privacy of our chamber, he took his Bible and read that beautiful chapter in Corinthians beginning with the sublime hope of the resurrection—"For we know that if our earthly house of this tabernacle be dissolved, we have a building of God, a house not made with hands, eternal in the heavens;" and then kneeling down, he committed himself and her whom he loved to the protecting care of his Father in heaven. Never was a prayer more fervent, tender, and touching. His voice was so choked with emotion that he could scarcely utter the words, and one of his most earnest petitions was that "If consistent with His will, God would still avert the threatening danger and grant us peace!" . . . Ah! How the light went out of his home when he departed from it on that beautiful spring day! But in painful separation it was well for us that we could not know that this was the final breaking-up of our happy home, and that his footstep was never again to cross its threshold! . . . It was well that I could not foresee the future. It was in mercy that He who knew the end from the beginning did not lift the veil.*[119]

> Yet you do not know what your life will be like tomorrow. You are just a vapor that appears for a little while and then vanishes away.
> —JAMES 4:14

Little did Jackson know, when he walked out his door to go to war, that he would never return. The Bible tells us that our lives on this earth are temporary. Sometimes we take life too much for granted. Even though we may not be going to war like Jackson, we still do not have the promise of living another day. How will you spend your final days?

A Cowardly Chaplain

A LTHOUGH MOST CHAPLAINS of the Civil War were brave, a few disgraced the office by their cowardice and unconcern for the men. James Robertson, in his book, *The Blue and the Gray*, quoted from a story about a cowardly chaplain.

We got into a little row with the Yankees a few days ago and our parson, deeming, no doubt, that discretion was the better part of valor, took to his heels when the shells commenced flying and I have not seen him since. A New England officer who had witnessed the same misbehavior insisted that "undue susceptibility to cannon fever were ample grounds for the disqualification of a chaplain."[120]

Leaders of the church must demonstrate their faith by godly actions. Undoubtedly, the chaplain mentioned in Robertson's book was big on talk but little on the right actions.

Cowardly Peter denied Jesus around the enemy's campfire out of fear for his life. Later, he repented of his denials, and the Lord restored him to the ministry. The grace of the Lord made Peter a greater man of God than he could have ever hoped to be. As humans, we all fail and slip up in the area of leadership. When we are willing to repent of those mistakes, the Lord promises restoration and reconciliation.

Peter sat down with them. A servant girl saw him seated there in the firelight. She looked closely at him and said, "This man was with him." But he denied it. "Woman, I don't know him," he said. A little later someone else saw him and said, "You also are one of them." "Man, I am not!" Peter replied. About an hour later another asserted, "Certainly this fellow was with him, for he is a Galilean." Peter replied, "Man, I don't know what you're talking about!"

—LUKE 22:54–60

The Arm of Flesh Will Fail You

PASTOR E. P. POWELL said in a sermon on April 23, 1865, following the death of President Abraham Lincoln,

The work to be done was to watch the foul fiend of slavery in its death struggle; to hold the helm of State in a most terrible Civil War; to proclaim liberty to the captive; to enshrine himself in the hearts of his people next to Washington; and after a laborious, saddening administration in the hour of victory, also to die for his people and his country . . . He was battered by Providence into a nobler and deeper character . . . and above all, he learned that his only hope was in God. What could be our consolation if we should not feel that we should meet our dear President among the saved of Jesus? Sweet to us are those treasured words of his, "I love Jesus" . . . Oh how much we thank God, that in the hour of trial . . . and with the almost visible care and presence of God, he led us through the darkest hours, full up to the dawn of peace, with all the love of the nation centered in him, and then in the very hour of triumph, when we thought him for the first time safe . . . the horrible deed was done. May we never suffer again what we suffered one week ago. The word flew on the telegraph wire, "The President is shot" . . . But who could gain by it? We needed it to rely on God and not on the arm of the flesh.[121]

> Our God, won't you please judge them? We don't have the power to face this huge army that's attacking us. We don't know what to do. But we're looking to you to help us.
>
> —2 CHRONICLES 20:12

Far too often we rely on visible securities of this world rather than on God. Powell presented an important point to ponder: did the Lord allow Lincoln to die immediately following the Civil War so that we as a nation would not lean on him?

Is there anything in your life that is preventing you from depending on the Lord?

Does God Answer Prayer?

URING THE CIVIL WAR Mary Bethell missed her children and wrote:

This is a trying time for me, I have not heard from my daughter, Mrs.
Williamson, in six weeks I expect she is confined in childbed. I feel very
anxious to hear from her. . . . I am cast down and sorrowful, I cannot
hear from my dear children, but my hope and trust is in the Lord. I
find some relief in prayer, and reading my precious bible. I will try and
be patient and resigned. I believe that God will hear my prayers. . . .

We have received a long letter from our daughter. Mr. Williamson
wrote that our daughter was confined on the 14th of April, had given
birth to a son, and was doing tolerable well . . . I feel so thankful to
God for blessing my dear daughter. I had faith to believe she would do
well, the Lord heard and answered my prayer, glory and honor to his
name. I will praise him with joyful lips, if I had a thousand souls I
would give them all to God . . . "I called upon him in the day of trou-
ble, and he delivered me, now I will glorify his name."[122]

A dedicated mother can be sound asleep in
the deepest rhythms of the sleep cycle, but when
her baby cries, she can be at the crib in a single
bound. In a similar way, our God hears the slightest cries of his children and will answer prayer
whenever we call to him. David knew from experience that every time he had a problem, the Lord
stood ready to help.

Our God never slumbers or sleeps.

> In the day of my
> trouble I will call to
> you, for you will
> answer me.
> —PSALM 86:7

Committing Our Loved Ones to the Lord's Care

STONEWALL JACKSON had a special relationship with his wife Anna. The mighty Jackson must have felt helpless to care for his wife while consumed in the cause of the South. Yet, he did not rely on human ability; he relied on the power of God to take care of his beloved Anna. Jackson wrote the following to his wife:

> *April 25th, 1857,*
>
> *It is a great comfort to me to know that although I am not with you, yet you're in the hands of one who will not permit any evil to come nigh you. What a consoling thought it is to know that we may, with perfect confidence, commit all our friends in Jesus to the care of our Heavenly Father, with an assurance that all will be well with them! . . .*[123]

> Cast all your anxiety on him because he cares for you.
> —1 PETER 5:7

When I was young, every Saturday or Sunday afternoon in the fall we played football in our neighbor's long, flat yard. One day a huge storm moved to our area; I noticed hundreds of sparrows flying to a huge cedar. They happily chirped inside, feeling secure from the coming elements.

God, who is so interested in the intricate details of this universe, is just as mindful of us. In times of distress, we can run to him in prayer, and he will secure us from the coming storms.

GENERAL ULYSSES S. GRANT
The Library of Congress

Grant's Theology

IN AN INTERVIEW with Ulysses S. Grant, Dr. M. J. Cramer asked the general if he prayed to God for success in battle. Cramer said of his interview with Grant:

> To my question whether he ever prayed to God for assistance and success he replied that he often prayed to God mentally, but briefly, for strength and wisdom to enable him to carry to a successful termination the task expected of him. He further said that, like his mother, he never talked much about religion, but thought much on this all-important subject; that he believed in an overruling Providence; that the destiny of individuals and of nations is in God's hands; and that, while man has freedom of will and action, God overrules men's actions for the good of mankind. He further said that he could not see how anyone, in view of the history of the world, could be an atheist . . .[124]

Grant's statements are powerful since history does not often cite Grant as having faith in God as did Jackson and Lee. But apparently leadership in both the North and South shared the same view of the overruling providence of God.

> For it is God who works in you to will and to act according to his good purpose.
>
> —PHILIPPIANS 2:13

Grant showed great insight into theological understanding in his statement "man has freedom of will and action." God has granted the freedom of choice, yet he still reserves the right to intervene in matters that pertain to his ultimate will for nations and individual lives. God shapes our destinies, for he knows our end even before our beginning. He knows what is best for us. If we understand this, we will be far less anxious when unexpected tragedies and emergencies come our way.

Ultimately, these truths will lead a believer to find complete rest in the security of a God who can overrule in any situation.

Lincoln's Favorite Poem

ABRAHAM LINCOLN said of the following poem:

I would give all I am worth, and go into debt, to be able to write so fine a piece as I think that is. . . .[125]

Lincoln memorized the entire poem and recited it so often that some folks mistakenly thought he was the author. The poem's melancholy tone appealed to Lincoln and is here in edited form for brevity:

> I have seen all the things that are done under the sun; all of them are meaningless, a chasing after the wind.
>
> —ECCLESIASTES 1:14

Mortality
Oh, why should the spirit of mortal be proud?
Like a swift-fleeting meteor, a fast-flying cloud,
A flash of the lightning, a break of the wave,
He passes from life to his rest in the grave.
The leaves of the oak and the willow shall fade,
Be scattered around, and together be laid;
And the young and the old, the low and the high,
Shall molder to dust, and together shall lie.
. . . The eye of the sage, and the heart of the brave,
Are hidden and lost in the depths of the grave . . .
For we are the same that our fathers have been;
We see the same sights that our fathers have seen;
. . . To the life we are clinging, they also would cling—
But it speeds from us all like a bird on the wing.
. . . Yea, hope and despondency, pleasure and pain,
Are mingled together in sunshine and rain;
'Tis the wink of an eye 'tis the draught of a breath—
From the blossom of health to the paleness of death,
From the gilded saloon to the bier and the shroud
Oh, why should the spirit of mortal be proud?

—Author Unknown[126]

The Genius of Lincoln

AUTHOR THOMAS ASHBY describes Abraham Lincoln as follows:

> *Mr. Lincoln was a giant in height, with a frame as rugged as it was homely and striking in manner and personality . . . Lincoln was not a man of scholarly education, of wide learning, or of great oratorical power, yet he had the genius of common sense, the faculty of saying and doing the right thing at the right time. His knowledge of men, his clear views of the political situation, his powers of leadership were phenomenal. His clear, concise, and patriotic oration at Gettysburg placed him in the front rank of the world's great orators. Neither Demosthenes nor Cicero, Burke nor Sheridan, Webster nor Clay ever touched the hearts of nations as did Mr. Lincoln by his great classic.*[127]

For a man who has gone down in history as one of the greatest presidents of the United States, Abraham Lincoln did not have the qualifications of genius. He had no formal education. He was not attractive in his appearance nor striking in his personality or mannerisms. Neither did Lincoln have oratorical training, yet, he had the God-given ability of impeccable timing, and practical, everyday good sense.

> But God chose the foolish things of the world to shame the wise; God chose the weak things of the world to shame the strong.
> —1 CORINTHIANS 1:27

Even though Lincoln did not have oratorical training, his Gettysburg Address went down in history as one of the greatest speeches of all time. How do we account for such genius in a common man? We can make only one conclusion: Lincoln depended on God, and the Lord used his weaknesses to show the world that a person touched by God can be used in extraordinary ways.

Our disabilities can become great abilities if we will yield ourselves completely to God.

Antietam, Md., Allan Pinkerton, President Lincoln,
and Maj. Gen. John A. McClernand
The Library of Congress

A Wake-Up Call to Duty

J. P. CROWDER, a Confederate soldier, was reminded of his own mortality when he received the news that General Stonewall Jackson had died in battle. He wrote the following letter to his mother:

> *Mother, I have heard a good sermon preached this morning by a good preacher I think or at least I have heard several sermons preached since I have been at the hospital . . . Jackson is dead, though I do expect you will hear of it long before you get this letter. Though you will doubt it, he was wounded by his own men . . . It was not his wound that killed him. His death was caused by the attacks of pneumonia . . .*[128]

Stonewall Jackson's death came as a wake-up call to many Confederate soldiers who revered him as almost immortal. It is said that Jackson earned his nickname by standing solid like a "stone wall" in the face of enemy fire. When he was wounded by friendly fire, the Confederate soldier mentioned above came face-to-face with his own mortality. For the young soldier, a good sermon was the right medicine.

> My days are swifter than a weaver's shuttle . . . Remember, O God, that my life is but a breath.
>
> —JOB 7:6, 7

Near-death escapes serve a definite purpose in God's plans. They shake us to our senses and help us to realize that our purpose is to serve the Captain of our faith. Life at best is temporary. We need to serve our God like there will be no tomorrow.

A Dying Soldier Kisses His Bible

WILLIAM W. CRUMLEY was a chaplain in the Georgia hospitals during the Civil War. Crumley was given a Bible belonging to a soldier who died at the hospital from battle wounds. His mother had written in the front: "A present to my dear son, on his fifteenth birthday." Crumley wrote the following recollections of the young man's experience:

His first night in camp was trying one, surrounded, as he was, by many that were thoughtless and gay, as if they were merely on a holiday campaign; but Albert was more serious and felt that he must maintain his religious character, and that to begin right was of great importance in his new position.—By the camp fire he read a chapter in his Bible and knelt on the ground and prayed . . . he entered the Sharpsburg fight . . . he was struck by a ball and carried back to the rear a wounded man; from profuse hemorrhage, a sick, dreamy sensation stole over him; the light faded from his eyes . . . As soon as he was sufficiently restored, he drew from his pocket his neglected Bible, kissing it many times over, and bathing it in tears . . . His bloody fingers searched out the old-cherished promises of God, leaving many a gory stain on the blessed pages of inspiration . . . a new life was infused into his soul, which enabled him to bear his sufferings with true Christian heroism . . . Reduced by a secondary hemorrhage and amputation, Albert, with a calm, steady faith, came down to the cold waters of Jordan, where he lingered for a short time, and dictated a letter to his mother, which, I wrote for him, in which he gave an appropriate word to each one of the family, . . . Then, in a low, sweet voice, he repeated: Give joy or grief.

> Then he said to me, "Son of man, eat this scroll I am giving you and fill your stomach with it." So I ate it, and it tasted as sweet as honey in my mouth.
> —EZEKIEL 3:3

> *Take life or friends away, so I but find them all again, in that eternal day.*[129]

The Bible was so precious to the young soldier that he kissed it. Ezekiel discovered that the Word of God tasted like honey. Reading the Bible can sweeten your life and change you from the inside out.

Breaking the Chords of This Life

THE FOLLOWING poem was copied by Meta Morris Grimbal from a graduation ceremony at Charleston College sometime between 1860–1866. The poem was written and quoted by a Rev. Miles who gave the graduation address:

Fair faces beaming round the household hearth,
Young joyous tones in Melody of Mirth.
The sire doubly living in his boy,
And she, the Crown of all that wealth of joy;
These make the home like some sweet lyre given
To sound on earth, the harmonies of Heaven.
A sudden discord breaks the swelling strain,
One chord has snapped; the harmony again
Subdued & slower moves, but never more
Can pour the same glad music as of yore;
Less & less full the strains successive wake.
Chord after chord must break—and break—and break
Until on earth the lyre dumb
Finds all its chords restrung to loftier notes in heaven.[130]

Over time the Lord weans us from attachments to this life and gives us a longing for heaven. In youth we see our lives full and our futures bright, but as trials come, chord after chord is broken until we look forward to the glories of heaven.

> I know that my Redeemer lives, and that in the end he will stand upon the earth. And after my skin has been destroyed, yet in my flesh I will see God; I myself will see him with my own eyes— I, and not another. How my heart yearns within me!
> —JOB 19:25, 26

Pardoned by the President

PRESIDENT LINCOLN was a kind president with a heart full of mercy and compassion toward others, especially when he felt the cause was just. One Union soldier became the recipient of Lincoln's mercy near Washington, D.C., during the Civil War:

> *A private was court-martialed for sleeping on his post out near Chain Bridge on the Upper Potomac . . . his sentence was death . . . he did not beg for pardon, but was willing to meet his fate . . . the case reached the ears of the President; he resolved to save him; he signed a pardon and sent it out; the day came. "Suppose," thought the President, "my pardon has not reached him." . . .*
>
> *The telegraph was called into requisition; an answer did not come promptly. "Bring up the carriage," he ordered . . . through the hot broiling sun and dusty roads he rode to the camp, about ten miles, and saw that the soldier was saved! He doubtless forgot the incident, but the soldier did not.*[131]

> But God demonstrates his own love for us in this: While we were still sinners, Christ died for us.
> —ROMANS 5:8

President Lincoln wanted to be sure that the soldier who was condemned was pardoned. He went out of his way to find the soldier and show him mercy. In a similar sense, Jesus left the glories of heaven to come to earth to personally give us his pardon. May we never forget what Jesus has done for us.

God Honors a Mother's Prayers

NO CHILD can ever escape the prayers of a godly mother. One young soldier attributed his salvation to his mother's persistent prayers. Author Gordon Leidner said:

> *Soldiers often talked of their mothers. During one prayer meeting, a young soldier cried aloud, "O that my mother was here!" When asked why he wanted to see his mother, he replied, "Because she has so long been praying for me, and now I have found the Saviour." Another wounded Christian soldier asked a friend to "Tell my mother that I read my Testament and put all my trust in the Lord . . . I am not afraid to die."[132]*

We often say that the apostle Paul mentored Timothy in the ministry. But Paul recognized that Timothy's mother and grandmother had an even greater influence. Paul was simply influential in helping Timothy become stronger in his faith.

Paul recognized that Timothy was not a novice in the faith. The young man demonstrated his maturity in heeding Paul's wisdom and Paul loved him as his own son in the faith. Timothy would not have had an opportunity to serve with the greatest apostle of the New Testament had it not been for the godly, faithful prayers of his mother Eunice and grandmother Lois.

> I have been reminded of your sincere faith, which first lived in your grandmother Lois and in your mother Eunice and, I am persuaded, now lives in you also.
>
> —2 TIMOTHY 1:5

As parents we're usually anxious in the raising of our children, wondering if they will grow to become strong Christians and responsible citizens. We can take the guesswork out of childrearing if we will pray for them and teach them God's commandments.

The Influence of a Godly Mother

THE FOLLOWING account of a dying soldier was written by nurse Hannah Ropes to her mother from the Union hospital in Washington, D.C.:

September 18, 1862

My Dear Mother,

> Her children rise up and bless her.
> —PROVERBS 31:28

The young man who was shot through the lungs, to our surprise and, as the surgeons say, contrary to all "science" lived till last night, or rather this morning. We considered him the greatest sufferer in the house, as every breath was a pang. I laid down last night and got asleep, when I was roused by hearing him cry, very loud, "Mother! Mother! Mother!" I was out of bed and into my dressing gown very quickly, and by his side. The pressure of blood from the unequal circulation had affected the brain slightly, and, as they all are, he was on the battlefield, struggling to get away from the enemy. I promised him, that nobody should touch him, and that in a few moments he would be free from all pain. He believed me and, fixing his beautiful eyes upon my face, he never turned them away; resistance, the resistance of a strong natural will, yielded; his breathing grew more gentle, ending softly as an infant's. He was a brave soldier and a truthful boy.[133]

Who can put a price on the virtues and influence of a godly Christian mother? The average age of a Civil War soldier was twenty-two. Many of these young lads knew little of the perils of war. For an adventurous young man, the lure of heroism and adventure awakened a desire to "join up." Many, like the young man under nurse Hannah's care, had never traveled far from home. Yet in their moments of suffering and near-death experiences, young men cried out like desperate children for the comfort of their godly mothers.

My first cousin, Dr. William J. Tuley, helped my wife deliver our firstborn son Jonathan. Jonathan has grown into a fine Christian young man and has a close relationship with his mother. This kind of love has power to sustain a son through life's many battles.

God's Grace in Our Trial

MARY BETHELL depended on God's grace to see her through many trials. Mary could always thank and praise the Lord for something God was doing in her life. She did not quibble over the things she lacked; rather she praised God for his blessings during hard times.

May 9, 1864

Went to Union a few days ago to hear our dear Minister, brother Gannon, he is an able preacher. Oh how it grieves me that I cannot hear him, I am so deaf in one ear. I am the child of affliction. I have lately passed through a fiery trial, it was my constant prayer that God would give me grace to bear with meekness and patience all that he might see fit for me. I have been greatly tempted and cast down for many days, but 'tis all for the best. My Saviour designs to make me holy I give myself into his gracious hands, and pray that I may be able to do his blessed will.

I was 43 years old last Sunday, the Lord has spared my life, I hope for some good. Goodness and mercy have followed me all the days of my life, though I have had some fiery trials, and passed through deep waters, yet I have always found God's grace sufficient for every extremity, he has always been with me, and comforted me in all my trials. I will praise him for his wonderful goodness to me, who am so unworthy. I was greatly blessed in my childhood, for I had a good pious Father who led me in the way to Heaven. I had the advantage of a good Christian education, eternity will show the great blessing of pious parents.

I was converted and joined the church when I was 16 years old. I have grown in grace, God has given me strong faith, he has answered my prayers. I thank and praise him. Hallelujah for the Lord will reign "til all enemies are put under his feet."[134]

> Rejoice in the Lord always. I will say it again: Rejoice!
> —PHILIPPIANS 4:4

Paul praised God even though he was imprisoned for his faith. He had plenty to complain about, but he realized God's grace could sustain him through the worst circumstances. So rather than worry, he just praised! We can rejoice in circumstances on the outside if we have joy on the inside.

Lee's Self-Denial

GENERAL ROBERT E. LEE demonstrated good leadership with his self-control. Humanity taught Lee that he must expect others to fail, but as a Christian and a gentleman Lee expected even more of himself. Lee said, "I cannot consent to place in the control of others one who cannot control himself."

Lee gave advice to a lady in the care of her infant son and said, "Teach him to deny himself."[135] Douglass Freeman, Lee's biographer, said, "Had his life been epitomized in one sentence of the book he read so often, it would have been in the words, 'If any man will come after me, let him deny himself and take up his cross daily and follow me' " (Matt. 16:24)[136]

We live in a very selfish world. A preacher friend of mine once said, "The church has become so worldly and the world has become so churchy that one cannot tell the difference in our day." It is said that Lee's men were in constant awe of his self-control in the heat of battle. In our need for revival in a postmodern world, we need a renewal of self-denial and self-discipline. Jesus took up a cross and suffered humility and shame for our sakes. His sacrifice was one of self-denial and self-discipline. We are called to be "imitators" of Christ. When we deny ourselves to meet the needs of others, we become more like Jesus.

> 'If any man will come after me, let him deny himself and take up his cross daily and follow me' "
> —MATTHEW 16:24

Robert E. Lee's Opinion

WEBSITE AUTHOR Phil Melar shared an insightful look into Lee's opinion of those who criticized him.

General Robert E. Lee was asked what he thought of a fellow officer in the Confederate Army who had made some derogatory remarks about him. Lee rated him as being very satisfactory. The person who asked the question seemed perplexed. "General," he said, "I guess you don't know what he's been saying about you." "I know," answered Lee. "But I was asked my opinion of him, not his opinion of me!"[137]

As a Christian gentleman, Lee would not allow himself to return criticism toward those who criticized him. The spirit, discipline, and attitude Lee displayed are found in Matthew 5:44. Jesus taught us to love our enemies. When we do so, we exemplify Jesus' sacrifice on the cross. He loved those who hated him and forgave those who persecuted him.

> "But I tell you: Love your enemies and pray for those who persecute you."
> —MATTHEW 5:44

I tested this verse once when I was a young man. While I was working for the city of Boonville, Indiana, I was approached by a man who cursed me with extreme foul language. I had just read Matthew 5:44. So instead of getting angry at the man, I bought him a soft drink. Looking at me with a puzzled look in his eyes, he thanked me, and walked off mumbling. I never heard him curse in my presence again, and after that day I seemed to have his friendship and respect.

God's Word has been tried and proven. Using this godly principle of Scripture is our best weapon against those who criticize us.

Lee Identifies with His Men

URING THE COLD WINTER of December 1862, provisions had been denied Robert E. Lee's armies so long that many were barefooted. He wrote a letter to the proper authorities but got no results. As commanding general, Lee could occupy a comfortable house along with his commanders, but he chose to identify with the hardships of his men. The following account by author James McCabe gives evidence of Lee's self-denial:

> *The winter was intensely cold, and as early as the middle of December several of the Federal pickets were frozen to death. The Confederate troops suffered severely They were badly clothed and poorly provided for the winter . . . General Lee fared little better than his men. Later in the winter he steadily refused to establish his headquarters in a house and throughout the entire campaign, from Richmond to Fredericksburg, his quarters were in the field, and many of his staff slept under tent-flies, only until the weather became too cold for them to do so. This was fully appreciated by the men who were resolved that their commander should hear no murmurs from them, since he generously shared their privations . . .*[138]

As the adopted son of Pharaoh's daughter, Moses could have enjoyed all the advantages and comforts Egypt had to offer. Instead he chose to suffer with the rest of the Hebrew people because he felt the responsibility of leadership. If Moses had not denied himself these pleasures, he would never have led them out of bondage.

General Lee knew this secret of leadership and denied himself comfortable quarters because he would not ask his men to do what he was not willing to do himself.

We cannot lead others until we first identify with them.

> By faith Moses . . . chose to be mistreated along with the people of God rather than to enjoy the pleasures of sin for a short time. He regarded disgrace for the sake of Christ as of greater value than the treasures of Egypt, because he was looking ahead to his reward.
> —HEBREWS 11:24–26

A Drummer Boy Writes Home

Felix Voltz
Dear Brths,

I take the pen in Hand to write you ounce more that I an thank God all well yet Hoping these few lines will reach you the same the reason I say ounce more is because We are all thinking of being Home in A few Days . . . I beg you to excuse me for not writing sooner. the reason was because we was on such hard camping and I was most all the way sick the Day we marched through Richmond it was so dreadful Hot that nobody hardly could stand it and I was sun struck and was taken to the hospital.

I will close my writing with sending my best Regards and love to you all in the Family tell Mother not weary herself about me because I am as healthy as ever I was and tell Father that I beg him to forgive me for being so Ugly and Headstrong tell him that I have found out what A home is and that there is nobody on this world like Father & Mother and A Home and tell him if God save my Health and lets me get Home Safe again that I will try and behave and mind my Parents better than I have.[139]

The story of the Union drummer boy, Felix Voltz, reminds us of the Prodigal Son, who after leaving home, realized how good he had it with his father. War has a way of helping boys grow into men. Many a young man went off to war with less than a realistic attitude of its horrors. Once they experienced the weather conditions in camp, the scarcity of food, and the sheer terror of men baptized in blood on the battlefield, their young hearts turned toward home. Such was the

> The son said to him, "Father, I have sinned against heaven and against you. I am no longer worthy to be called your son."
> —LUKE 15:21

case of Felix Voltz. He gained a new appreciation for his father and mother and thanked God for them and was sorry for his disobedience.

Is your home the kind of place to which a child would long to return?

"No Excellence without Great Labor"

JOSEPH SLAGG
(1839–1929)

U NION SOLDIER and Christian, Joseph Slagg wrote home to his cousin in Wisconsin to encourage her during the Civil War.

Dear Cousin Margret. I will take time to write a few lines to you hoping it will find you enjoying that great blessing health. You said in your letter to Joe that the Sunday school had commenced on the Prairie. I was very glad to hear that. I have fancied I have seen you about ten o'clock going upon the Prairie on Hank to school. I have heard you in imagination singing those good old hymns and wondered who your teachers were. I know you go has often has you can. I have spent many happy hours in old Chapel. Cousin, persist and persevere in so good a cause. There is no excellence without great labor. You have not had so a chance has some but their are better times coming. Cousin, keep up your spirits. While I am writing Joe is lying on my right Alex on my left they are laughing and joking with our comrades. The report is that we shall take up our winter here but I do not know whether it is true or not. I should like to receive a letter from you Margaret. I remain your affectionate Cousin,
Edward Slagg[140]

> Whatsoever thy hand findeth to do, do it with thy might
> —ECCLESIASTES 9:10 (KJV)

Slagg's statement, "There is no excellence without great labor," is true both for success in life and spiritual growth. Solomon labored for everything under the sun and found that living for material possessions was emptiness.

When Your Heart Bleeds

MARY BETHELL prayed with a broken heart for the conversion of her son Willy.

All day after my dear son Willy left my soul was overwhelmed with sorrow; my heart seemed almost to bleed. I prayed to God to comfort me, and he heard and answered, he did comfort me and give me faith to believe that he would bless my son, glory! and honor! and praise to his name forever! He is my refuge in the day of trouble, he is my best friend, I will love him and praise him as long as I live. I think of Willy every day, but I do not sorrow and grieve for him, because God comforts my heart, and has taken away sorrow from my heart. The Lord has said ask and ye shall receive. I do ask him to convert all of my children, and that his kingdom may come, his will be done on earth as it is in Heaven. I am looking for my dear George to come home, I do pray that God may bring him safely home to my arms.[141]

> Go, and say to Hezekiah, "Thus saith the LORD, the God of David thy father, I have heard thy prayer, I have seen thy tears: behold, I will add unto thy days fifteen years."
>
> —ISAIAH 13:5

Hezekiah had just received news to get his house in order for the Lord had told him, through the prophet, that he was to die shortly. Hezekiah began to weep and pray when he heard the bad news, and the Lord granted him fifteen more years.

Mary Bethell prayed that the Lord would save all her children. We do not know whether they were eventually converted, but we have no cause to doubt it. Mary knew how to get things from God. She poured out her heart until God heard and answered her prayers.

Let us not grow tired in praying. Determination in prayer brings positive results.

A Baby So Longed For

OCTAVIA
STEPHENS IN HER
LATE TEENS
*P. K. Younge
Library of
Florida History*

OCTAVIA STEPHENS, a young wife and mother, suffered much during the Civil War, yet she retained her faith in God.

Near Thomasville—March 15, 1864 With a sad heart I begin another journal. On Sunday, February 28, dear Mother was taken with a congestive chill. On Friday, Mar. 4, Davis came with the news of the death of my dear, dear husband. He was killed in battle near Jacksonville on the first of March. Mother grew worse and on Sunday, Mar. 6th, she was taken from us between 12 and 1 O'clock. She passed quietly away, (Typhoid pneumonia). At 7 p.m. I gave birth to a dear little boy, which although three or four weeks before the time, the Lord still spared to me. Mother was buried on the 7th and Rosa was taken with fever, but recovered after two days . . . I have named my baby Winston, the sweet name of that dear lost one, my husband, almost my life.

God grant that his son, whom he longed for, but was not spared to see, may be like him. I now begin as it were a new life and I pray that the Lord will give me strength to bear up under this great affliction and with His help and the example of those two dear ones now with Him I may be enabled to do my duty in this life and be prepared when the Lord calls me to meet them in that better world, where there will be no parting and no more sorrow.[142]

> These have come so that your faith—of greater worth than gold, which perishes even though refined by fire—may be proved genuine and may result in praise, glory and honor when Jesus Christ is revealed.
>
> —1 PETER 1:7

Thomas R. Fasulo made a touching observation. "We often think of the Civil War as having 622,000 soldiers killed in action dying of wounds or diseases. What we forget is that the casualties numbered in the tens of millions among civilians who suffered heartache."[143]

The Famous Letter
of Sullivan Ballou

IN JULY OF 1861, General Irvin McDowell led his Union army of 28,452 men from Manassas, Virginia, to Bull Run Creek to meet 21,000 Confederates under General Beauregard. Because of their inexperience the Union soldiers were stopped in their tracks by Stonewall Jackson's armies. Even though the Union army was defeated, Northern patriotism still soared. Thirty-two-year-old Major Sullivan Ballou of the Second Rhode Island Volunteers wrote to his wife concerning his faith in God and his love for her. His letter stands as one of the most famous letters written during the Civil War.

Washington, D.C.,
14 July 1861

The indications are very strong that we shall move in a few days—perhaps tomorrow. Lest I should not be able to write you again, I feel impelled to write lines that may fall under your eye when I shall be no more. . . .

> Then Paul answered, "What are you doing, weeping and breaking my heart? For I am ready . . . to die at Jerusalem for the name of the Lord Jesus."
> —ACTS 21:13

Not my will, but thine O God, be done. If it is necessary that I should fall on the battlefield for my country, I am ready . . . My dear wife . . .
I cannot describe to you my feelings on this calm summer night, when two thousand men are sleeping around me, many of them enjoying the last, perhaps, before that of death—and I, suspicious that death is creeping behind me with his fatal dart, am communing with God, my country and thee.
Sarah, my love for you is deathless, it seems to bind me to you with mighty cables that nothing but Omnipotence could break . . . The memories of the blissful moments I have spent with you come creeping over me, and I feel most gratified to God and to you that I have enjoyed them so long . . .[144]

One week after Ballou wrote this letter he died in battle at First Manassas. Sullivan Ballou and the apostle Paul were ready to meet the Lord. How about you?

Jackson's Principles of Leadership

GENERAL THOMAS "STONEWALL" JACKSON attended four years at West Point as an army cadet before the Civil War. While at West Point, Jackson began to develop his strong sense of Christian character as revealed in the pages of a private book that he kept for personal use. The rules, morals, manners, dress, choice of friends, and goals in life show the standards Jackson had for his own conduct and character.

1842–1846

> The fear of the LORD is the beginning of wisdom, and the knowledge of the Holy One is understanding.
>
> —PROVERBS 9:10

Through life let your principal object be the discharge of duty. Disregard public opinion to be at peace with all men. Sacrifice your life rather than your word. Endeavor to do well everything which you undertake. Never speak disrespectfully of any one without a cause. Spare no effort to suppress selfishness, unless that effort would entail sorrow. Let your conduct towards men have some uniformity . . . Speak but what may benefit others or yourself; avoid trifling conversation. Resolve to perform what you ought; perform without fail what you resolve . . . A man is known by the company he keeps. Be cautious in your selection. There is the danger of catching the habits of your associates . . . Seek those who are intelligent and virtuous; and if possible, those who are a little above you, especially in moral excellence.[145]

Jackson's Christian character, humility, and confidence were shaped through his fear of God and reading the Bible. His creation of maxims for himself was evidence of his daily walk with the Lord. Through the wisdom and knowledge of God, Jackson chose to live a holy life governed by the Word of God and the leadership of the Holy Spirit.

My grandfather was a farmer in southern Indiana. He used to say, "The Lord will provide the 'taters,' but you've got to dig them." If we are to acquire the characteristics that made Jackson great, then we must be willing to work for them.

A Prayer-Answering God

THE FOLLOWING is an example of the anxieties many women on the home front suffered while their husbands and sons fought in the Civil War. Yet, for strong Christian women like Mary Bethell, enduring meant clinging to the Lord in prayer.

May 9th
I have just heard of a terrible battle near Yorktown, our loss is 1200 in killed, wounded and missing. The enemy loss is great. I am in anxiety and suspense of mind about dear Willie, he was in the battle, his company suffered, was cut up. Oh my Heavenly Father, help to bear this great trial. I am so concerned about my dear boy, I do not know what his situation . . . Oh! this suspense of mind is so unpleasant, I never had such trials before in all my life, I pray for grace to bear it.

May 14th
I have heard from the battle at Williamsburg, my dear son was not hurt, he was sick in the hospital at Richmond during the battle, he has got better and gone to the army again. I thank God for preserving my child. I feel like praising him today for his goodness. I have received comfort from the Lord, I am cheerful again, the glory of God illuminates my soul, glory and honor to his name . . .

> But those who hope in the LORD will renew their strength. They will soar on wings like eagles; they will run and not grow weary, they will walk and not be faint.
> —ISAIAH 40:31

August 6th
My dear soldier boy Willie got home safe last night at 1 o'clock. I do thank and praise my God for bringing him home, he is in good health, looks well, while thousands of soldiers have died, some from disease, some by the enemy, my dear boy's life has been preserved by my Heavenly Father. Glory! and Honor! and praise, and might be ascribed unto Jesus Christ.[146]

As Christians, our hope should always be in the Lord. Then we will not grow weary or faint in tough times.

A Revival on Ship

T HE FOLLOWING occurred on board the steamer, *Canada*, during the Civil War. Union soldiers sailed on her passage from Dubuque to St. Louis. While on board, a prayer meeting turned into a refreshing experience through the godly prayers of young soldiers and an elderly gentleman.

> *In the evening while many of the passengers were engaged in conversation, others whiling away their times . . . a young man seated himself at one of the tables, and engaged in reading his Bible. Another, and still another took their places around this temporary altar, until nearly all of that little band of soldiers, numbering about twenty, were reading the Scriptures. An aged man took his station in their midst. He had a pious and venerable air, for his hoary [silver] locks proclaimed that many a winter had passed over his head. There, those farming boys, with that old man, formed a group, whose actions indeed were worthy of all commendation. The creaking machinery of the boat, the dirge-like music of the wind, was loud; yet, above the clatter, all things else, we know those boys were heard in heaven, and their prayers will be answered! . . . parents and friends of home, fear not for such brave sons, who, relying on Heaven, are not ashamed nor afraid to praise God, and do battle for the Star-Spangled Banner.*[187]

> Therefore confess your sins to each other and pray for each other so that you may be healed. The prayer of a righteous man is powerful and effective.
> —JAMES 5:16

When Christian people gather to pray, good things happen. In the story above, it all started with one young man reading his Bible in public. Others came around the table joining the soldier boy. Soon an elderly gentleman sat down with them and their Scripture reading turned to prayer. Then their prayers turned to praise.

Next time you visit someone in a hospital, nursing home, or restaurant, try taking your Bible. Interesting things happen in the presence of God's powerful Word.

Jackson Gives Glory to God

STONEWALL JACKSON took the time to write a pastor friend expressing his gratitude for the many prayers that had gone up for him.

July 31st, 1862
My dear Doctor,

I am very grateful to you for your prayers to God for the success of the operation which God has entrusted to me. Please continue to pray for me and for the success of the troops entrusted to me. It cheers my heart to think that many of God's people are praying to our very kind Heavenly Father for the success of the army to which I belong. Without God's blessing I look for no success, and for every success my prayer is, that all the glory may be given unto Him to whom it is properly due. If people would but give all the glory to God, and regard his creatures as but unworthy instruments, my heart would rejoice. Alas too frequently the praise is bestowed upon the creature. Whilst we must not forget the superior importance of spiritual victories, yet I trust that you will under God's direction do what you can in securing the prayers of His people for the success of our arms, especially for the success of them which are entrusted to me, an unworthy servant, but who desires to glorify His name even in my present military calling. My trust is in God for success. Praying for a continuation of your usefulness I remain your much attached friend,

T. J. Jackson[148]

> And lead us not into temptation, but deliver us from evil: For yours is the kingdom, and the power, and the glory, for ever. Amen.
> —MATTHEW 6:13

Jackson wanted God to get all the credit for his success. "Too frequently the praise is bestowed upon the creature" reflects Jackson's attitude toward self-glorification. Jackson believed in a sovereign, omnipotent God. He frequently referred to himself as an "unworthy servant." Likewise, our goal should be to give God all the glory and honor for our successes.

Anna Jackson Encourages
Her Husband

My precious husband,

I will go to Hanover and wait there until I hear from you again, and I do trust I may be permitted to come back to you again in a few days. I am much disappointed at not seeing you again, but I commend you, my precious darling, to the merciful keeping of the God of battles, and do pray most earnestly for the success of our army this day. Oh! that our Heavenly Father may preserve and guide and bless you, is my most earnest prayer.

I leave the shirt and socks for you with Mrs. Neale, fearing I may not see you again, but I do hope it may be my privilege to be with you in a few days. Our little darling will miss dearest Papa. She is so good and sweet this morning. God bless and keep you, my darling

ANNA JACKSON

Your devoted little wife.[149]

JOB TOLD HIS FRIENDS that if they were suffering like him, he would want to encourage them, yet Job found no encouragement in his affliction from them.

Jackson was strong and courageous in battle and an able leader, but he was just human. Who would know this better than his wife, Anna? They had a close relationship with each other and a mutual faith in God. From the many letters they wrote to each other during the war, it is apparent that they continually encouraged one another.

> "But my mouth would encourage you; comfort from my lips would bring you relief."
> —JOB 16:5

A Compassionate President

ABRAHAM LINCOLN was a tender and compassionate president, especially when ministering to wounded soldiers. His compassion is illustrated in the following story:

Despite his busy schedule during the Civil War, Abraham Lincoln often visited the hospitals to cheer the wounded. On one occasion he saw a young fellow who was near death. "Is there anything I can do for you?" asked the compassionate President. "Please write a letter to my mother," came the reply. Unrecognized by the soldier, the Chief Executive sat down and wrote as the youth told him what to say. The letter read, "My Dearest Mother, I was badly hurt while doing my duty, and I won't recover. Don't sorrow too much for me. May God bless you and Father. Kiss Mary and John for me." The young man was too weak to go on, so Lincoln signed the letter for him and then added this postscript: "Written for your son by Abraham Lincoln." Asking to see the note, the soldier was astonished to discover who had shown him such kindness. "Are you really our President?" he asked. "Yes," was the quiet answer. "Now, is there anything else I can do?" The lad feebly replied, "Will you please hold my hand? I think it would help to see me through to the end." The tall, gaunt man granted his request, offering warm words of encouragement until death stole in with the dawn.[150]

> Be kind and compassionate to one another, forgiving each other, just as in Christ God forgave you.
> —EPHESIANS 4:32

One of the characteristics of godly leaders is their humility and willingness to help those who are weak and hurting. Lincoln never forgot his roots as a poor, humble, barefoot boy in Kentucky and southern Indiana. He could identify with the trials and hurts of others. Thus, he took the time to minister to those society overlooked. This was the true secret of his greatness.

A person of greatness condescends to those who are less fortunate.

A Slave Speaks on Slavery

MARTHA GRIFFITH BROWNE was a slave in the middle 1800s. As a young girl, Martha suffered the pains of being torn from her mother while living on a slave plantation. The owner of the plantation had died, and the slaves were sold to pay off debts. Martha was sold to an evil man who delighted in beating his slaves. While under this oppression, she spoke of a time when slavery would be judged and those who perpetrated it would be brought into accountability.

> *There can be no argument or fact adduced, whereby to justify slavery as a moral right. Serving and being a slave are very different. And why may not Ham's descendants claim a reprieve by virtue of the passion and death of Christ? Are we excluded from the grace of that atonement? No; there is no argument, no reason, to justify slavery, save that of human cupidity. But there will come a day, when each and every one who has violated . . . others . . . will stand with a fearful accountability before the Supreme Judge. Then will there be loud cries and lamentations, and a wish for the mountains to hide them from the eye of Judicial Majesty.*[151]

Martha Browne's statement was almost prophetic when she said that a day would come when those who supported slavery would be brought into "accountability before the Supreme Judge." Her prediction came true with the advent of the Civil War. Many from both the North and South admitted that the War between the States was God's judgment for over two hundred years of slavery.

May we have the courage to stand against the evils and injustices of our day. Thank God a courageous African-American woman like Martha Browne stood for righteousness no matter the consequences. The late Peter Marshall Sr., former chaplain of the U.S. Senate said, "Lord, help us to stand for something, lest we fall for anything."

> Then we cried out to the LORD, the God of our fathers, and the LORD heard our voice and saw our misery, toil and oppression.
> —DEUTERONOMY 26:7

General J. E. B. Stuart

J. E. B. STUART was another great Christian general of the Civil War. The Virginia Military Institute describes his character as follows:

J. E. B. STUART
The National Archives

J. E. B. Stuart was cut out for a cavalry leader. In perfect health, but thirty-two years of age, full of vigor and enterprise, with the usual ideas imbibed in Virginia concerning State Supremacy, Christian in thought and temperate by habit, no man could ride faster, endure more hardships, make a livelier charge, or be more hearty and cheerful while so engaged . . . He commanded Lee's cavalry corps—a well-organized body, of which he was justly proud.

On May 11, 1864, Major General James Ewell Brown Stuart was mortally wounded at the Battle of Yellow tavern. He died the next day. Confederate General J. E. B. Stuart's last words were spoken on May 12, 1864, shortly before he died from a mortal wound received at the Battle of Yellow Tavern the day before. After asking two attending ministers to sing his favorite hymn, "Rock of Ages," Stuart made this statement: "I am going fast now. I am resigned; God's will be done."[152]

General Stuart's strength and vigor in battle can be directly ascribed to his Christian faith. God gives his men and women the ability to do things others may find difficult because they trust in him who gives them strength for the battle. At the end of Stuart's life, he said only "God's will be done." He could accept even death as long as he knew it was God's will.

> I can do everything through him who gives me strength.
> —PHILIPPIANS 4:13

Willingness to Sacrifice

CAPTAIN RICHARD W. BURT

CAPTAIN RICHARD BURT wrote in a letter from the Seventy-sixth Ohio Volunteer Infantry, which was camped ten miles from Pittsburgh Landing, May 10, 1862. One can hardly imagine the sacrifices that both the North and South made during the Civil War in the name of freedom:

Our present camp is in a hard looking place, and we don't care how soon we move forward. We were ordered last night to put three day's cooked rations in our haversacks and fall in line of battle, with blankets, knapsacks and arms, and 40 rounds of cartridges in cartridge boxes, and 60 rounds about the person. This seems to be a load sufficient for a pack mule, but the soldier has to stand it. Our brave soldiers, who have to endure these hardships and bear these burdens, richly deserve the sympathy of those whose homes and government they are fighting to protect.

Very many of them are sacrificing their lives for their country, not only on the battlefield, but in their tents, from diseases caused by exposure and sometimes by the fatigue of rapid marches. Besides four companies of our regiment have never yet received a cent of pay, which certainly seems like very ill usage, after having been in two great battles. Who is to blame, I am unable to say?[153]

> Therefore, I urge you, brothers, in view of God's mercy, to offer your bodies as living sacrifices, holy and pleasing to God— this is your spiritual act of worship.
>
> —ROMANS 12:1, 2

The early disciples of Christ suffered persecution and martyrdom for the cause of Christ. They literally sacrificed their bodies because they would not deny his name.

Resisting Evil

I N STRAWBERRY PLAINS, Tennessee, a captain on General Sheridan's staff told of a man dressed in semi-military garb riding in a carriage drawn by a team of mules. The captain, who was tired and thirsty, asked him for a drink of whiskey. The man in the carriage replied,

> *"I am not your wet nurse . . . I do not frequent the society of intemperate men." "Well," said the Captain, looking hard at him . . . "perhaps we have both mistaken your calling; are you not a sutler?"* [A person who follows an army and sells provisions and liquors.] *"Sutler? no sir . . . I am a follower of the Lord Jesus Christ; the chaplain of the Ohio cavalry" . . . The Captain stopped not to hear more, but putting spurs to his horse, left in a twinkling.*[154]

The hardships of war revealed many vices among the enlisted men, but thank God many lived clean lives for the name of Christ during the worst of times.

Alcohol is the number one drug problem in America among both teenagers and adults. The scourge of alcohol has destroyed the lives of countless men and women. As followers of the Lord, we cannot afford to partake of this world's vices.

> Submit yourselves therefore to God. Resist the devil, and he will flee from you.
> —JAMES 4:7

The soldier in our story was a man of moral convictions who was not afraid to let the arrogant captain know where he stood with Jesus. The Bible says, "The righteous are as bold as a lion" (Prov. 28:1).

The Encouragement of a Mother

WOMEN PLAYED an important role in the Civil War. They often stood by their spouses and sons with courage, stamina, and sacrifice. Charles C. Jones was stationed at Camp Claghorn, Georgia, while preparing for battle. His mother, Mary, wrote to encourage him that whether he lived or died, he was fighting for a righteous cause.

> *I know that you are now every moment exposed to the attack of our perfidious and merciless enemy; but your sword will be drawn in a righteous cause, and I fervently implore my God and my Redeemer to protect and save you in the day of battle, and to encourage your heart and hearts of our commander and all of our noble company, and to strengthen your arms for the conflict . . .*[155]

Mothers and wives played the important role of praying and encouraging their men on the battlefield. While women feared for their sons' or husbands' lives, they let them know they were supporting and praying for them behind the scenes.

In Jesus' day, a band of women followed him and ministered to his needs. They were encouragers. As you read the Gospels you may not immediately see their influence, but they were always willing and ready to help Jesus however they could. Thank God for women who stand by their men in the battles of life. As a minister for over twenty-seven years, the Lord has blessed me with a godly wife. And the women in the church have helped me in my ministry.

If you know someone of the feminine gender that has been a blessing to your life, take time to write a note of thanks to them today.

> In Galilee these women had followed him and cared for his needs. Many other women who had come up with him to Jerusalem were also there.
> —MARK 15:41

Suffering Hardships

THE FOLLOWING is from a letter by Lieutenant Nathaniel Macon Dudley to his mother on the rigors of military life:

We left Winchester . . . about 3 o'clock p.m. without dinner and marched until 4 o'clock the next morning over as rough a road as there is in Virginia. About 12 o'clock at night we came to the Shenandoah River . . . and waded through. The . . . rocks at the bottom cut my feet . . . As soon as we had [climbed] the Shenandoah Mountains . . . the troops laid down on each side of the road and slept until 6 o'clock a.m. When we were aroused . . . we marched . . . to Piedmont . . . [where we] remained . . . without much to eat and . . . slept on the ground every night and one night it rained all night. We left Piedmont . . . on top of the boxes [railroad box cars], as there were only 7 cars for our Regiment. It commenced raining shortly after we left and we had to take it all day long [until] we arrived at [Manassas] Junction . . .

From Richmond, Virginia, Dudley writes:

Our Brigade marched about ten miles the first evening [out of Williamsburg] and camped for the night. I had command of the company. Capt. King and Lt. Sparks are both marching in advance of the army sick. On the 2nd day I was quite sick myself from diarrhea and as it rained all day I got very wet and had a chill . . .

Lt. Dudley was wounded in the head at 2nd Manassas, and died from those wounds on 28 Sept., 1862[156]

Our Lord never promised an easy pathway when we began to follow him. We can expect hardships along the way. But heaven will make it worth the journey.

> They preached the good news in that city and won a large number of disciples. Then they returned to Lystra, Iconium and Antioch, strengthening the disciples and encouraging them to remain true to the faith. "We must go through many hardships to enter the kingdom of God."
> —ACTS 14:21, 22

Another Chance at Home

UNION PRIVATE Absolom A. Harrison served at Camp Anderson, Kentucky. His wife was Susan Allstun Harrison. Susan's grandmother was Nancy Lincoln Brumfield, Thomas Lincoln's sister and President Abraham Lincoln's aunt. Harrison wrote to his wife and said:

Dear Wife,

You wrote to know whether you must sell that corn or not. . . . I would like to be at home to manage for you. I want you to stay where you are at and be as content as you can. And put your trust in One who is able to guide us all through all our difficulties. I think if the Lord will spare me to get home once more I will do better than I ever done before. I never go to bed without a prayer at heart that He will permit me to see my lovely wife and children once more and if it is His will He is able to carry us all through all difficulties and if it is His will that I shall never see you again I pray that He will take care of you and the children. I must bring my letter to a close so nothing more at present but remaining your affectionate husband until death. A. A. Harrison

P.S. You must write as often as you can . . . Be sure and take good care of our sweet little children. God bless their little hearts.[157]

Job was feeling separated from his wife when he received news that all of his children had been killed. Job was a family man. He loved his wife and children deeply. Job does not indicate that he has any regrets of how he treated his family before these things happened. Job was a man who had harmony with his children and peace with God.

Private Harrison had a deep love for his wife and family. Yet, when a man is called from his home, he begins to think about what he had. Harrison's longing was for the Lord to give him another chance to go home.

> While he was still speaking, yet another messenger came and said, "Your sons and daughters were feasting and drinking wine at the oldest brother's house, when suddenly a mighty wind swept in from the desert and struck the four corners of the house. It collapsed on them and they are dead, and I am the only one who has escaped to tell you!"
>
> —JOB 1:18, 19

Hope for the Troubled Heart

A LANSA STERRETT ROUNDS wrote of stirred emotions as cavalry-men galloped into the night to join the army of Northern Virginia.

May 1861

Saddest day I ever saw . . . Mr. Arnold (Methodist minister) offered prayer. Then followed the sad farewells of mothers, wives, sisters, sweethearts and friends! Many a strong man quivered with emotion and tears fell from eyes unused to weep! We watched the cavalrymen as they mounted, whirled into line, waved their hats, and galloped out of sight, leaving aching hearts to mourn their departure. They belonged to the army of Northern Virginia and were bound for Virginia.[158]

My godly grandmother told the following story about my uncle in World War II:

Roland Tuley fought in strategic battles against Nazi Germany. On one occasion, he camped with his army buddies on the banks of the Rhine River. Word came that the Germans were advancing up the river. The Americans were outnumbered. The officers asked the soldiers to burn their identification because they would either die or be captured. During those crucial hours my grandmother in southern Indiana had a strong feeling that her son was in great danger. She wept and prayed for him until early morning. She later said, "I prayed until I got peace and arose to fix coffee. When I walked into the hallway, I heard a deep voice say, "Let not your heart be troubled!" She stood there for a moment, realizing that she had just heard God speak. From then on she knew that Roland was going to be alright. Later she received a letter from Roland talking of the events that took place and assuring her that he was safe.

> Do not let your hearts be troubled. Trust in God; trust also in me.
> —JOHN 14:1

COMMISSIONED AND NONCOMMISSIONED OFFICERS OF COMPANIES
C & D, FIRST MASSACHUSETTS CAVALRY, PETERSBURG, VA, 1864
The Library of Congress

A Correct View of Life

GENERAL ROBERT E. LEE wisely said,

> *Get correct views of life, and learn to see the world in its true light. It will enable you to live pleasantly, to do good, and, when summoned away, to leave without regret.*[159]

Although Robert E. Lee was a man of great faith, he was also a realist. He viewed life through the lens of the Bible and learned to be content within the parameters of reality. He could accept both victory and defeat with patience because he had learned to trust in the providence of almighty God.

We often live with exaggerated expectations and put others on pedestals. But humans are human, which means they are subject to weaknesses as part of the human race. At times the best people will disappoint us. However, if we have a realistic view of life, we learn to accept things that normally would confuse us.

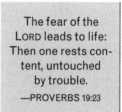

The fear of the LORD leads to life: Then one rests content, untouched by trouble.
—PROVERBS 19:23

The apostle Paul lived with life's harsh realities. The Roman government opposed his ministry, and the scribes and Pharisees saw him as an enemy of Judaism. Paul learned that God's grace was sufficient to sustain him through the tough times. Before his death he could say with no regrets that he had "fought a good fight."

Women Heroes of the Civil War

FRANK MOORE, in his book *Women of the War,* wrote of the loyalty and sacrifice of women who supported their men in the Civil War:

American mothers, with more than Spartan patriotism, sent forth their sons to fall by rebel bullets, or to languish in rebel prisons. Many loyal women along the vexed border, and within the lines of the enemy, exhibited a more than human courage for the Union and its glorious banner, in the face of persecution and danger. In the hospital, and amid the stormy scenes of war, they displayed heroism as brilliant as that of Grace Darling, surpassed the charity of Florence Nightingale, and repeated the humility and gentle sacrifices recorded of Mary in the sacred Scriptures.

Every one, thoughtful and true, must admire and appreciate the memorable conduct of the young wife Gertrude, of medieval times, who knelt at the foot of the wheel upon which, her unfortunate husband hung in excruciating torture, praying for the wretched sufferer, whispering words of consolation, and sustaining him with exhortations to look at the joys beyond. "He had ceased to try to send her away," says the historian, "and still she watched when morning came again, and noon passed over her, and it was verging to evening when for the last time he moved his head, and she raised herself so as to be close to him. With a smile, he murmured, 'Gertrude, this is faithfulness till death,' and died."[160]

> Near the cross of Jesus stood his mother.
> —JOHN 29:25

Mary stood below the cross near her son, Jesus, watching him suffer, feeling helpless to do anything but weep. A loving mother's tears can arouse sympathy, compassion, confession, and conviction. Through her tears, we see the very heart and compassion of a loving God.

Stonewall Jackson and Prayer

STONEWALL JACKSON was a sincere man of prayer. When he entered the battlefield his men could be confident that he was "prayed up." This was the secret of his calmness in the midst of flying missiles. The following is a quote about Jackson's prayer life by an unknown Virginian:

> *Prayer was like breathing with him—the normal condition of his being. Every morning he read his Bible and prayed, and the writer will not soon forget the picture drawn by one of his distinguished associates, who rode to his headquarters at daylight, last November, when the army was falling back to Fredericksburg from the Valley, and found him reading his Testament, quietly in his tent, an occupation which he only interrupted to describe, in tones of quiet simplicity, his intended movements to foil the enemy. Before sitting down to table he raised both hands, and said grace. When he contemplated any movement, his old servant is said to have always known it by his wrestling in prayer for many hours of the night; and on the battle-field thousands noticed the singular gestures with the right arm, sometimes both arms, raised aloft. Those who looked closely at him at such moments saw his lips moving in prayer. Like Joshua, he prayed with uplifted hand for victory.[161]*

> Be joyful in hope, patient in affliction, and faithful in prayer.
> —ROMANS 12:12

Historians revere Jackson as one of the nation's greatest generals. His humbleness, steadfastness, and absolute dependency on almighty God can be attributed to his prayer life. He prayed with uplifted hands to God, which in turn gave him the confidence to strike fear into the hearts of the enemy. Even though the South did not win the war, Jackson won the respect and admiration of both the North and South for his amazing leadership and strategic maneuvers.

Christians need to have a prayer life that honors God; and he will give us abilities beyond ourselves.

A Strange Place to Write a Letter

ISAAC WHITE was an assistant surgeon in the Confederate army. The following letter was written to his wife on June 4, 1864:

My Dear Jinnie,

> In this you greatly rejoice, though now for a little while you may have had to suffer grief in all kinds of trials.
> —1 PETER 1:16

We have had a very hard fight today + the slaughter of the enemy is terrible. We have repulsed them at every point. We have had only one nights sleep out of seven. We are all very much prostrated + I am sick enough to be in bed with the Dysentery; but have not left the field for fear some one might say I was cowardly. . . . Our division has been engaged every day since I wrote you + through the blessings of God I am still alive though I have been in danger on every hand. Oh it is terrible to hear the constant roar of canon + musketry + to know that we are in so much danger but I hope through blessing of God we may be permitted to meet again. The balls are still flying in every direction but it is called a skirmish here. The enemy may try it again but if they do will meet with the same fate. The slaughter of to day is said to be greater than it was at Spotsylvania Court House. I received a letter from you yesterday.

Love to all, Your devoted
Isaac
PS Strange place to write a letter[162]

The Lord never promised that we would not suffer trials in our service for him. Isaac White witnessed sickness and pain as a physician in the Confederate army. He realized it was by God's grace that he was still alive.

When I was four years of age I contracted scarlet fever. My temperature soared, and I almost died. My mother and father prayed in those uncertain moments and said, "Lord, if you will preserve Terry's life, we will give him to you." God spared my life and called me to ministry years later.

In the Hands of a Merciful God

MARY BETHELL wrote in her diary:

Last Thursday the 30th my dear son George left us to join the army; he joined the same company of his brother Willy. I suppose they have gone to Richmond, where there are 40,000 soldiers so 'tis said, it is a consolation to believe that my sons are in the hands of a merciful God. I hope and pray that they may be permitted to return home, if consistent with the Lord's will, I pray to God every day in their behalf, it is a trial to me, but I pray that our Country may enjoy peace and be independent. The thought of a bloody war is awful to contemplate.[163]

Many mothers sent their sons off to war not knowing if they would ever see them again. My wife and I wept when our daughter Ashley left for college. It is hard to comprehend the courage the mothers must have had to send their sons into a bloody war not knowing if they would return.

Mary Bethell said it was consolation to "believe that her sons were in the hands of a merciful God." She prayed for them every day. Solomon pleaded for mercy in his prayer. The Lord has mercy on them who pray and humble themselves before him.

For many parents and soldiers in the Civil War, it was God or nothing.

Where can we go but to the Lord?

> Yet give attention to your servant's prayer and his plea for mercy, O LORD my God. Hear the cry and the prayer that your servant is praying in your presence.
> —2 CHRONICLES 6:19

An Old-Time Brush Arbor Revival

Converts from Jackson's corps numbered in the thousands, many being "saved" at great outdoor meetings. One of these meetings places was a large sloped clearing with log seats for some 2,000, and a platform at the lower end. Wire baskets were hung in a circle around the platform and were lined in front of the seats. They held chunks of light wood which burned in the night.[164]

It is not surprising that Jackson's corps were among the many being saved at the outdoor "brush arbor" revivals. Jackson was a mighty man in battle, but a very humble man when it came to his faith. His attitude toward prayer and the providence of God must have had a profound influence on his men. We can imagine Jackson on his knees by a tree stump somewhere in the woods, on the eve of a great battle. His men must have heard his petitions coming from his tent in the night as he beseeched the Lord to strengthen him for leadership.

> For this is what the high and lofty One says—he who lives forever, whose name is holy: "I live in a high and holy place, but also with him who is contrite and lowly in spirit, to revive the spirit of the lowly and to revive the heart of the contrite."
>
> —ISAIAH 57:17

We will not see true and lasting revival in America until we are willing to take the path of contriteness and humility in our attitude toward Almighty God. God delights in hearing the prayers of those who are willing to confess and forsake their sins. The Lord takes pleasure in bending his ear to those who are willing to bow their knee and earnestly seek his face.

Are you going through a spiritual dry spell? Developing a contrite heart and an attitude of humility can bring great changes in one's life.

General Lee Refuses Bitterness

R OBERT E. LEE had a God-given ability to forgive his enemies and not harbor any bitterness against them. The following is evidence of that fact:

> *His house on Pamunky river was burnt to the ground, and the slaves carried away, many of them by force, while his residence on Arlington Heights was not only gutted of its furniture, but even the very relics of George Washington were stolen from it, and paraded in triumph in the saloons of New York and Boston. Notwithstanding all these personal losses, when speaking of the Yankees, he neither evidenced any bitterness of feeling, nor gave utterance to a single violent expression, but alluded to many of his former friends and companions among them, in the kindest terms.*[165]

Lee's virtue of self-control was rare in his day. The Scripture tells us that a patient man is better than a soldier who captures an entire city. People who lose their temper never win, but those who can control their temper have qualities of great leadership. To keep your head while others around you are losing theirs comes from the Holy Spirit's power. Controlling your temper means yielding yourself completely to God.

> Better a patient man than a warrior, a man who controls his temper than one who takes a city.
> —PROVERBS 16:32

When we react to the words of angry people, we fall prey to Satan's tactics. But if we are slow to react and quick to listen, the Lord will give us words that will make a difference. Next time you are confronted with an angry person, try listening and using as few words as possible. If you do so, you will find Lee's secret of self-control.

Lincoln's Tribute to the Brave Women of America

LINCOLN HAD a high regard for faithful women during the war. He recognized their faithfulness and care as vital to the relief of suffering soldiers and their families.

Ladies and Gentlemen: I appear, to say but a word. This extraordinary war in which we are engaged falls heavily upon all classes of people, but the most heavily upon the soldier. For it has been said, "All that a man hath will he give for his life;" and while all contribute of their substance, the soldier puts his life at stake, and often yields it up in his country's cause. The highest merit, then, is due the soldier.

In this extraordinary war extraordinary developments have manifested themselves, such as have not been seen in former wars; and among these manifestations nothing has been more remarkable than these Fairs for the relief of suffering soldiers and their families. And the chief agents in these Fairs are the women of America.

I am not accustomed to the use of language of eulogy; I have never studied the art of paying compliments to women; but I must say, that if all that has been said by orators and poets since the creation of the world in praise of woman were applied to the women of America, it would not do them justice for their conduct during this war. I will close by saying, God bless the women of America.[166]

> Then Mary took about a pint of pure nard, an expensive perfume; she poured it on Jesus' feet and wiped his feet with her hair. And the house was filled with the fragrance of the perfume.
> —JOHN 12:3

Lincoln was correct in his summation of women. Women have always played a prominent role in our nation and our churches. The courage and strength of godly women in America is phenomenal. As a husband and father, I'm habitually amazed how my wife ministers to the needs of her family. Never underestimate the strength of a Christian woman.

Take some time to appreciate your wife, mother, sister, or some other godly woman in your life today.

The Need for Accountability

R OBERT E. LEE felt accountable to God for his actions in behalf of
others. This characteristic motivated him to handle his decisions with
great care and attention to detail. The following observation by Lee's
wartime aide, Walter Taylor, is evidence of the general's motivation:

> *I had excellent opportunities at that time to observe General Lee as a
> worker, and I can say that I have never known a man more thorough
> and painstaking in all that he undertook. Early at his office, punctual
> in meeting all engagements, methodical to an extreme in his way of dis-
> patching business, giving close attention to details—but not, as is
> sometimes the concomitant if not the result of this trait, neglectful of
> the more important matters dependent upon his decision—he seemed
> to address himself to the accomplishment of every task that devolved
> upon him in a conscientious and deliberate way, as if he himself was
> directly accountable to some higher power for the manner in which he
> performed his duty . . .[167]*

Christians must give an account to God someday for how they lead others. General Lee had a
profound awareness of this scriptural truth.

We are responsible for how we follow and
submit to godly leadership. Let your pastor and
church staff know that you support and pray for
them. Not only will you be encouraging them, but
your submission to their leadership will be profitable for you.

> Obey your leaders
> and submit to their
> authority. They keep
> watch over you as
> men who must give
> an account. Obey
> them so that their
> work will be a joy, not
> a burden, for that
> would be of no
> advantage to you.
> —HEBREWS 13:17

When Your Father and Mother Forsake You

WILLIAM HEYSER, born in Pennsylvania in 1796, was a shopkeeper in Chambersburg's South Ward. Heyser also supervised his family farm until he sold it in 1862. He remained in Chambersburg with his wife, adult children, and grandchildren until his death on November 5, 1863. His diary provides insight into wartime life on the Franklin County home front.

> B. Wolff and myself spent a couple hours in the Lutheran graveyard where an interment was being made. This churchyard is in much disarray and scattered about. Many of the graves are lost thru negligence of friends and the church. Part of John Maderia's family is in one place, and part in another. A Mr. Humphrie's lay beside Mary Maderia, then John Maderia. Then a stone with the inscription, "Our Sister." This was Catherine Maderia, one of their daughters who was a little backward, and received little attention from the family. She was kept out of society and led a life with the servants. I knew her well in my boyhood days by the name of Kit. I believe the sin of this injustice was visited upon the rest of the family, for none of them prospered in life. Reading her epitaph finds only the word Sister, someone who knew her history wrote beneath in pencil, "When my Father and Mother forsake me, the Lord will take me up." May she have that rest beyond this life, which was denied in this.[168]

> Though my father and mother forsake me, the LORD will receive me.
> —PSALM 27:10

Many lonely people do not have the comforts of close family and friends. Jesus received the despised and rejected of society. Scripture tells us that when no one else understands or loves us, the Lord will care for us. Christians must do the same. Do you know a lonely widow or a homeless person that needs care? A meal, a kind letter, or a phone call could make an eternal difference in someone's life today.

The Power of the Sword
Shall Not Hurt Thee

J. K. STREET wrote the following letter to his wife, Ninnie. Street was a part of the Ninth Texas Infantry, Company A:

Head Quarters, Camp Iuka Tishomingo Co
Feb 25, 1862

Now darling come let us reason together, 1st What good does it do my dear to grieve 2nd What harm does it do? I think darling it does you no good at all; that you will admit it surely does you harm—think my love of your condition. My love my own sweet Ninnie, will you make me happy? Darling shall our anticipated little one be an idiot!! Darling will you comfort me in my hours of loneliness and sorrow? O then dear please write me one cheerful letter that I may read it and find there words of solace. Darling don't become grieved and think that I do not sympathize and feel that truly you have sorrows! Dear you know I love you and would give my very existence for you. . . . Then my dear please do not sign and weep so much for me. Again don't write cheerfully while truly the heart feels differently. I know you will be ever happy—why not love is not God pledged to take cared of me? . . . God is my trust. I feel fully confident that God, our God, will fulfill the promise he has made and as ere long I shall again be with my Ninnie. Then dear I shall have the consciousness of knowing that I have done what I felt to be my duty to my country.[169]

What a wonderful promise. No weapon that is used against us by the enemy will ever prosper. Do you have someone who is attacking your life at this moment? Is there someone in your life who is deliberately trying to make your life miserable? Remember, no one who is trying to destroy your life or ministry will prosper. You have God's promise on it.

> "No weapon that is formed against thee shall prosper; and every tongue that shall rise against thee in judgment thou shalt condemn. This is the heritage of the servants of the LORD, and their righteousness is of me," saith the LORD.
>
> —ISAIAH 54:17 (KJV)

The Spirit of "Little Giffen"

FRANCIS O. TICKNOR, a surgeon during the Civil War, treated wounded soldiers who came through his hospital in Columbus, Georgia. Sixteen-year-old Isaac Newton Giffen from Tennessee was wounded in battle and brought to Ticknor's hospital. Ticknor and his wife respected the boy's courage and brought him to heal at their home. After he recovered, the boy returned to the Confederate army and was killed in battle. In memory of the boy, the doctor wrote the poem "Little Giffen of Tennessee." The doctor published many poems after the Civil War, but "Little Giffen" remains his best-known poem.

LITTLE GIFFEN

Out of the focal and foremost fire,
Out of the hospital wall as dire,
Smitten of grape shot and gangrene,
(Eighteenth battle and he sixteen!)
Spectre! Such as you seldom see,
Little Giffen of Tennessee

"Take him and welcome!" the surgeons said;
Little the doctor can help the dead!
So we took him and brought him where
The balm was sweet in the summer air;
And we laid him down on a wholesome bed—
Metter Lazarus, heel to head!

And we watched the war with bated breath—
Skeleton boy against skeleton death.
Months of torture, how many such
Weary weeks of stick and crutch,
And still a glint of the steel-blue eye,
Told of a spirit that WOULDN'T die.

And didn't. Nay, more! in death's despite
The crippled skeleton "learned to write."
"DEAR MOTHER," at first, of course; and then
"DEAR CAPTAIN," inquiring about the men.
Captain's answer; "of eighty and five,
Giffen and I are left alive."

Word of gloom from the war one day:
Johnston pressed at the front, they say.
Little Giffen was up and hurried away;
A tear—his first—as he bade goodbye,
Dimmed the glint of his steel-blue eye.
"I'll write, if spared!" There was news of the fight,
But none of Giffen—he did not write.

I sometimes fancy that, were I king
Of the princely knights of the Golden Ring,
With the song of the minstrel in mine ear,
And the tender story that trembles here,
I'd give the best on his bended knee,
The whitest soul of my chivalry,
For "Little Giffen" of Tennessee.

—Francis O. Ticknor[170]

The Experience of Soldiers on the March

CARLTON McCARTHY tells what it was like to be a Civil War soldier on the march.

> *Troops on the march were generally so cheerful and gay that an outsider, looking on them as they marched, would hardly imagine how they suffered. In summer time, the dust, combined with the heat, caused great suffering. The nostrils of the men, filled with dust, became dry and feverish, and even the throat did not escape. The grit was felt between the teeth, and the eyes were rendered almost useless. There was dust in eyes, mouth, ears and hair. The shoes were full of sand, and the dust penetrated the clothes. The heat was at times terrific, but the, men became greatly accustomed to it, and endured it with wonderful ease. Their heavy woolen clothes were a great annoyance; . . . indeed, there are many objections to woolen clothing for soldiers, even in winter.*
>
> *If the dust and heat were not on hand to annoy, their very able substitutes were: mud, cold, rain, snow, hail and wind took their places. Rain was the greatest discomfort a soldier could have; it was more uncomfortable than the severest cold with clear weather. Wet clothes, shoes and blankets; wet meat and bread; wet feet and wet ground; wet wood to burn, or rather not to burn; wet arms and ammunition; wet ground to sleep on, mud to wade through, swollen creeks to ford, muddy springs, and a thousand other discomforts attended the rain. There was no comfort on a rainy day or night except in bed—that is, under your blanket and oil-cloth. Cold winds, blowing the rain in the faces of the men, increased the discomfort. Mud was often so deep as to submerge the horses and mules, and at times it was necessary for one man or more to extricate another from the mud holes in the road . . .[171]*

> Jesus replied, "Foxes have holes and birds of the air have nests, but the Son of Man has no place to lay his head."
> —MATTHEW 8:20

We can hardly imagine that the King of Kings had no home on earth. In a similar way, soldiers in the Civil War suffered many hardships, yet because of their loyalty, they would not neglect their duties. We must not allow hardships to divert us from our Christian duties.

The Conversion of Josiah the Slave

J OSIAH, a black slave during the Civil War, was not acquainted with the Scriptures. One day after listening to the passionate words of a preacher at a camp meeting, Josiah heard the gospel for the first time and was converted. He wrote details of his conversion as follows:

> When I arrived at the place of meeting, the services were so far advanced that the speaker was just beginning his discourse from the text, Hebrews ii. 9: "That He, by the grace of God, should taste death for every man." This was the first text of the Bible I had ever listened to, knowing it to be such. I have never forgotten it, and scarcely a day has passed since in which I have not recalled it, and the sermon that was preached from it.
>
> "Who can describe my feelings, and the strange influence that came upon and overwhelmed me, as I listened to those wondrous words?" . . . O, the blessedness and sweetness of the feeling that then came over me! I was LOVED! I could have died that moment with joy for the compassionate Saviour about whom I was hearing. "He loves me. He looks down from heaven in compassion and forgiveness on me, a great sinner. He died to save my soul" . . .
>
> I seemed to see a glorious Being in a cloud of splendour smiling down from on high. In sharp contrast with the experience of the contempt and brutality of my earthly master, I seemed to bask in the sunshine of the benignity of this glorious Being! He'll be my dear refuge—He'll wipe away the tears from my eyes! Now I can bear all things. Nothing will seem hard after this! I felt sorry that my master, Riley, did not know this loving Saviour; sorry that he should live such a coarse, wicked, cruel life. Swallowed up in the beauty of the Divine love, I could love my enemies, and prayed for them that did despitefully use and entreat me . . . Religion became to me, indeed, the great business and concern of my life . . .[172]

> Therefore, if anyone is in Christ, he is a new creation; the old has gone, the new has come!
> —2 CORINTHIANS 5:16, 17

It is remarkable how the gospel has power to totally transform a life. Josiah's conversion led him to love his enemies, even after terrible beatings.

The Breath of Faith

A UNION SOLDIER from southern Indiana wrote his wife, Ellen, describing his first experience in battle:

My Dear, Dear Ellen:

Right here you may wish to know how I "stood fire". I will tell you while laying on the ground and just before we reced. Orders to fire I simply breathed faith: "Ever kind Father preserve me." When I arose and the firing [began I] was as cool and composed as if sitting down for a chat or shooting squirrels. The bullets whistled over our heads, shells bursting all around us, balls whiz [zi] ng past, tearing trees . . . While I was laying on my face a bullet whistled over my head and passed through my Haversack.[173]

Jesus rebuked his disciples because they lacked faith. Just a little faith brings big results in the kingdom of God.

It's not the longevity of our prayers, it's the sincerity of our prayers that get through to God. Notice that the soldier "simply breathed faith" in his prayer to God. When he prayed, he was "cool and composed" even though bullets whizzed over his head. Faith should be as normal to the Christian as breathing.

> He replied, "Because you have so little faith. I tell you the truth, if you have faith as small as a mustard seed, you can say to this mountain, 'Move from here to there' and it will move. Nothing will be impossible for you."
>
> —MATTHEW 17:20

Love Each Other

CONFEDERATE SOLDIER Phillip Wallace from Kentucky was in General Braxton Bragg's army. He wrote the following letter from Grenada, Mississippi, to his wife:

July 27, 1864

After nearly three years of bitter and cruel separation, my darling wife, on tomorrow we must separate again, you to a life of loneliness and privation and I to one of danger and sorrow . . . There is but one thing left us and that is trust in God's providence which has done so much for us, and the hope that it may not desert us in the future . . . "And, behold a new commandment I give unto you, that ye love one another." Through the coming time of our separation your image and our dear boy's shall be ever with me, sleeping or waking, in sickness, in health, in quiet or in danger, to bless and cheer me and not recalled in order to bring to mind some unpleasant reminiscence of the past. I pray God it may be so with you. Each succeeding year robs us of some loved friend or some cherished hope. Let us then cling the closer together and build new hopes on the ruins of the fallen . . . I have but one wife and one darling boy to whom my heart clings as its anchor and to whom it will continue to cling while I live.[174]

> My command is this: Love each other as I have loved you.
> —JOHN 15:12

Wallace reminded his wife of Jesus' commandments to love one another. Wallace had a deep love for his wife and family whom he missed. He was an example of a man who believed in clinging to his wife and family in the worst of circumstances.

A revival of love in our homes will help us to endure life's greatest challenges.

Trusting God in the
Midst of Flying Shells

R ACHEL CORMANY was born in Canada and later moved to Chambersburg, Virginia, with her husband, Samuel. During the war, he served as a Union soldier. She wrote diaries both before and during the war, and they vividly describe her life as a woman on the home front.

June 15, 1863

Monday. This morning pretty early Gen Milroys wagon train (so we were told) came. Contrabands on ahead coming as fast as they could on all & any kind of horses, their eyes fairly protruding with fear—teams coming at the same rate—some with the covers half off—some lost—men without hats or coats—some lost their coats as they were flying . . . There really was a real panic. All reported that the rebels were just on their heels . . . Soon followed 100–200 cavalry men—the guard. Such a skedadling as there was among the women & children to get into the houses. All thought the Rebels had really come. The report now is that they will be here in an hour. If I could only hear of My Samuels safety—Many have packed nearly all of their packable goods—I have packed nothing. I do not think that we will be disturbed even should they come. I will trust in God even in the midst of flying shells—but of course shall seek the safest place possible in that case—which I hope will not come to us. I have just put my baby to sleep & will now sit at the front door awhile yet—then retire, knowing all will be well.[175]

> You will not fear the terror of night, nor the arrow that flies by day.
> —PSALM 18:5

Diaries give examples of devotion, courage, and patriotism during the Civil War. They were written by fighting men and faithful Christian women who remained at home. Rachel Cormany, a woman of great courage, learned to put her trust in God in spite of flying shells.

Peace Which Flows like a River

STONEWALL JACKSON was promoted to Brigadier General of the Army of the Confederacy in June of 1861. Surprised by this promotion, he was deeply grateful to his country and the Lord. His concluding statements in a letter to his wife, Anna, reveal the deep faith and trust he had in Jesus as his Savior. His directed her to the one from whom he drew his strength.

> *I have been officially informed of my promotion to be a brigadier-general of the Provisional Army of the Southern Confederacy . . . My letter from the Secretary of War was dated 17th of June. Thinking it would be gratifying to you, I send the letters of Generals Lee and Johnston . . . My promotion was beyond what I anticipated . . . One of my greatest desires for advancement is the gratification it will give my darling, and the [opportunity] of serving my country more efficiently . . . I should be very ungrateful if I were not contented, and exceedingly thankful to our kind Heavenly Father. May his blessing ever rest on you is my fervent prayer. Try to live near to Jesus, and secure that peace which flows like a river.*[176]

The peace that Christ brought through his death on the cross was extended to the world through the missionary efforts of the apostle Paul who became known as the Apostle to the Gentiles. That peace is still available to our postmodern world. Notice Jackson's final remarks to Anna when he admonished her to "live near to Jesus and secure that peace which flows like a river." Having God's peace is always preceded by drawing near to Jesus. When we seek to live close to him, he gives us the inner peace that surpasses anything the world can comprehend.

> For this is what the Lord says, "I will extend peace to her like a river, and the wealth of nations like a flooding stream."
>
> —ISAIAH 66:12

Are you searching for peace today? Then draw near to Jesus, and you will find it flowing like a river.

A Confederate Pastor and Shiloh

PREACHERS WHO were in sympathy with the South often spoke on themes relating to its cause. After a victory at Shiloh, John Burrows preached a message entitled, "The Lord Appeared Again; in Shiloh" (1 Sam. 3: 1, KJV).

> *God has revealed Himself as our shield and defense. "THE LORD appeared again; in Shiloh." Can we take the praise to ourselves? I would withhold none of the honor due to our brave sons for their fidelity and courage. They deserve our gratitude and praise; all the rewards and honors which a grateful country can bestow. But they were the willing agents through whom GOD wrought. . . . An army comparatively poorly clad and poorly armed, has met and mastered an army of at least equal numbers, said to have been one of the best equipped and prepared for battle that the world has ever seen. What with such differences has turned the victory to our side? After admitting the operation of all secondary causes, what other conclusion can we reach than this—the God of battles favored our cause? Now, let us keep God on our side by recognizing and praising Him—by self-distrust; and confidence in Him—by obedience and love. Let us remember—"When thy brethren go up to battle then keep thee from every wicked thing."[177]*

Both Northern and Southern pastors must have found it difficult to remain neutral in what they believed to be a righteous cause for their country. They felt God was on their side. Often, churches became the rallying points for morale in communities during the war. Some conclude that the Lord was on both sides, working out his sovereign will for the good and unity of our great nation.

At the conclusion of the Civil War, some Southern leaders, including Robert E. Lee, admitted that all things worked according to God's overall plan for the greater unity of the United States.

Let us not forget to pray for our country. Many issues and factions divide us. Pray that God will give us courage to remain one nation under him.

Our Heavenly Parent

I N RACHEL CORMANY'S diary entry, she told about the Union forces fleeing from the Confederates (see June 15th). She continued with this entry four days later:

> *June 19, 1863, the excitement is still high. I have slept well every night so far knowing that my Heavenly Parent watches over me at all times. Ironed this morning & baked a loaf of brown bread. Feel a little blue. I feel troubled about Mr. Cormany—we are penned up so here that we can hear nothing. All kinds of reports are flying about—still the excitement has abated considerably. Mended all my clothes & put every thing away. Read about the great revivals of, 56 &, 57 Felt much happier than in the forenoon, enjoyed a sweet season of prayer.*[178]

> He will have no fear of bad news; his heart is steadfast, trusting in the LORD.
> —PSALM 112:7

Our greatest fears come from the unknown. We fear most what we cannot understand. In our modern society, information flies like lightning through the Internet, on radio, and television. One can view the major news events of the world in a matter of seconds. In Rachel's day, information traveled slowly and rumors preceded factual news by weeks. So families must have been fearful and frustrated concerning the fate of husbands and sons in battle.

Rachel Cormany put her trust in the Lord and declared he was like a "heavenly parent" who watched over her at all times. She did not dwell on the things she could not know, rather she contented herself in thinking on the things she did know. And Rachel knew God was watching over her every minute. As she read about great revivals in the past, she was reminded of the power of prayer. She enjoyed "a sweet season of prayer." Prayer can lift us from the cares of this life to a firm confidence that our heavenly Father is watching over us.

Hold Fast to Your Profession

HARDIN AND MARGARET BOSTIC, who lived in Williamson County, Tennessee, were the proud parents of four sons, Litton, Joe, Tom, Abe, and a daughter, May. When Tennessee seceded from the Union in May, 1861, Abe was convinced of the great cause of the South and joined the Confederate army with a hunger for adventure.

Not long after, Abe boarded a railroad train and left for Virginia to help reinforce the army of G. T. Beauregard and Joseph E. Johnston at Manassas, Virginia. On June 30, 1862, near Drury's Bluff, Virginia, Abe lost his life charging Union forces. The following letter was written by a close friend and comrade to his sister:

Miss May Bostick

This note is to inform you of the death of your brother Abe who fell on the evening of [the 27th] *while gallantly charging the enemy's fortifications with* [the] *7th Tennessee Regt. The shot which proved fatal took effect just above his left knee passing through and cutting the artery. He might have been saved if he could have received attention at once but we were repulsed on the first charge and before we could rally and drive the enemy from his works he had expired from loss of blood . . .*

> Let us hold unswervingly to the hope we profess, for he who promised is faithful.
> —HEBREWS 10:23

It is painful to us to make the communication to you because we who have been intimately associated with him for twelve months past know something of the sorrow you must feel at the loss of a brother, whom it must have been so great a pleasure to have loved but we can heartily recommend two sources of consolation.

First, he was a Christian and maintained his profession amid the temptations of the army. He has therefore exchanged the turmoil's of this inhuman warfare for a world of peace and happiness.

The second is he was a brave and chivalrous soldier and fell while gaining a noble victory for the South . . . We felt like we had lost one like unto a brother and will long cherish him in our memories.[179]

Absolute Surrender

T HE ABSOLUTE SURRENDER of Mary Bethell to the will of God stands as a testimony of the strength of women on the Civil War home front. Notice in the opening paragraph that Mary rejoiced that she had lived to see her forty-fourth birthday. The average life span was not very long in the late 1800s. With the threat of sickness and disease many could not hope to live past fifty.

I have lived to see another birthday; I am 44 years old today. The Lord has spared me for something, I hope he will enable me to finish the work which he has given me to do, I feel that I am an unprofitable servant have come short of my duty, I feel weak and vile in mine eyes. I can do nothing without his help. I am humbled under the hand of God; I will continue to look to him as my Savior, my Lord and my God. I will now offer up myself to him, with every thing I have, I offer up my husband, children, servants, property, influence, all I give to him, and ask him to use them all, for his glory. I do feel that God is mine, and I am his, I hope he will guide me with his counsel and afterwards lead me to Glory. My soul doth magnify the Lord, and my spirit hath rejoiced in God my Savior . . .[180]

We may be willing to give our time, talents, and abilities to many organizations, but none is as rewarding as spreading the gospel. A surgeon, wielding his knife, makes the difference between life and death. A politician makes life-changing decisions for his state or country. Yet, what Christians do for God's kingdom will last for eternity.

> "But be very careful to keep the commandment and the law that Moses the servant of the LORD gave you: to love the LORD your God, to walk in all his ways, to obey his commands, to hold fast to him and to serve him with all your heart and all your soul."
> —JOSHUA 22:5

When a Man Loves a Woman

IN THE FOLLOWING letter, we see Stonewall Jackson's tender heart toward his beloved wife. Duty demanded Jackson remain with his men, but he longed for home and the love of his sweet wife.

May 16th

> *There is something very pleasant in the thought of your mailing me a letter every Monday; such manifestation of regard for the Sabbath must be well-pleasing in the sight of God. Oh that all our people would manifest such a regard for his holy day! If we would all strictly observe his holy laws, what would not our country be? . . . When in prayer for you last Sabbath, the tears came to my eyes, and I realized an unusual degree of emotional tenderness. I have not yet fully analyzed my feelings to my satisfaction, so as to arrive at the cause of such emotions; but I am disposed to think that it con-sisted in the idea of the intimate relation existing between you, as the object of my tender affec-tion, and God, to whom I looked up as my Heavenly Father. I felt that day as if it were a communion day for myself. . . .*[181]

> A man will leave his father and mother and be united to his wife, and the two will become one flesh.
> —MATTHEW 19:5

We need a revival of the Christian marital relationship in a postmodern world. Satan's greatest attack target is the home. Divorce increases and dysfunctional families demoralize our nation. The Bible teaches that husbands must love their wives as Christ loved the church and gave himself for it. Jesus allowed himself to be humiliated, persecuted, and crucified because he loved the church.

If Christian men would love their wives as Christ loved the church, our country would see a steep decline in divorce. Women would feel secure in their marriages and in their relationship with their husbands. General Jackson set a good example of a godly husband leading a secure marriage.

An Admonition to the Confederate Soldiers from the Baptists

CHURCHES AS A WHOLE tried to explain the spiritual implications of the Civil War. The following is an excerpt of an admonition to Southern soldiers from a leader of the Baptist General Association of Virginia:

> *Soldier of the cross! Remember that you have a victory to achieve, a reward to gain, an inheritance to enter upon, transcendently more glorious than any to which your country calls you. The captain of our salvation has enlisted us for a warfare whose "weapons are not carnal, but mighty through God to the pulling down of strongholds; casting down imaginations and every high thing that exalteth itself against the knowledge of God, and bringing into captivity every thought to the obedience of Christ." And there is no discharge in that war; neither does it allow any relaxation of discipline. Religion makes the same demands upon us in the camp as at home. The perils which environ us, far from lessening the obligation of Christian duty, rather require us to walk more "circumspectly, not as fools, but as wise, redeeming the time, because the days are evil."[182]*

> Be very careful, then, how you live—not as unwise but as wise.
> —EPHESIANS 5:15

As soldiers of Christ we wage a war against an awesome enemy in the spiritual realm. We must always be on our guard and alert to the devil's tactics and schemes. We cannot afford to waste our time on trivial things, but must be about the business of our Commander in Chief—Jesus Christ. We must not relax our standard if we are going to wage this spiritual war successfully.

Words of Comfort

CONCERNED CHRISTIANS spoke words of comfort and compassion to the soldiers in the Civil War during the Baptist General Convention.

It is sad to think that this address may find many of you prostrate with disease, or disabled by wounds, in the hospital, or among strangers, far from home. This is among your sorest trials. The sense of duty, the active employments and responsibilities of the service, which, in health, buoy up your spirits to endure cheerfully privations and toils, stay not the languor and helplessness of the sick-bed. And though kind nurses may attend you, though some of those many noble hearted women, who have relieved the darkest scenes of this hour of trial by the beauty of their love, may hover like ministering angels around your couch, still you feel a void is there.

It is now that you would lean your head again, as in the hour of childhood's weakness, upon a fond mother's arm, or upon that tender bosom which has hid its life and love in yours; you long for a sister's gentle touch and sweet soothing voice; or to hear the little prattlers at your bedside: calling you father and brother. And yet, dear Christian brother, there is one standing by who loves you more than all these,

> Cast your cares on the LORD and he will sustain you; he will never let the righteous fall.
> —PSALM 55:22

saying to you, "Be of good cheer, it is I, be not afraid" . . . Oh! lean upon Him, for He is a "friend that sticketh closer than a brother." It is He "who forgiveth all thy iniquities; who healeth all thy diseases; who redeemeth thy life from destruction." He speaks to you in such words as these: "Can a woman forget her suckling child, that she should not have compassion on the son of her womb? yea, they may forget, yet, will I not forget thee." Why then should you doubt or fear? In the absence of earthly comforts find them all in Jesus; and leave all with Him; assured that He will richly supply your every need . . .[183]

The Word of God is timeless. The same Bible that comforted the Civil War soldier can bring comfort and consolation to hurting hearts today.

Jackson's Remarkable
Faith in God

STONEWALL JACKSON stands as a godly Christian general during the Civil War. His diaries and letters to his beloved wife show his firm faith in the providence of God. Jackson was a good friend of Rev. Robert Dabney. Dabney's inspirational tribute to Jackson is well deserved and depicts Jackson as an example of a Christian leader.

> *Such was the foundation of the courage of Jackson. He walked with God, in conscious integrity; and he embraced with all his heart "the righteousness of God which is by the faith of Jesus Christ." His soul, I believe, dwelt habitually in the full assurance that God was his God, and his portion forever. His manly and vigorous faith brought heaven so near, that death had slight terrors for him.—While it would be unjust to charge him with rashness in exposure to danger, yet whenever his sense of duty prompted it, he seemed to risk his person with an absolute indifference to fear. The sense of his responsibilities to his country, and the heat of his mighty spirit in the crisis of battle, might sometimes agitate him vehemently; but never was the most imminent personal peril seen to disturb his equanimity for one moment. It is a striking trait of the impression which he has made upon his countrymen, that while no man could possibly be farther from boasting, it always became the first article of the belief of those subject to his command, that he was of course, a man of perfect courage.*[184]

> Enoch walked with God; then he was no more, because God took him away.
> —GENESIS 5:24

What greater comment could be made about a Christian than he or she walked with God? There was no doubt that Jackson did walk with God. Integrity is what we do when no one else is looking. May we so live that our families and friends can engrave on our tombstone someday, that we walked with God.

Lincoln and a Cup
of Cold Water

AFTER LINCOLN'S nomination for president of the United States, he attended a reception and the following account revealed Lincoln's preference in drinking:

> *Mr. Lincoln remarked to the company, that as an appropriate conclusion to an interview so important and interesting as that which he had just transpired, he supposed good manners would require that he should treat the committee with something to drink; and opening a door that led into a room in the rear, he called out, "Mary! Mary!" A girl responded to the call, whom Mr. Lincoln spoke a few words to in an under-tone; and closing the door, returned again to converse with his guests. In a few minutes the maiden entered, bearing a large waiter, containing several glass tumblers, and a large pitcher in the midst, and placed it upon the centre-table. Mr. Lincoln arose and gravely addressing the company, said, "Gentlemen, we must pledge our mutual health's in the most healthy beverage which our God has given to man; it is the only beverage I have ever used or allowed in my family, and I cannot conscientiously depart from it on the present occasion; It is pure Adam's ale from the spring!" and taking a tumbler, he touched it to his lips and pledged them his highest respects in a cup of cold water . . .*[185]

> And if anyone gives even a cup of cold water to one of these little ones because he is my disciple, I tell you the truth, he will certainly not lose his reward.
> —MATTHEW 10:42

Lincoln's love for pure water and his desire for others to partake of it reminds us of Jesus' words. When we have compassion and love for God's servants, we are assured of a special reward in heaven. We help God's people when we give them cups of cold water in the name of Jesus.

You Can't Kill the Soul

I T IS REGRETTABLE that many African-American men and women suffered in the bonds of slavery in the United States. Many who were stolen away from their native lands had to make the best of bad circumstances as they lived on Southern plantations.

Fortunately, a few plantation owners did treat their slaves with care. If a slave had a kind master, often good relationships were formed between them and their families. Hence, some slaves actually felt a loyalty for the South because of the fair, humane, and loving treatment of their Southern owners.

Oppression and prejudice unfortunately were not limited to the South. In the following story, Nancy Emerson wrote about a Union soldier who tormented a Southern slave because he would not renounce his secession from the Union:

> *An old negro who was kept on nothing but water for three days because he refused to work & said he was 'secesh.' The fourth day an officer went to him with the inquiry "Are you secesh yet?" His reply was "Bless de Lord, Massa, I is secesh yet." He was then set to splitting wood with iron balls attached to his hands & feet . . . The old fellow went on splitting saying "Bless de Lord, massa, any where you can put 'em. You can kill de body but you can't kill de soul, & when dat gets to heaven, it will be secesh yet." Noble fellow. It does one good to hear such instances. I do not know how I could stand the starving process myself, but think I would have to be right hungry before I would give in. She adds that her brother called to the officer saying, "Hello Grant, is that what you call freedom."*[186]

> I am not ashamed of the gospel, because it is the power of God for the salvation of everyone who believes.
> —ROMANS 1:16

The old African-American slave in the story should convict and inspire us because he would not compromise his convictions. May the Lord give us men and women in our day who are virtually unashamed to stand up for the sake of the gospel.

A Sacred Anonymous Prayer

THE FOLLOWING prayer was written by an unknown member of the Lenoir family in October of 1863 during the Civil War:

> *Fit us we pray Thee for any trials which may await us. If it should be thy will that we are driven from our home, and deprived of temporal comforts, give us strength to bear it and to look forward to those eternal blessings which are promised to the truly faithful; Oh! strengthen our faith that we may trust thee in the darkest hour of our trials here. We pray thee to look in much mercy upon our afflicted country, and stay the strife which imbues a brothers hand in a brothers blood . . . Have mercy we pray thee on the sick and wounded soldier. Give him patience in his afflictions and be blessed to restore him to health and usefulness . . . Hear we pray thee the wailing and moans that proceed from thousands of bereaved hearts united in one common cause and sympathizing each with others woes. Oh! that this together with the shrieks of the wounded and dying soldiers might penetrate the hearts of those who have it in their power to stop this cruel war. If our cause is unjust, be pleased to open the eyes of our rulers before it is too late, and prepare us as a people for any trials to which we may be subjected . . . Watch over us this night as a family, refresh us with sleep and fit us for the duties of another day . . . And prepare us for thy Kingdom above, we ask for Christ's sake.*

> *Amen . . .*

> *October AD 1863*[187]

You know that the testing of your faith develops perseverance.
—JAMES 1:3

The Lenoir family had a mature view of their Christian faith. Rather than asking the Lord to keep them from trials, they prayed for strength to bear them. They also asked God to prepare them for his kingdom above.

The Source of Jackson's Courage

I N THE FOLLOWING account, author George Eggleston speaks on the sources of Jackson's courage:

Nobody ever understood him, and nobody has ever been quite able to account for him. The members of his own staff, of whom I happen to have known one or two intimately, seem to have failed, quite as completely as the rest of the world, to penetrate his singular and contradictory character. His biographer, Mr. John Esten Cooke, read him more perfectly perhaps than any one else, but even he, in writing of the hero, evidently views him from the outside. Dr. Dabney, another of Jackson's historians, gives us a glimpse of the man, in one single aspect of his character, which may be a clew to the whole. He says there are three kinds of courage, of which two only are bravery. These three varieties of courage are, first, that of the man who is simply insensible of danger; second, that of men who, understanding, appreciating, and fearing danger, meet it boldly nevertheless, from motives of pride; and third, the courage of men keenly alive to danger, who face it simply from a high sense of duty. . . . Whatever other mysteries there may have been about the man, it is clear that his well-nigh morbid devotion to duty was his ruling characteristic.[188]

Jackson's courage was drawn from his attention to duty. Yet, his sense of duty came from a much stronger spiritual conviction. He believed he was being used by God in a plan which was too high for human comprehension.

Things do not always go as we plan, but if we will continue with God, we can face life's difficulties without fear, knowing that God sees the bigger picture.

> Now all has been heard; here is the conclusion of the matter: Fear God and keep his commandments, for this is the whole duty of man. For God will bring every deed into judgment, including every hidden thing, whether it is good or evil.
>
> —ECCLESIASTES 12:13, 14

A Way of Escape

THE ANXIETY of the mothers of young soldiers in the Civil War was often more than they could bear. Communication traveled slowly, and it was often weeks before concerned mothers heard of their sons' fate from the battlefields. Mothers could only pray that the Lord would protect their sons from death.

Bettie Kimberly was one such mother who expressed her feelings in a letter of to her family:

> *. . . I am all anxiety for the termination of the battle of Murfreesboro* [Tennessee] *hoping we may gain some advantage from a great victory there, though I am in fear and trembling for the boys. They are all there I expect and God grant that they may all escape."*
> *Bettie M Kimberly*[189]

We often face trials and fear we have no way of escape, yet the Lord has promised us that he will not allow anything to come into our lives that we will not be able to bear. He will either make a way of escape or else give us the grace to endure it.

> No temptation has seized you except what is common to man. And God is faithful; he will not let you be tempted beyond what you can bear. But when you are tempted, he will also provide a way out so that you can stand up under it.
> —1 CORINTHIANS 10:13

I Will Look to the Hills

A NNA MELLINGER, a farmer's wife, kept a diary throughout the year of 1864 on the burning of Chambersburg, Pennsylvania, by Confederate troops. Most of Anna's diary was written about everyday life. Yet the burning of Chambersburg prompted her to write the following:

Anna Mellinger [1st] *January. O Lord preserve us in thy ways that we turn not to the right nor left keep us beneath thy cross bestow us A willing heart and mind while all things Cometh from thee keep us In thy narrow path and in thy Love and union with all thy Children and peace with all men. I will lift up mine eyes unto the hills from whence cometh my help my help cometh from the Lord which made heaven and earth. He will not Suffer thy foot to be moved he that keepeth thee will not slumber Behold he that keepeth Israel shall neither Slumber nor Sleep The Lord is thy keeper the Lord is thy shade upon thy right hands the sun shall not smith thee by day nor the moon by night The Lord shall preserve thee from all evil he shall preserve thy soul.*[190]

God's grace sustained the needy Mellinger family through one of the most trying times in history. Anna Mellinger drew her strength from Psalm 121. Our support as Christians is found by walking daily in the presence of Christ. Anna reminded herself of the sacrifice that Christ made on the cross. In light of that sacrifice, Anna's prayer was that the Lord would always keep her ready to accept God's will for her life.

> I lift up my eyes to the hills where does my help come from? My help comes from the LORD, the Maker of heaven and earth. He will not let your foot slip—he who watches over you will not slumber; indeed, he who watches over Israel will neither slumber nor sleep. The LORD watches over you— the LORD is your shade at your right hand; the sun will not harm you by day, nor the moon by night. The LORD will keep you from all harm— he will watch over your life; the LORD will watch over your coming and going both now and forevermore.
> —PSALM 121:1–8

Peace Proclaimed!
But at What a Price!

JUDGE J. M. HARRIS married Mary Lum and moved to Avenel plantation near Vicksburg, Mississippi, where they operated a family cotton
plantation business. When the Civil War began in 1861, their lives changed
dramatically. Daughter Annie Laura Broiderick wrote the following account
30 years after the war:

> *Peace proclaimed at last! But how dearly
> bought! Death had entered almost every house-
> hold in the land, and I could write of women
> traveling miles over the different battle-fields
> seeking for their dead.*
>
> *Some never knew where their loved ones
> lay. . . . Hundreds sleep the eternal sleep unclaimed,
> and their deeds of glory are buried with them;
> but they are not forgotten . . .*
>
> *My enthusiasm and love of country grow
> stronger, as the old scenes spring into life, the
> ruined homes, poverty, distress and death; and
> yet I feel that the War was inevitable. The Union
> could not have been separated, and from heart-aches, bitterness and
> pain, has been born a newer feeling, a newer love for the old Flag; the
> new South in loving reconciliation holds fast the hand of her Northern
> brother, and feels that though reconstructed they are Stronger in affec-
> tion and more united in thought . . .*
>
> *'This was written by my Sister, Annie Laura Harris.'*

signed Carrie L. Harris. I have kept it all these years. I loved her.[191]

> Then God said,
> "Take your son, your
> only son, Isaac,
> whom you love, and
> go to the region of
> Moriah. Sacrifice
> him there as a burnt
> offering on one of
> the mountains I will
> tell you about."
> —GENESIS 22:2

Abraham knew the meaning of sacrifice. When called upon to sacrifice
his only son, Abraham obeyed, but the Lord provided a substitute.

The price the soldiers of the Civil War paid for their cause was astounding. We can only imagine the heartache of sorrowful mothers as they traveled miles along the lines of battle after the Civil War, looking for the
remains of their fallen sons.

The Escape of Henry "Box" Brown

THE BLACK SLAVES in the South often used desperate measures to escape. Henry Brown lived as a slave in Richmond, Virginia, in the 1840s. William Still, a well-known abolitionist, tells the story of an ingenious plan that he and Brown devised to gain the slave's freedom. He would climb into a wooden crate and have himself shipped to William H. Johnson in Philadelphia.

> *The size of the box and how it was to be made to fit him most comfortably was of his own ordering. Two feet eight inches deep, two feet wide, and three feet long were the exact dimensions of the box, lined with baize . . . His resources with regard to food and water consisted of the following: One bladder of water and a few small biscuits. His mechanical implement to meet the death-struggle for fresh air, all told was one large gimlet (a small tool for drilling holes) . . . He entered his box, which was safely nailed up and hoped with five hickory hoops, and was then addressed by his next friend, James A. Smith, a shoe dealer, to Wm. H. Johnson, Arch street, Philadelphia . . . The witnesses will never forget that moment. Saw and hatchet quickly had the five hickory hoops cut and the lid off, and the marvelous resurrection of Brown ensued. Rising up in his box, he reached out his hand, saying, "How do you do, Gentlemen?" The little assemblage hardly knew what to think or do at the moment.[192]*

> It is for freedom that Christ has set us free. Stand firm then, do not let yourselves be burdened again by a yoke of slavery.
> —GALATIANS 5:1

In this age of equal rights we can't imagine the atrocities that many African-Americans suffered during a disappointing time in U.S. history. For black slaves, the prospect of freedom was only a dream until the beginning of the War between the States. Henry Brown was one of the few who escaped the bonds of slavery unscathed. Many slaves, less fortunate than Brown, found freedom in Christ that sustained them through the perilous experiences.

Victory, Honor, and Independence

THE CONFEDERATE Congress chose Constance Cary along with two other ladies to sew the first flags of the Confederacy for the Culpepper Courthouse in Culpepper, Virginia. Constance sent her first flag to a dashing young cavalry general named Van Dorn.

November 10, 1861

Will General Van Dorn honor me by accepting a flag which I have taken pleasure in making, and now send with an earnest prayer that the work of my hand may hold its place near him as he goes out to a glorious struggle—and, God willing, may one day wave over the re-captured batteries of my home near the down-trodden Alexandria? . . .

> But the plans of the LORD stand firm forever, the purposes of his heart through all generations.
> —PSALM 33:11

"Constance Cary."
Army of the Potomac, Manassas, November 12, 1861[193]

* * * * *

To Miss Constance Cary, Culpepper C.H.
Dear Lady:

The beautiful flag made by your hands and presented to me with the prayer that it should be borne by my side in the impending struggle for the existence of our country, is an appeal to me as a soldier as alluring as the promises of glory; but when you express the hope, in addition, that it may one day wave over the re-captured city of your nativity . . . Be assured, dear young lady, that it shall wave over your home if heaven smiles upon our cause, and I live, and that here shall be written upon it by the side of your name which it now bears, "Victory, Honor and Independence." . . .

Very truly and respectfully, dear lady, I am your humble and obedient servant.
"Earl Van Dorn, Major-General, P. A. C. S."

Even though General Van Dorn did not see his dream realized for the South, his spirit for "victory, honor and independence" lives in the hearts of brave men and women who have defended our great country.

No Fear at Gettysburg

ABRAHAM LINCOLN spent time in prayer and depended on God's guidance during the war-torn years of his presidency. President Lincoln made the following statement to General Dan Sickles who had fought at Gettysburg:

> *Well, I will tell you how it was. In the pinch of the campaign up there (at Gettysburg) when everybody seemed panic stricken and nobody could tell what was going to happen, oppressed by the gravity of our affairs, I went to my room one day and locked the door and got down on my knees before Almighty God and prayed to Him mightily for victory at Gettysburg. I told Him that this war was His war, and our cause His cause, but we could not stand another Fredericksburg or Chancellorsville. And after that, I don't know how it was, and I cannot explain it, but soon a sweet comfort crept into my soul. The feeling came that God had taken the whole business into His own hands and that things would go right at Gettysburg and that is why I had no fears about you.*[194]

> I prayed to the LORD and said, "O Sovereign LORD, do not destroy your people, your own inheritance that you redeemed by your great power and brought out of Egypt with a mighty hand."
> —DEUTERONOMY 9:26

Moses faced an overwhelming task in delivering over two million people from the bondage of Egypt, but he took his problems to the Lord in prayer and saw a mighty deliverance all because he dared to place the task in God's hands.

As Lincoln faced Gettysburg he felt the great weight of responsibility on his shoulders for the final fate of the Union. Like Moses, Lincoln knew where to take his burdens when faced with this nearly impossible task. History bears witness to the fact that God heard Lincoln's prayer that day. Even though great loss occurred on both sides, Gettysburg became the turning point of the Civil War. We often fight unnecessary battles because we refuse to turn them over to the capable hands of the Lord. Prayer still changes things.

Lee Wept over Jackson's Death

ROBERT E. LEE'S personal servant, William, was with Lee when the general learned of the death of his dear friend General Jackson.

I have even seed him cry. I never seed him sadder dan dat gloomy mownin' when he tol' me 'bout how Gineral Stonewall Jackson had been shot by his own men. He muster hurd it befo' but he never tol' me til' nex' mawnin'.

"William," he says ter me, "William, I have lost my right arm."

"How come yer ter say dat, Marse Robert?" I axed him. "Yo ain't bin in no battle sence yestiddy, an' I doan see yo' arm bleedin' ".

"I'm bleeding at the heart, William," he says, and I slipped out'n de tent, 'cause he looked lak he wanted to be by hisself. A little later I cum back an' he tol' me dat Gineral Jackson had bin shot by one of his own soljers. The Gineral had tol' 'em to shoot anybody goin' or comin' across de line. And den de Gineral hisself puts on a federal uniform and scouted across de lines. When he comes back, one of his own soljers raised his gun. "Don't shoot. I'm your general," Marse Jackson yelled. Dey said dat de sentry was hard o' hearin'. Anyway, he shot his Gineral an' kilt him. . . .[195]

> My flesh and my heart may fail, but God is the strength of my heart and my portion forever.
> —PSALM 73:26

Even though William was not exactly clear over the events that surrounded Jackson's death, Jackson did eventually die from wounds inflicted by his own soldiers.

Lee felt as if his heart was bleeding, and that he had lost his right arm when he received news that Jackson had fallen in friendly fire. In spite of this great loss, Lee continued to fight trusting in the Lord until the conclusion of the war. Lee, like Jackson, had learned to draw his strength from the Lord.

Little Eddie, the Drummer Boy

G ENERAL LYON of the Union army lost his drummer boy to sickness
and was seeking a new one. He soon learned of a young boy who
would like to enlist in his company.

> *The next morning a nice-looking middle-aged woman appeared with
> her young thirteen year old son. She was from East Tennessee. Her
> husband had been killed by the rebels . . . In the process of finding a
> way to earn a living she came up with a plan to allow her boy to use
> his talent in the army for a short time until she could obtain gainful
> employment.*
>
> *The captain was about to express determination not to take the
> young boy when he blurted out, "Don't be afraid captain, I can
> drum." Admiring the young boy's confidence
> and discovering his very talented ability to play
> the drum, the captain accepted the mournful
> mother's offer. The mother's parting words to
> the captain were very emotional as she said,
> "Captain, you will bring him back with you,
> won't you?" "Yes", he replied, "we will be cer-
> tain to bring him back" . . . It wasn't long until
> word was passed along that General Lyon had
> been killed. One soldier upon listening for the
> footsteps of the enemy heard a low drum beat
> coming from the underbrush of the ravine which sound much like lit-
> tle Eddie's drum. Upon investigating the noise, one of the soldiers from
> the First Iowa came upon little Eddie who had his back against a tree.
> It was apparent that both his feet had been blown off by a cannon ball.
> Lying next to him was a dead rebel soldier. The rebel soldier had been
> mortally wounded and fell next to Eddie. In compassion he had taken
> off his leather suspenders and tied them around the lower part of
> Eddie's legs to keep him from bleeding to death. The rebel soldier then
> turned over on the ground and died. . . .*[196]

> I tell you the truth,
> anyone who will not
> receive the kingdom
> of God like a little
> child will never
> enter it.
> —MARK 10:15

Little Eddie's courage in battle reminds us of Jesus' illustration of children in relation to the kingdom of God. The desire of Little Eddie, the drummer boy, to bravely follow his commander into battle, no matter the cost
should inspire us to follow our Lord with equal dedication.

A Slave's Prayer

A VIRGINIA SLAVE set himself to pray after he learned of Lincoln's promise of emancipation.

A Virginia slave, who had heard of the President's [Lincoln's] promise concerning the proclamation to be issued on the 1st of January, then only a few days in the future, was heard praying, and with great earnestness and a deeply affected heart thus;

"O God Almighty! Keep the engines of the rebellion going till New Year's! Good Lord! Pray, don't let off the steam; Lord, don't reverse the engine; don't back up; Lord, don't put on the brakes! But pray, good, Lord, put on more steam! Make it go a mile a minute! Yes, Lord, pray make it go sixty miles and hour! ('Amen!' 'Do good Lord!' responded the brethren and sisters.) Lord, don't let the express train of rebellion smash up till the 1st of January! Don't let the rebels back down, but harden their hearts as hard as Pharaoh's and keep all hands going, till the train reaches the Depot of Emancipation!"[197]

Christians should pray with the fervency of the slave in the South who longed for freedom. We read about the prayers of the Civil War leaders, but we seldom consider the cries of African-American slaves who prayed day and night with a determination that rivaled that of New Testament saints.

What could be accomplished spiritually in our churches and our nation if believing men and women would pray with fervency and determination until God opens the floodgates of heaven?

> Therefore confess your sins to each other and pray for each other so that you may be healed. The prayer of a righteous man is powerful and effective.
>
> —JAMES 5:16

Free at Last

TO BLACK SLAVES, the Yankees battling their way through the South meant a long-awaited deliverance.

A couple of officers were advancing some distance apart from their men, when they were hailed by an old Negro woman standing in the door of her rude cabin. 'Bless de Lord, bless de Lord,' she exclaimed as loud as she could, 'yer's come at last, yer's come at last! I've looked for yer these many years, and now yer's come. Bless de Lord.' Nothing could exceed the old woman's delight at seeing the Yankees . . . long years she had waited to see this deliverance. Slave she was, and the slow years dragged their weary lengths past her youth, and still hope whispered that the hour would come when the bondage would be broken.[198]

Simeon had longed and prayed for the coming Messiah. When he finally realized his prayers had been answered, he rejoiced and said that he could now die in peace. The slave woman in the above account prayed and longed for freedom. With the coming of the Union soldiers, her prayers became reality.

Continuing in prayer will bring results in due time.

> Moved by the Spirit, he went into the temple courts. When the parents brought in the child Jesus to do for him what the custom of the Law required, Simeon took him in his arms and praised God, saying: "Sovereign Lord, as you have promised, you now dismiss your servant in peace."
> —LUKE 2:27–29

The Morning Just before Eternity

GENERAL HAYES was about to enter the conflict in the wilderness where he would lose his life. That morning he wrote down his thoughts, not knowing that the wilderness battle would be his last:

This morning was beautiful, for

Lightly and brightly shone the sun,
As if the morning was a jocund one.

Although we were anticipating to march at eight o'clock, it might have been an appropriate harbinger of the day of the regeneration of mankind; but it only brought to remembrance, through the throats of many bugles, that duty enjoined upon each one, perhaps, before the setting sun, to lay down a life for his country.[199]

Could this be our final day of life on earth? What a sobering thought. As we rush about at a busy pace, we scarcely think about the nearness of eternity. Jesus promised that he would return and take us to heaven.

When my dad came home from the hospital after he learned he had terminal cancer, his whole attitude drastically changed. Temporal values lost their allurement, while eternal values became the most urgent. His ultimate goal was to prepare himself and others for meeting Jesus Christ at any time.

What would you do differently if you faced imminent eternity because of a terminal illness?

> "Men of Galilee," they said, "why do you stand here looking into the sky? This same Jesus, who has been taken from you into heaven, will come back in the same way you have seen him go into heaven."
>
> —ACTS 1:11

Lincoln Invited the Influences
of the Holy Spirit

PRESIDENT ABRAHAM LINCOLN called upon the people of the United States to pray, and he said the following:

July 15, 1863

> *I invite the people of the United States . . . to invoke the influence of His Holy Spirit . . . to guide the counsels of the government with wisdom adequate to so great a national emergency, and to visit with tender care and consolation throughout the length and breadth of our land all those who, through the vicissitudes of marches, voyages, battles, and sieges have been brought to suffer in mind, body, or estate, and finally to lead the whole nation through the paths of repentance and submission to the Divine will back to the perfect enjoyment of union and internal peace.[200]*

> But the Counselor, the Holy Spirit, whom the Father will send in my name, will teach you all things and will remind you of everything I have said to you.
>
> —JOHN 14:26

Lincoln urged the people of the United States to ask God for wisdom in the face of a great national emergency. His prayer was that God would lead the nation to repentance and complete submission to God, which would inspire peace.

Already the North and South had suffered tremendous losses. Lincoln believed that America was reaping God's chastisement because she had not repented and submitted to his divine authority. He also believed the only way to peace in the hearts of people was through a spiritual revival.

Lincoln's observation of a war-torn nation is just as true of our country today. We have drifted from depending on the Lord's guidance in our national life.

Pray for a spiritual revival in the leadership of our great nation.

Mrs. Bickerdyke

A BELOVED ARMY NURSE, Mrs. Bickerdyke, was a remarkable woman of moral fortitude. All the Union officers, including General Sherman admired her. She always had the best interest of the soldiers in mind when she attended to them in the hospital where she worked. The following story shows her influence in doing what was necessary and right:

On one occasion, visiting one of the wards at nearly eleven o'clock A.M., where the men were very badly wounded, she found that the assistant surgeon-in-charge, who had been out "on a spree" the night before and had slept very late, had not yet made out the special diet list for the ward, and the men, faint and hungry, had had no breakfast. She at once denounced him in the strongest terms. He came in meanwhile, and on his inquiry, "Hoity, toity, what's the matter!" She turned upon him with, "Matter enough, you miserable scoundrel! Here these men, any one of them is worth a thousand of you, are suffered to starve and die, because you want to be off upon a drunk! . . . you shall not stay in the army a week longer." The surgeon still laughed, but he turned pale, for he knew her power. . . . Within three days, she had caused his discharge. He went to headquarters and asked to be reinstated. General Sherman, who was then in command, listened patiently, and then inquired who had caused this discharge . . . said the surgeon, hesitatingly; "I suppose it was that woman, that Mrs. Bickerdyke." "Oh," said Sherman. "Well, if it was her, I can do nothing for you. She ranks me."[201]

Mrs. Bickerdyke would not tolerate immoral behavior, especially when it came to caring for wounded soldiers. She is an example of the honesty and morality that is needed in people of our communities today. A revival of old-fashioned morals would do much to bring our nation back into God's favor. Pray earnestly for a spiritual revival in America.

> Now we know that whatever the law says, it says to those who are under the law, so that every mouth may be silenced and the whole world held accountable to God.
> —ROMANS 3:19

The Great Day of Judgment

M. B. BROUGHTON, a Confederate soldier from Alabama, wrote some detailed accounts of the results of war on famous battlefields, including a firsthand account of the battle of Gettysburg:

> One of the saddest sights I ever witnessed was on the field of Gettysburg. We had captured some fifteen hundred prisoners and I was one of the guards marching them to the rear. Passing along where there were hundreds dead, wounded and mutilated I saw a soldier with a North Carolina regiment mark in his cap leaning against a fly tent. A fragment of a shell had struck him above the breast bone and tore the whole stomach lining away leaving exposed his heart and other organs which were in motion and he seemed alive and conscious. I lingered a moment for I had never seen any thing so shocking before nor have I seen the countenance of a dying man so peculiar and unearthly. The artillery fire at the battle of Gettysburg was something terrific. The battle field abounded in mounds and hills which were advantageous for planting and operating the cannon and the batteries on both sides were the pride of either army. I do not know the number operated at the same time but it was said to be five hundred; but I do know the roar was awful and the heavens surcharged with hissing, roaring balls screeching, screaming, bursting shells enveloped in sulphurous smoke that clouded the July sun. When the heavens are rolled together as a scroll in the last days I doubt whether it will present a more awe-inspiring spectacle than that historic field presented on that fatal day.[202]

> The sun will be turned to darkness and the moon to blood before the coming of the great and dreadful day of the Lord.
> —JOEL 2:31

The prophet Joel preached that in the future God will judge the earth. No other day in history (including Gettysburg) will compare to the awfulness of that great day.

Barefoot in the Snow

CIVIL WAR SOLDIER and author W. R. Broughton wrote:

On the East Tennessee campaign, we were cut off three months from railroads, mails and supplies. I saw hundreds of bare-footed men marching over frozen snow near Dandridge on the French Broad River, and saw the blood from their feet mark the snow. Sometimes an order would come for the barefooted to go to the butcher's pen. A man would put his foot on the hairy side of a fresh cow hide and a piece heart-shaped would be cut out. Then holes were cut near the edges, and it was sewed with thongs of the same material over his feet. They were better than nothing for a time, but when near the fire they shrank amazingly, and when wet by the rains, they became too large. Yet men clad in this fashion on empty stomachs, drove the enemy, and after dark we felt among the shucks where the enemy had camped and picked and ate raw corn that had dropped from the horses mouths.[203]

The Confederate soldiers were poor and often ill equipped. Many wore out their shoes so they had to walk barefooted in the snow. In spite of hunger and lack of clothing, these dedicated men continued to do their duty.

The sacrifice of these soldiers reminds us of Jesus making himself poor so that we might become spiritually rich. We are a rich country indeed, in light of the sacrifices that have been made by God-fearing, courageous men and women in uniform. Let us thank God for their sacrifices and let us also thank God for Jesus who sacrificed his all for our salvation.

> For you know the grace of our Lord Jesus Christ that though he was rich, yet for your sakes he became poor, so that you through his poverty might become rich.
>
> —2 CORINTHIANS 8:9

A Union Soldier's Love
for His Country

UNION SOLDIER Thomas W. Leach wrote to his church family in Warrick County, Indiana, as follows:

I love my Country its free institutions and privileges which we have always enjoyed from our youth up and which our forefathers shed their blood on the field of battle for us their posterity and I for one feel willing if necessary to sacrifice my life and my all of a worldly nature to leave the same legacy to my children and their posterity for without it what would our Country be . . . I am one that believes in putting down this rebellion let it cost what it will. I enlisted in this war to fight the battles of our Country not for mere pay but because I love our free and noble government which has protected our rights and made our nation respected over the whole world therefore my brethren I feel glad to say to you that I am a soldier fighting in defense of the old stars and stripes which has floated over our happy land of America and I pray God that it may still continue to wave while time shall last.[204]

> Suppose one of you wants to build a tower. Will he not first sit down and estimate the cost to see if he has enough money to complete it?
> —LUKE 14:28

Private Leach counted the cost of serving his country and decided he would serve the Union no matter what cost. His attitude came from a deep sense of a debt owed to the forefathers of America by the sacrifice of their blood.

We owe a great debt to Jesus Christ who paid the price on the cross that we might be free from the bondage of sin and Satan. Jesus reconciled us to God so we would reconcile others to him. Out of gratitude for Jesus' sacrifice, we owe him our sacrificial service in reaching a lost generation in a postmodern world.

A Soldier Feels Rejected

DEWITT CLINTON GALLAHER was a provost guard in the First Virginia Cavalry. When he marched into Richmond, he was dirty, tired, and hungry. It was Sunday, and everyone around him was dressed in their finest clothes, including the officers he encountered.

August 7th (Sunday)

Left camp and marched to and through Richmond—up Pearl to Main St., to 3rd to Broad and to Brooke Turnpike. As we were riding along at corner of Franklin and 3rd St., someone called my name. I found it was Miss Laura Kent, whom I had met and known in Waynesboro. She begged me to accompany her to her home, corner of 1st and Franklin and get something to eat. . . . Tried to beg off, though terribly hungry, but she insisting, I yielded. The streets were full of Church goers at the time. I tied my horse in front of her home and entered with her to the parlor, where entertaining some well dressed officers in flashy uniforms and shining boots, evidently swivel-chair sissy officers around Richmond, who looked almost shocked to see a private, dusty and not very neat sitting at a marble top table eating from silver and china! I was so fussed and felt so awkward, I really could eat but little. So I told Laura I "had a sick comrade" and if she would fix up a lunch I would take it to him. . . . Needless to say, that soon after leaving, I threw my reins on the neck of my horse and the "sick comrade" ate and enjoyed that lunch. I ate every crumb of it. I overtook my command at the Yellow Tavern (where our old Commander General J. E. B. Stuart was killed in the May previous) . . .[205]

> When the teachers of the law who were Pharisees saw him eating with the 'sinners' and tax collectors, they asked his disciples: "Why does he eat with tax collectors and 'sinners?' "
> —MARK 2:16

When the Pharisees saw Jesus associating himself with the rejected of society they passed judgment on him. Soldier Gallaher did not feel comfortable in Richmond around people in their Sunday best. He was hungry, dirty, and felt alone among all the churchgoers. In the spirit of Christ, the church needs to love and receive sinners.

Leadership in the Home

CONFEDERATE SOLDIER Samuel M. Potter wrote to his wife, Cynthia, on July 20, 1863, expressing his love for her and his home.

I will still leave you in the hands of our Great Preserver who has kept us all so long in the midst of dangers & preserve us from harm. Oh how I would like to be sitting beside you in the old church on the hill listening to Mr. McKee. Those were among the most pleasant hours of my life there to have them with the children & me there & oh how I would like to enjoy them again. I hope God will preserve & protect us & permit us to meet again to enjoy the service of his sanctuary again on earth. Pray for me dear Cynthia that I may grow in grace maybe more sanctified & that I may be more acceptable to my Creator & I will still pray for my dear wife that she may be kept in the hollow of Gods hand, that no harm may befal her that she may be made holy & righteous that we all parents & children may be accepted by the Almighty through his son the Lord Jesus Christ. That will bless you all in the prayer of your most affectionate husband.

> For I have chosen him, so that he will direct his children and his household after him to keep the way of the LORD by doing what is right and just, so that the LORD will bring about for Abraham what he has promised him.
> —GENESIS 18:19

S. M. Potter.[206]

Potter's desire was to sit beside his dear wife in church. From this, we gather he was a dedicated Christian husband who took his spiritual leadership seriously.

The Lord knew he could trust Abraham to be the spiritual leader of his home. We need a revival of manly leadership today to secure our homes against the onslaughts of the enemy.

Jackson Stood Firm
like a Stone Wall

AT MANASSAS, Virginia, General Thomas Jackson fought a famous battle in which he was wounded and earned his historic nickname "Stonewall."

At one moment it seemed as if all was lost, The troops of Southern Carolina, commanded by General Bee, had been overwhelmed, and he rode up to Jackson in despair, exclaiming, "They are beating us back!" "Then," said Jackson, "we will give them the bayonet!" This cool reply showed the unconquered mind of one who never knew that he was beaten, and put fresh courage into the heart of him who was almost ready to acknowledge defeat; and, as he rode back to his command, he cried out to them to "look at Jackson!" saying, "There he stands like a stone wall! Rally behind the Virginians!" The cry and the example had its effect, and the broken ranks were reformed, and led to another charge, when their leader fell dead with his face to the foe. But with his last breath he had christened his companion in arms, in the baptism of fire, with the name that he was henceforth to bear, not only in the Southern army, but in history, of STONEWALL JACKSON, while the troops that followed him on that day counted it glory enough to bear on their colors the proud title of the "Stonewall Brigade." [207]

> Therefore, take up the full armor of God, so that you will be able to resist in the evil day, and having done everything, to stand firm.
>
> —EPHESIANS 6:13, 14

Jackson was a God-fearing leader in the Confederacy and relied on God's armor to protect him in battle. He amazed his men by his calmness, absolute courage, and resolve in battle—so much so that he earned the nickname, "Stonewall." He could stand firm in battle because he first spent time on his knees in prayer.

Saved by the Bible

SOON AFTER THE BATTLE of Manassas, Stonewall Jackson wrote an amazing account of a Confederate soldier whose life was saved by a Bible.

> *Mr. James Davidson's son, Frederick, and William Page (son of my dear friend) were killed. Young Riley's life was saved by his Bible which was in the breast-pocket of his coat . . .*[208]

How ironic that a soldier's life was literally saved by carrying his Bible into battle. Notice that he carried it in a pocket which covered his heart. Little did this soldier know that his habit of keeping the Word of God near his heart would one day save his life.

We need more than just a head knowledge of Scripture. It needs to rest deeply in our hearts. When that happens, the Bible becomes a shield of truth protecting us from the enemy's fiery arrows. It brings salvation, protection, comfort, and a shield against temptation.

> Your word I have treasured in my heart, that I may not sin against you.
> —PSALM 119:11

A Patriotic Maryland
Woman's Sacrifice

W HILE MAKING entrenchments for battle near Washington, D.C., some soldiers came upon a little home directly in the line of battle at Bladensburg. This beautiful cottage stood on the brow of a hill, surrounded by shrubbery and flowers. It was a little paradise on earth. This posed a problem for the Union army.

Calling upon the lady, therefore, the officers explained, in the most delicate manner, the object of their visit, and the military necessity which doomed her beautiful ground to destruction. The lady listened in silence. Tears rose to her eyes. She arose, walked to the open window, looked for a moment upon the lovely scene, and then, turning to the officers, said: "If it must be so, take it freely. I hoped to live here in peace and quiet, and never to leave this sweet spot, which my husband has beautified for years past. But if my country demands it, take it freely. You have my consent." Then offering refreshments to the officers, she said no more on the subject.[209]

This sweet lady in the story recognized there was a cause greater than her sentimental feelings, so she sacrificed her beautiful home to help ensure the future of the United States. Reaching a new generation with the gospel may mean we will have to give up our traditional methods. Doctrinal truth should never change, but methods should fit the needs of a changing generation.

According to the Scripture, when we are willing to give up houses and lands for the sake of the gospel, we can expect to be rewarded by God.

> "I tell you the truth," Jesus replied, "no one who has left home or brothers or sisters or mother or father or children or fields for me and the gospel will fail to receive a hundred times as much in this present age (homes, brothers, sisters, mothers, children and fields—and with them, persecutions) and in the age to come, eternal life.
> —MARK 10:29, 30.

Joshua Chamberlain's Message

JOSHUA CHAMBERLAIN'S legacy speaks to us long after Gettysburg. Nearly a quarter of a century after the Civil War, Chamberlain stood on hallowed ground to dedicate a memorial in honor of the battle that made him a hero. On a stone is written, "Honor abides here." The following is part of the speech he gave in 1889 at the dedication of the Twentieth Maine Monument at Gettysburg:

I am certain that the position of this monument is quite to the left of the center of our regimental line when the final charge was ordered. Our original left did not extend quite to the great rock which now supports this memorial of honor . . . It was entirely fitting to mark it with that honor, as it became so conspicuous an object during the terrible struggle, the center and pivot of the whirlpool that raged around . . .

> A good name is more desirable than great riches; to be esteemed is better than silver or gold.
> —PROVERBS 22:1

The lesson impressed on me as I stand here and my heart and mind traverse your faces, and the years that are gone, is that in a great, momentous struggle like this commemorated here, it is character that tells . . . What I mean by character is a firm and seasoned substance of soul. I mean such qualities or acquirements as intelligence, thoughtfulness, conscientiousness, right-mindedness, patience, fortitude, long-suffering and unconquerable resolves. . . .

We know not of the future, and cannot plan for it much. But we can hold our spirits and our bodies so pure and high, we may cherish such thoughts and such ideals, and dream such dreams of lofty purpose, that we can determine and know what manner of men we will be whenever and wherever the hour strikes, that calls to noble action, this predestination God has given us in charge. No man becomes suddenly different from his habit and cherished thought. We carry our accustomed manners with us. And it was the boyhood you brought from your homes which made you men; which braced your hearts, which shone upon your foreheads, which held you steadfast in mind and body, and lifted these heights of Gettysburg to immortal glory.[210]

General Beauregard's Wise Advice

GENERAL GUSTAVE BEAUREGARD, on a visit to his battalion, shook hands with all his soldiers and addressed them as follows:

GENERAL GUSTAVE
TOUTANT
BEAUREGARD
*The National
Archives*

"Boys, be patient. The spider is patient; it takes him a long time to weave his web, but he never fails to catch his fly. We must imitate the spider; our web is nearly complete. In a few days you will have work to do. My advice to you is, to keep cool; don't be in too great a hurry; take your time when the fight comes . . . load and shoot slow, and aim low. Follow this, and history will have another victory to record for you."

After another warm shake of the hands, and a cordial "God bless you," the General left amid the wildest applause.[211]

One who rejects God is weaving for himself a web that will eventually trap him. The atheist in his disbelief has fallen prey to the enemy who is like a spider that traps his prey through deception.

Beauregard hoped to trap the enemy in much the same way and reminded his men that patience would win the day.

> What he trusts in is fragile; what he relies on is a spider's web.
> —JOB 8:14

Do Your Best to Read Your Bible

URBAN GRAMMER OWEN wrote the following encouraging letter to his young wife, Laura:

Tazewell, Claiborne County Tennessee, August 11th, 1862

Dear Laura, the little testament that Sallie Burns gave me I have read carefully through & another Bible nearly. I read the Bible a great deal several chapters every day. Your Daguerreotype [picture] & my little bible I carry in my side pocket.

I have lived honestly, morally & virtuous since I saw you. I left Cumberland Gap 17 of June since have been in ten miles of the railroad above Knoxville about 40 miles . . . Do your best you can to read your bible is the fervent prayer & wish of your devoted & unworthy servant.

U.A. Owen
Surgeon 4th Tenn
Col. J.A. McMurry's Regiment[212]

> It is to be with him [a king], and he is to read it all the days of his life so that he may learn to revere the LORD his God and follow carefully all the words of this law and these decrees.
>
> —DEUTERONOMY 17:18

Dr. Owen's love for the Bible, his wife, and his child became sweeter on the battlefield. Sometimes it takes the battlefield experiences of life to awaken us to the importance of family. Owen's admonition was for his wife to read the Bible. Undoubtedly, Owen found how precious the words of Scripture are in times of uncertainty. He longed for his wife to have the same blessing and comfort.

When things go smoothly, we may neglect our Bibles, but in tough times the Bible becomes as sweet as honey. Then we can prove its promises.

J. E. B. Stuart's Trampling of the Corn

MYRTA AVARY was a young Southern girl who recorded the following event during the Civil War. She met and knew some of the great leaders of the war, including J. E. B. Stuart.

> It was while I was at Mr. Bradford's that one of the most stirring events in Confederate history occurred. This was the trampling down of John Minor Botts's corn. Very good corn it was . . . but a field of corn, however good, and a private citizen, however estimable, are scarcely matters of national or international importance. The trouble was that John Minor Botts was on the Northern side and the corn was on the Southern side, and that Stuart held a grand review on the Southern side and the corn got trampled down. The fame of that corn went abroad into all the land. Northern and Southern papers vied with each other in editorials and special articles, families who had been friends for generations stopped speaking and do not speak to this day . . . and I can testify that General Stuart went there to review the troops, not to trample down the corn.
>
> Afterward John Minor Botts came over to see General Stuart and to quarrel about that corn. All that I can remember of how the general took Mr. Botts's visit and effort to quarrel was that Stuart wouldn't quarrel—whatever it was he said to Mr. Botts he got to laughing when he said it. Our colored Abigail told us with bated breath that "Mr. Botts ripped and rarred and snorted, but Genrul Stuart warn't put out none at all."[213]

> A fool gives full vent to his anger, but a wise man keeps himself under control.
> —PROVERBS 29:11

J. E. B. Stuart displayed great Christian character in his ability to take criticism and remain calm and unresponsive. Sometimes leaders must do things others may not understand or agree with. If a Christian leader has found his direction from the Lord, he must be calm, quiet, and firm in his decision.

Loyalty to the Union

HERMANN BOKUM was a chaplain in the Union army and wrote of events in East Tennessee:

It was at that time that a great Union meeting was held in the vicinity of Knoxville. Horace Maynard was occupied in another part of the State, but Andrew Johnson and other leading Union men were there, and the question was seriously debated whether East Tennessee should take up arms and destroy the bridges in order to prevent the sending of rebel troops from Louisiana, Mississippi and Alabama to Virginia. Less extreme measures prevailed, the bridges were not burnt, the troops from the Southern States rushed into East Tennessee, and the Union men of East Tennessee were singly overpowered and disarmed. In the meantime Fort Sumter had fallen and some of the secessionists came to me and asked me to join the Southern Confederacy. "You remind me," said I, "of a good old bishop, when he was led to the stake he was advised to abjure the Savior and save his life. 'Eighty and five years, was the answer of the bishop, has my Savior graciously protected me, and should I now forswear him?' So say I to you; thirty and five years has the flag of the Union with the help of God nobly protected me, and should I now forswear it?"[214]

> I eagerly expect and hope that I will in no way be ashamed, but will have sufficient courage so that now as always Christ will be exalted in my body, whether by life or by death.
> —PHILIPPIANS 1:20

As followers of the Lord Jesus Christ, we should not be ashamed to identify with his name. Jesus hung on the cross in public humiliation in order to reconcile us to God. We should never let the world, peer pressure, or any other opposing force keep us from proclaiming the good news of Jesus boldly.

The Struggle of East Tennesseans

CHAPLAIN HERMANN BOKUM spoke of the terrible hardships Tennesseans endured during the Civil War in Knoxville.

When . . . I on my missionary tours was passing through the fruitful valleys and over the pleasant hill sides of East Tennessee . . . I asked myself, whether indeed it was possible, that the mad ambition of men would go so far as to desolate these scenes of beauty. It has proved possible indeed . . . There is now misery and wretchedness the most fearful, and the rule of an armed mob bent upon indiscriminate plunder. Do you see yonder wretch? He has been a drunkard and a vagabond all his life-time, yet he has thousands of dollars in his pocket now, and he rides the most beautiful horse in that whole region of country. I could take you to the industrious farmer from whom he took the horse, and whom he robbed of his money . . . Do you see yonder girl? How beautiful she would be, if it were not for the loss of that eye! That eye she lost in successfully defending her honor against the assault of a Confederate soldier . . . Ah, my reader, you who live here so comfortable and so undisturbed, have little knowledge of what is going on but a few hundred miles from here. I have seen the man of eighty, the oldest and the wealthiest man of a loyal district, who at his age had joined the Home Guards, raise his trembling hands to heaven, and ask God whether there was no curse in store for deeds so cruel . . . Who could remain cold at the sight of enormities like these . . . Neither Brownlow nor myself, nor any, nor all of us can give a full record of cruelties which have been perpetrated and are now being perpetrated in the recesses of the mountains and valleys of East Tennessee. . . .[215]

> Do not take revenge, my friends, but leave room for God's wrath, for it is written: "It is mine to avenge; I will repay," says the Lord.
> —ROMANS 12:19

As children of God we often cry, "Is there no justice on earth?" How do we answer those who would look at the present atrocities in our world and ask, "Where is God?" The answer is that vengeance belongs to God.

Belle Boyd, Confederate Spy

ALTHOUGH WOMEN were not officially allowed to join the army during the Civil War, many of them performed a vital service as spies. Belle Boyd was a Confederate spy who showed great courage in her efforts to help the South. She gave the following account:

> *The night before the departure of General Shields, who was about, as he informed us, to "whip" Jackson, a council of war was held in what had formerly been my aunt's drawing-room. Immediately above this was a bedchamber, containing a closet, through the floor of which I observed a hole had been bored, whether with a view to espionage or not I have never been able to ascertain. It occurred to me, however, that I might turn the discovery to account; and, as soon as the council of war had assembled, I stole softly up-stairs, and, lying down the floor of the closet, applied my ear to the hole, and found, to my great joy, I could distinctly hear the conversation that was passing below. . . .*
>
> *I remained motionless and silent until the proceedings were brought to a conclusion, at one o'clock in the morning. As soon as the coast was clear I crossed the courtyard, and made the best of my way to my own room, and took down in cypher everything I had heard which seemed to me of any importance.*
>
> *I felt convinced that to rouse a servant, or make any disturbance at that hour, would excite the suspicions of the Federals by whom I was surrounded; accordingly I went straight to the stables myself, saddled my horse, and galloped away in the direction of the mountains* [to inform Confederate Colonel Ashby of her findings].[216]

> Greater love has no one than this, that he lay down his life for his friends.
>
> —JOHN 15:13

Belle Boyd's main concern was the protection of the Confederate armies. She was willing to put herself in harm's way to ensure the safety of those she loved dearly.

The Son of God laid down his life for his "friends." What a friend we have in Jesus.

A Confederate Girl's Thoughts on War

SARAH DAWSON did not care for the bitterness she witnessed from many men and women around her in 1862. With the innocence of a young girl's mind, she looked past the hatred. She felt that all who fought in the Civil War were Americans and should not be enemies.

I see some of the holiest eyes, so holy one would think the very spirit of charity lived in them, and all Christian meekness, go off in a mad tirade of abuse and say, with the holy eyes wondrously changed, "I hope God will send down plague, yellow fever, famine, on these vile Yankees, and that not one will escape death." O, what unutterable horror that remark causes me as often as I hear it! I think of the many mothers, wives, and sisters who wait as anxiously, pray as fervently in their faraway homes for their dear ones, as we do here; I fancy them waiting day after day for the footsteps that will never come, growing more sad, lonely, and heart-broken as the days wear on; I think of how awful it would be if one would say, "Your brothers are dead"; how it would crush all life and happiness out of me; and I say, "God forgive these poor women! They know not what they say!" O women! into what loathsome violence you have abased your holy mission! God will punish us for our hard-heartedness. Not a square off, in the new theatre, lie more than a hundred sick soldiers. What woman has stretched out her hand to save them, to give them a cup of cold water?[217]

> Keep yourselves in God's love as you wait for the mercy of our Lord Jesus Christ to bring you to eternal life. Be merciful to those who doubt; snatch others from the fire and save them; to others show mercy. . .
> —JUDE 21–22

Sarah Dawson saw the Civil War through the eyes of childlike innocence. Children can get to the root of a situation. I have often said that "a child can spot a hypocrite a mile away!" May Sarah's words convict us to have more compassion toward others.

General Pickett and God's Guidance

MAJOR GENERAL George E. Pickett wrote many intimate letters home to his dear wife. In this particular letter, Pickett was nearing the end of the war and Appomattox was just ahead. Defeat was inevitable, yet Pickett's men exhibited extraordinary faith.

> *It is long past the midnight hour and, like a boy, I have been reading over your dear, cheery letter, caressing the written page because it has been touched by your hand.*
>
> > You guide me with your counsel, and afterward you will take me into glory.
> > —PSALM 73:24
>
> *All is quiet now, but soon all will be bustle, for we march at daylight. Oh, my darling, were there ever such men as those of my division? This morning after the review I thanked them for their valiant services yesterday on the first of April, never to be forgotten by any of us, . . . Their answer to me was cheer after cheer, one after another calling out, "That's all right, Marse George, we only followed you." Then in the midst of these calls and silencing them, rose loud and clear dear old Gentry's voice, singing the old hymn which they all knew I loved*
>
> *"Guide me, oh, thou great Jehovah,*
> *Pilgrim through this barren land."*
>
> *Voice after voice joined in till from all along the line the plea rang forth:*
>
> *"Be my sword and shield and banner*
> *Be the Lord my righteousness."*
>
> *I don't think, my Sally, the tears sounded in my voice as it mingled with theirs; but they were in my eyes, and there was something new in my heart.*
>
> *When the last line had been sung, I gave the order to march, proceeding to this point where I had expected to cross the Appomattox and rejoin the main army.*[218]

Life can be filled with disappointments. In each we can depend on God's Word to give us the right counsel until the great day when there will be no disappointments.

In Memory of a Fellow Soldier

THE FOLLOWING was written in a manual by Confederate Chaplain
C. T. Quintard in memory of Thomas Edward King of Roswell, Georgia,
who fell at the battle of Chickamauga, on Saturday, September 18, 1863:

> *Whatever be the intensity of sorrow that bows
> and presses the heart of man, remember that,
> for every grief you suffer, the meek and Holy
> One suffered a thousand—that there is not in
> the spirit a dungeon or recess of anguish, how-
> ever untrodden or lonely, in which the Lord of
> glory was not a mourning inhabitant before
> you. Does the victim know the loss of earthly comforts? Christ knew
> not where to lay his head. Does he regret the fall from wealth or
> power? . . . Does he deplore the loss of friends? Christ was friendless
> in his most trying hour. Does he bewail the ingratitude of friends?
> Christ was betrayed by his own familiar one. Finally, does he fear the
> coming of death—the torture of the separation? What death can we
> anticipate which shall approach the horror of the last days of his
> Redeemer? Thus, wherever we turn, whatever be our shade of grief, we
> are but feeble copyists of the great sufferer, who, in His own person,
> exhausted every variety of human sorrow.*

> | There is a friend who sticks closer than a brother. |
> | :-- |
> | —PROVERBS 18:24 |

> *Christ leads me through no darker rooms
> Than He went through before;
> He that unto Christ's kingdom comes,
> Must enter by His door.
> "Come, Lord, when grace has made me meet
> Thy blessed face to see;
> For if Thy work on earth be sweet,
> What will Thy glory be?"*

—Baxter[219]

May we choose the kind of friends whom we can commend to the
Lord. An old proverb says, "A man is known by the company he keeps."

He Stood Alone

NATHANIEL D. RENFROE, Lieutenant of the Fifth Alabama Battalion of A. P. Hill's Division, fell in the battle of Fredericksburg on December 13, 1862. The following are quotes from his letters by his brother, Rev. J. J. D. Renfroe, who revealed Nathaniel's faith and readiness to meet the Lord:

> *In another letter he says: "And now, my brother, I have some reason to fear that you have not prepared yourself to meet the news of such a fate as may befall me . . . Let us be prepared for the worst—nay, rather for the best, for, though life is sweet, Heaven is infinitely sweeter! I am willing to go when God calls . . ."*
>
> *The last words he ever said to me [were] . . . "Well, brother, now we part, and unless you visit the army soon, we will not meet again on earth; but shed no tears for me—we will meet in heaven." How often have these words flashed through my memory, and carried solemn music deep into my soul! O that joyous meeting in heaven! Thank God, for the hope of heaven!*
>
> *His last day's work. He had offered up fervent prayer to God, and with the dawn of day the battle opened . . . The enemy rushed on and was too strong. An order came to retreat. It is supposed by his comrades that brother did not hear the order. The first Tennessee retreated, and the battalion retreated, except a few of his company who stood by him. The enemy coming up a few steps ordered surrender. He turned to his few men, with a gentle smile, and said: "Boys, this is a pretty hot place, and you must get out the best you can." Then turning to the enemy with his Repeater in hand he began to fire, and was unhurt, and firing his piece with cool deliberation, when his "boys" left him! And here he was found dead. No friend saw him die . . . In the last moments he stood alone on that part of the field of carnage with his face to the enemy giving him battle.*[220]

> Jesus called out with a loud voice, "Father, into your hands I commit my spirit." When he had said this, he breathed his last.
>
> —LUKE 23:46

Jesus died on the cross alone, forsaken by all, but he won the battle for eternity.

General Morgan's Retribution

IRBY, WIFE of one of Southern General John H. Morgan's cousins, wrote in her book concerning his power of restraint:

GEN. MORGAN, *with a portion of his command, marched in the direction of Gallatin, on the 19th inst., and learning that the enemy was moving into the place he ordered Capt. Hutchison with his company to cut them off from Nashville by destroying the bridge, which he did.*

Gen. Morgan moved early on the morning of the battle to engage the Federals, whom he thought gallant enough to meet him. But what was our surprise to learn on reaching Gallatin that the cowards had contented themselves with visiting distress and misery upon the citizens of

> For God so loved the world . . .
> —JOHN 3:16

that town. These hirelings of the North had arrested every male citizen of the town that could be found. . . . The heartrending appeals of the distressed ones mourning for those who were hurried in the dead hour of night, on foot, to a distant prison, without crime, brought tears to the eyes of many a stout heart besides Morgan's.

If Morgan stays his hand when the invader treats our citizens thus, and tries still to abide the rules of civilized warfare, our consolation is that there is a God who looks deep into the heart, who will bless the noble patriot for his forbearance, while he will as surely curse the foul persecutors of quiet men, women, and children. Gen. Morgan could have swept more than one hundred and sixty of them that day from the face of the earth; but no, he captured them. He would not yet turn a deaf ear to their appeals, notwithstanding that they had murdered two of our men in cold blood after they had surrendered, and the cries of those who had appealed in vain were still ringing in his ears. Take care, invaders! . . .[221]

Morgan's restraint against his enemies reminds us of the restraint of our Lord Jesus Christ on the cross, who had power to wipe his enemies into oblivion but did not because he "so loved" the world.

Grant Speaks of the Influence of Christianity on a Nation

GENERAL ULYSSES GRANT's friend and pastor, M. J. Cramer, revealed insight into the general's philosophy and religion. From their close relationship, Cramer learned what Grant thought about morality and the reliance of a nation upon God.

> *We are in reality a Christian nation which owes much to the teachings of the Bible through the Churches and Sunday schools. There can be no question, in his opinion, as to the fact that the various humanitarian institutions in the several States owe their existence indirectly to the teachings of Christianity. He was glad to notice that there was so much religious activity in our country; and if the Churches and Sunday schools continue to do their duty, the danger growing out of lawlessness, anarchy, and the secret machinations of a countryless enemy will be diminished and overcome.*[222]

General Grant recognized that our nation owed much to the teachings of the Bible through churches and Sunday schools. To acknowledge that humanitarian institutions owed their existence to the teachings of Christianity should cause humanists to revisit their philosophy of the original intent of our nation's forefathers.

> Every word of God is flawless; he is a shield to those who take refuge in him.
>
> —PROVERBS 30:5

Grant concluded that if churches would continue to do their duty, we would have no threat of destruction from within. An enemy from without does not threaten a nation as much as moral deterioration from within. We can never vote our way back to God, but if we will proclaim God's Word and teach the moral and ethical principles found in it, our nation could and would turn back to its spiritual roots.

Clothed for a Cooler Climate

NOT ALL of the Civil War was made up of suffering and death. Some humorous incidents bear mentioning.

The Sergeant of the picket guard being stationed near Pohick Church, Va., had his attention drawn to the tinkling of a cowbell in the bushes. With visions of new milk running through his head, he examined carefully, and to his intense astonishment made the discovery as he advanced the cow bell retreated, The sergeant made a double quick retrograde movement, and imme-diately reported the affair to Colonel Hays. The Colonel secreted a squad of men in the woods, and the Sergeant again made himself conspicu-ous. He brushed about among the bushes, and the cow-bell approached. The squad soon had the satisfaction of see-ing-not the cow, but a "Secesher" [or rebel soldier] with a cow-bell hung to his neck, and a six shooter in his belt. When he got within easy range, and in sight of the squad, the Sergeant hailed him:

> A cheerful heart is good medicine, but a crushed spirit dries up the bones.
> —PROVERBS 17:22

"I say, old fellow, would you rather go to the devil or to Washington?"

The squad at the same time rushed forward. "To Washington, I reckon," drawled the rebel. "I ain't clothed for a warm climate" . . .[223]

Laughter is good medicine for a depressed spirit. At times we may take life too seriously. Find time to see the humor in events. There would be far less need for antidepressants if we would learn to laugh.

Union or Confederate?

AUTHOR FRANK MOORE shared the following story in his book on Civil War anecdotes and illustrations:

> A traveler, passing through one of the counties of Tennessee on horse-back, stopped at a modest cottage on the roadside, and asked for shelter, as it was quite dark and raining. The "head of the family" came to the door, and accosted the traveler with—
> "What do you want?"
> "I want to stay all night," was the reply.
> "What are yer?"
> This interrogatory was not fully understood by the traveler, and he asked an explanation. "I mean, what yer politics?" rejoined the former, "Air yer fur this Union, or agin it?" This was a poser, as the traveler was not certain whether the "man of the house" was a Union man or a secessionist [Confederate], and he was anxious to "tie up" for the night; so he made up his mind and said, "My friend, I am for the Union."
> "Stranger, you kin kum in."[224]

The traveler had a choice to make. To admit he was a Confederate sympathizer might mean he would be rejected. To say he was for the Union could end in less than desirable circumstances. He chose to be true to who he was, and he found acceptance.

> I am not ashamed of the gospel, because it is the power of God for the salvation of everyone who believes.
> —ROMANS 1:16

Paul was not ashamed of the gospel of Christ, nor of who he was. God has made each of us with a unique personality. To be self-deprecating does not bring glory to God. He has created us in his image so we can carry out his plan like no one else can. Do not be ashamed of who you are if you're a Christian. God has a great plan for your life that only you can fulfill.

Cultivate a Cheerful Spirit

MANY CHAPLAINS on both sides during the Civil War brought honor to the army chaplaincy by their inspiring messages and general high morale. One such chaplain is cited by Robertson in his book, *Soldiers, Blue and Gray*:

> *Comforting the homesick and sorrowful, as well as offering counsel of other kinds to individual soldiers, occupied much of a chaplain's time. He was expected to perform individual therapy as well as group presentations. In January 1863, a New England soldier wrote in his diary: "Our chaplain made a speech to us on dress parade last night, and its subject was, Cultivate a Cheerful Spirit;" and it is just so. If a man makes the best of everything, he will be much happier than if he looks on the dark side all the time.*[225]

Anyone can be negative, but it takes a special person to cultivate a cheerful spirit. Learning to make the best of any situation is better than complaining. Paul learned the secret of cheerfulness by being content in whatever befell him.

> A cheerful look brings joy to the heart, and good news gives health to the bones.
> —PROVERBS 15:30

We should limit our time with negative people and associate with positive, cheerful people. A positive atmosphere will cultivate a positive, pleasant attitude. Just as negativism has a negative effect on the lives of others, cheerfulness can have a positive effect on others.

The gospel, being good news, has a positive effect on others.

A Union Soldier Brings Manna from Heaven

A UNION SOLDIER risked his life to obtain food for his fellow soldiers during a hailstorm of grapeshot and missiles. Upon his return, he was greeted with a hero's welcome.

Oh, I shall never forget the thrill of pleasure which I experienced when I carried this food and set it before those famishing men and saw them eat it with sort of awe and reverence as if it had fallen from heaven. One of the men looked up, with moistened eyes and said: "Bob, do you know that this food has been sent us by our heavenly Father, just as much as the manna was sent to the Children of Israel?" That boy risked his life in procuring it for us, but he never would have returned from that burning building if God had not shielded him from bursting shell . . .[226]

The bravery of Bob, the Union soldier, is similar to the courage of the three mighty men who risked their lives to get David a drink of water from the well in Bethlehem. David was so touched that he would not drink the water.

We serve a God who has promised to meet our every need.

> David longed for water and said, "Oh, that someone would get me a drink of water from the well near the gate of Bethlehem!" So the three mighty men broke through the Philistine lines, drew water from the well near the gate of Bethlehem and carried it back to David. But he refused to drink it; instead, he poured it out before the LORD. "Far be it from me, O LORD, to do this!" he said. "Is it not the blood of men who went at the risk of their lives?" And David would not drink it. Such were the exploits of the three mighty men.
> —2 SAMUEL 23:15–17

Chaplain Quintard, the Servant

THE CHAPLAINS of the Civil War often did far more than preach and comfort the dying. Some fought along with their men and fulfilled roles outside their normal ministerial duties. While officers and soldiers cited some chaplains as being "scoundrels," other chaplains rose to Christian heroism. Such is the story of Charles T. Quintard of Connecticut.

Charles T. Quintard, a medically trained Episcopalian chaplain, set up practice in Athens, Georgia, and then moved to Memphis, Tennessee, to teach. When the war began he was serving in a church in Nashville, Tennessee. He went to Bull Run to accompany the "Rock City Guards." There Quintard became a full-fledged Confederate chaplain. As an assistant surgeon, he ministered to men's physical needs as well as their souls. He also filled the role of undertaker after the battle of Franklin where he collected several bodies of generals, giving them Christian burial rites. One soldier named Watkins said of Quintard, "He was one of the purest and best men I ever knew."[227]

The foundation of Quintard's testimony among his men, in contrast to the "scoundrels" of his day, was his willingness to be a servant. Not only did Quintard preach God's Word to his Southern soldiers, but also he lived its principles in front of them. He was not too proud to take on many roles as chaplain. His willingness to do what any other soldier might be asked to do won the respect and following of those to whom he ministered daily.

According to Jesus, the greatest position we can occupy is that of a servant.

> . . . Whoever wants to become great among you must be your servant, and whoever wants to be first must be your slave—just as the Son of Man did not come to be served, but to serve, and to give his life as a ransom for many.
>
> —MATTHEW 20:24–28

Jackson's Appreciation
for God's Creation

GENERAL STONEWALL JACKSON had a great love for God's creation. In a letter to his beloved wife, Anna, he described his appreciation for the things he observed on his daily walks.

> *In my daily walks I think much of you. I love to stroll abroad after the labors of the day are over, and indulge feelings of gratitude to God for all the sources of natural beauty with which he has adorned the earth. Some time since, my morning walks were rendered very delightful by the singing of the birds. The morning caroling of the birds, and their sweet tones in the evening, awaken in me devotional feelings of praise and thanksgiving, though very different in their nature. In the morning, all animated nature (man excepted) appears to join in expressions of gratitude to God; in the evening, all is hushing into silent slumber, and thus disposes the mind to meditation. And as my mind dwells on you, I love to give it a devotional turn, by thinking of you as a gift from our Heavenly Father. How delightful it is thus to associate every pleasure and enjoyment with God the Giver! Thus will He bless us, and make us grow in grace, and in the knowledge of Him, whom to know aright is life eternal.*[228]

My oldest daughter and I made a wonderful discovery when we moved to the countryside of rural Henderson, Kentucky, to pastor. With the absence of streetlights and glaring spotlights, we enjoyed the beauty and wonder of the stars from our back deck. We learned to identify the constellations of the stars by name and once in a while we witnessed the wonder of a falling star.

Are you tense and stressed? Find a dark area of the world and look to the stars.

> The heavens declare the glory of God; the skies proclaim the work of his hands. Day after day they pour forth speech; night after night they display knowledge. There is no speech or language where their voice is not heard. Their voice goes out into all the earth, their words to the ends of the world.
>
> —PSALM 19:1–5

A Sermon Preached and Lived

A
UTHOR JAMES ROBERTSON says, "Chaplains were judged far more for what they did than for what they said; but if they turned out to be good preachers as well, that was an extra point in their favor."[229] Chaplain Isaac T. Tichenor, who served during the battle of Shiloh, not only preached to his men, but also he practiced what he preached, as evidenced by the following:

REV. ISAAC TICHENOR
CHAPLAIN, PASTOR,
PRESIDENT OF
AUBURN UNIVERSITY
AND PRESIDENT OF
SOUTHERN BAPTIST
CONVENTION
*From the Auburn
University Website*

We were under a crossfire . . . from three directions. Under it the boys wavered. I had been wearied and was sitting down, but seeing them waver, I sprang to my feet, took off my hat, waved it over my head, walked up and down the line, and, as they say, "preached them a sermon." I reminded them that it was Sunday. That at that hour all their home folk were praying for them . . . I called upon them to stand there and die, if need be, for their country. The effect was evident. Every man stood to his post, every eye flashed, and every heart beat high with desperate resolve to conquer or die.[230]

Tichenor urged and inspired his men to stand firm in battle and be willing to die if necessary for their cause. The significant illustration here is that Tichenor not only preached to his men before the battle, but he also was with them in the battle.

Whatever you may be going through at the moment, you can be sure that the Lord is right there with you.

> He said, "Look! I see four men walking around in the fire, unbound and unharmed, and the fourth looks like a son of the gods."
> —DANIEL 3:25

A Friend Who Changes Not

THE FOLLOWING letter reveals that Stonewall Jackson had a close communion with his wife and God:

I wish I could be with you to-morrow at your communion. Though absent in body, yet in spirit I shall be present, and my prayer will be for your growth in every Christian grace . . . I take special pleasure in the part of my prayers in which I beg that every temporal and spiritual blessing may be yours, and that the glory of God may be the controlling and absorbing thought of our lives in our new relation. It is to me a great satisfaction to feel that our Heavenly Father has so manifestly ordered our union. I believe, and am persuaded, that if we but walk in His commandments, acknowledging Him in all our ways, He will shower His blessings upon us, How delightful it is to feel that we have such a friend, who changes not! The Christian's recognition of God in all His works greatly enhances his enjoyment."[231]

Jackson rejoiced in his marriage with Anna. His close communion with God kept him close to his wife, even though the war kept them apart from one another. Jackson promised her that by walking in God's commandments his blessings would be "showered on them." To Jackson, Jesus was his unchanging friend, and the more he sought to praise him, the greater his joy and delight in him.

> Jesus Christ is the same yesterday and today and forever.
> —HEBREWS 13:8

If we could learn to praise Jesus more, we would have less time to ponder our problems.

Warning People of What Is Ahead

MANY TENNESSEE WOMEN had a great loyalty and respect for the Union. In the summer of 1862, a trainload of Union soldiers left from Corinth and traveled in the direction of Jackson, Tennessee. Every place a man could stand or sit was occupied by the soldiers as the train traveled at a high rate of speed toward potential danger. If not for the courage of two patriotic women, hundreds of soldier's lives could have been lost:

> *Just before reaching the railroad bridge the engineer saw a couple of lanterns being waved in the distance directly on the track. He stopped the locomotive, and sent men ahead to ascertain the cause of alarm. They found the lanterns held by two women, who explained how a crew of guerrillas in that vicinity had been informed that a train thus loaded with Union soldiers was, and had fired the bridges at eight o'clock that evening, and allowed the main timbers to burn so that the bridge would break under the weight of the train, and then put out the fire. These noble women had heard of the act, and walked ten miles through the mud at midnight, carrying their lanterns, and taking their station on the track, where they had patiently waited for hours, with the determination of thwarting the dastardly plan of the villains . . .*[232]

> When I say to the wicked, "O wicked man, you will surely die," and if you do not speak out to dissuade him from his ways, that wicked man will die for his sin, and I will hold you accountable for his blood.
> —EZEKIEL 33:8

The women warned the Union soldiers that there was a bridge out a few miles down the track. To warn them, the women went to the right location and waved their lanterns.

God has told us to warn the world, lest they perish with no hope. We will be held accountable someday for how we have accepted our responsibility. We must not fail in our mission. Lives depend on it!

Baptism in Blood

CHAPLAIN NEILL delivered a sermon in the woods to a group of Civil War soldiers. The setting provided an excellent illustration for his message, as recorded by one of the Minnesota Army Volunteers:

The cold winds brought the dead leaves down in showers, and swept them in heaps. The chaplain could scarcely raise his voice above the rustling of the leaves; but we heard him say that death was essential to life and prosperity. It was so in the natural world. We could see around us that these trees, late densely covered with verdure, were all sapless and naked. But after storms of the coming winter of death, a renewed friend of life would clothe with brighter venue, these same trees. So it would be with our nation. Dangers and difficulties must be met. A long period of stormy adversity must be passed through to prepare the nation for greater excellence. Nations must be baptized in blood and subjected to defeat before sufficient strength of purpose and character is obtained to ensure permanent prosperity.[233]

Dangers and difficulties in life are inevitable. According to Chaplain Neill, these clarify our purpose and determination. When we go through hardships and struggles, we learn from our mistakes and defeats. We must depend upon the sustaining power of God's grace to experience growth and maturity in the process.

> They preached the good news in that city and won a large number of disciples. Then they returned to Lystra, Iconium and Antioch, strengthening the disciples and encouraging them to remain true to the faith. They said, "We must go through many hardships to enter the kingdom of God."
> —ACTS 14:21, 22

A Virtuous Wife

URING THE CIVIL WAR Lorenzo Dow Hylton enlisted in the Fifty-fourth Virginia Infantry in Abingdon, Virginia. He was wounded in action at Missionary Ridge, Tennessee, and died in the Marietta [Georgia] hospital on February 13, 1864. Before he died, Barbara Hylton wrote a letter to her husband, announcing the birth of their daughter:

To L. D. Hylton

Dear Husband,

This time affords me the pleasure of writing you a few lines to inform you that I am well as could be expected, and all the rest of the family are well, and hoping that these few lines may find you enjoying the same blessing. . . .

I can inform you that I have another Daughter, it was born April 17th. Nathan Hylton went for a Doctor, send the name that you choose that it should be called. . . .

I would like to know if you have received the coat and socks that I sent to you by Col. Shelor.

Dear husband thou art kind and true and every day I think of you. So my dear husband think of me while many a mile apart we be.

Yours truly,
Barbara E. Hylton[234]

Barbara Hylton loved her husband but was willing for him to fight. She had given her husband up to fight in the army to secure freedom for the South. Southern women had to have a toughness and resiliency to endure while their husbands were away. For many Christian wives in the South, separation meant learning to lean on the Lord more than they ever had in their lives. In Barbara Hylton's case, her husband would never come home again.

> A wife of noble character is her husband's crown, but a disgraceful wife is like decay in his bones.
> —PROVERBS 12:4

"Sweetest of the Sweet"

URBAN GRAMMER OWEN, a surgeon in the Confederate army, wrote this letter to his wife whom he loved deeply.

A letter from Jacksboro

Campbell City, August 17th 1861

I enjoy myself up here in the mountains. I stopped about an hour ago with John Jordan in a cabin at the foot of the Mountain and took a nice dinner on good cider & cakes. I don't think we will stay here long we will go back to Knoxville, as we don't think there will be much need of us minding the gap. Great many Union men in this part of the country. Dear Laura cheer up keep in fine spirits don't fear but what I will keep right. All the College Grove company are well & in fine spirits. I will write in a few days again and keep you posted up by writing often. We have had another big fight in Virginia, gained a great victory & took several thousand prisoners. I must close. God bless you my sweet lovely wife the sweetest of the sweet, dearest of the dear, & loveliest of the most lovely of all God's Creation.

My love to all enquiring friends
Your devoted husband
U.A. Owen[235]

Owen treated his wife in a way that brought honor to God. The King James version uses the words "weaker vessel" instead of "weaker partner." Husbands should handle their wives in the same way that one handles an expensive delicate vase.

> Husbands, in the same way be considerate as you live with your wives, and treat them with respect as the weaker partner and as heirs with you of the gracious gift of life, so that nothing will hinder your prayers.
>
> —1 PETER 3:7

Sticking to the Pathway of Duty

ROBERT E. LEE wrote to his son at West Point in 1852, instructing him on the importance of duty. The following letter is inspiring:

> *In regard to duty, let me in conclusion of this hasty letter, inform you that nearly a hundred years ago there was a day of remarkable gloom and darkness—still known as "the dark day"—a day when the light of the sun was slowly extinguished, as if by an eclipse. The legislature of Connecticut was in session, and as its members saw the unexpected and unaccountable darkness coming on, they shared in the general awe and terrour. It was supposed by many that the last day—the Day of Judgment—had come. Some one in the consternation of the hour, moved an adjournment. Then there arose an old Puritan legislator, Devenport, of Stamford, and said, that if the last day had come, he desired to be found at his place doing his duty, and, therefore, moved that candles be brought in, so that the house could proceed with its duty. There was quietness in that man's mind, the quietness of heavenly wisdom and inflexible willingness to obey present duty. Duty, then, is the sublimest word in our language. Do your duty in all things like the old Puritan. You cannot do more; you should never wish to do less.*[236]

> Now all has been heard; here is the conclusion of the matter: Fear God and keep his commandments, for this is the whole duty of man.
> —ECCLESIASTES 12:13

A basic principle of soldiering demands that each soldier fulfill their duty, otherwise they are not worthy to be soldiers. Doing one's duty may mean continuing through pain and darkness.

If we served God only when we felt like it, much of the work of his kingdom would not be accomplished. When we make up our minds to serve the Lord, no matter the difficulties, we join the company of New Testament disciples.

"O My Brother, My Brother!"

ISAAC WHITE was born in Charlottesville, Virginia, on January 29, 1837. He was appointed a Major in the Twenty-ninth Virginia Infantry Regiment. He married Mary Virginia Day and affectionately called her "Jinnie." Jinnie wrote her husband a series of three letters, one of which announced the death of his brother. The following letter is Isaac's response:

Camp Near Front Royal Va
August 19th/64

My Dear Jinnie

Day before yesterday while on the battlefield three letters were handed me. I hastily opened one of them hoping to hear good news from those I love. And oh what a shock. I there saw an account of my brother's death. I was not aware of his illness. God only knows the sorrow of my heart. Oh I was perfectly devoted to him. Oh my brother my brother. Many are the tears I have shed over thy sad fate.

I desire to come home + have made the effort as you can see + failed. It would be a great consolation to be with you all at this time. Write to me soon. Love to all

Your devoted
Isaac[237]

White's mourning over his brother's death reminds us of King David's sorrow over the death of his rebellious son Absalom. David was so involved in the business of his kingdom that he did not take time to be involved in his own son's life. Absalom's rebellious nature was a cry for much needed attention from his father.

God has given us our children for a short time. Let us not waste time on the temporary things of this life while our children cry for our attention.

> The king was shaken. He went up to the room over the gateway and wept. As he went, he said: "O my son Absalom! My son, my son Absalom! If only I had died instead of you—O Absalom, my son, my son!"
> —2 SAMUEL 18:33

The Test of a Christian

MAJOR ISAAC WHITE wrote the following to his wife, Jinnie, to encourage her in the Lord upon the loss of her father:

Harrisonburg, Va
August 20th/63

My Dear Jinnie

I suppose ere this you have heard (through Dick) of the death of our dear father. I do not know any of the particulars . . . I know dear Jinnie it is not and neither do I believe it is the power of any one on earth to console you; but there is a higher power + you must look to it for comfort . . . As adversity is the test of character so is affliction the test of the Christians We want some comforting more substantial than earthly ones I believe dear Jinnie that you are a Christian + that you will take the death of him that you loved so dearly as becomes a Christian. . . .

> Let us run with perseverance the race marked out for us.
> —HEBREWS 12:1B

I feel that I am unworthy to write as I have; but you may rest assured my dear Jinnie that every throb of my heart is a throb of sympathy for thee. I loved your father dearly + always looked with pleasure for the day to come that I might see him + enjoy his society once more but alas never again on earth will I have that pleasure; but hope to meet him in a better land . . .[238]

White mentioned in his letter that "adversity is the test of character." We can profess to be strong in the Christian faith until adversity strikes. It is then that our faith is put to the test. How we react to adversity and endure through it will bring out our true character. Dr. Bob Jones Sr., in a sermon, said, "The true test of a man's character is what it will take to stop him."

The Sweetness of a Christ-Centered Marriage

CIVIL WAR SURGEON U. A. Owen wrote to his wife, Laura, from Jacksboro, Tennessee:

Laura:

I have not been sick a minute since I left you but when I do get sick you will know it soon, and if you get bad sick let me know it also. If you were to get sick I would go to you if it sank the whole Southern Confederacy. God knows that is so. I have nothing in the Confederacy but you that is all I am here for—to protect you. The South is nothing to me if you were out of it. I don't know how long we will stay, probably a week or month and maybe not three days. Did you get my last letter? I wrote one at Clinton (Tennessee) did you get it? I want you to write to me to Jacksboro. Write soon tell me all the news. I hope to hear that you are well and not grieving about me. I am not worth grieving after so much by such a nice sweet and lovely woman as you. My love I will write to you often. God knows I love you better than all the world besides. God love & protect my dear sweet wife is my prayer.[239]

Successful marriages take three—the spouse, the Lord, and me! A disturbing problem in our day is an inability to keep the "honey" in the honeymoon. We live such fast-paced lives that we forget the importance of rekindling the fires of romance. In Dr. Owen's age, life moved at a much slower pace. The uncertainty of life during the Civil War prompted couples to cultivate their relationships with one another and with the Lord.

Taking time for your personal relationship with the Lord and your spouse is the key to success in marriage.

> Husbands ought to love their wives as their own bodies. He who loves his wife loves himself. After all, no one ever hated his own body, but he feeds and cares for it, just as Christ does the church . . . for we are members of his body. "For this reason a man will leave his father and mother and be united to his wife, and the two will become one flesh."
>
> —EPHESIANS 5:22, 30

"Come Home or We Die"

B Y THE END of the Civil War over 300,000 soldiers had deserted their armies and returned back home. Edward Cooper was court-martialed and placed on trial for deserting his fellow soldiers to return home to help his desperate wife. He then faced execution. Cooper's wife wrote the following letter which motivated him to desert:

> My dear Edward—I have always been proud of you, and since your connection with the Confederate army, I have been prouder of you than ever before. I would not have you do anything wrong for the world, but before God, Edward, unless you come home, we must die. Last night, I was aroused by little Eddie's crying. I called and said "What is the matter, Eddie?" and he said, "O Mamma! I am so hungry." And Lucy, Edward, your darling Lucy; she never complains, but she is growing thinner every day. And before God, Edward, unless you come home, we must die.
>
> Your Mary[240]

The home should become a priority once again in our nation. God's first institution was not the Church but the home. Even though we cannot condone a man who deserts, in this case we must admire Cooper because of his readiness to leave the army and take care of his desperate family.

> If anyone does not provide for his relatives, and especially for his immediate family, he has denied the faith and is worse than an unbeliever.
> —1 TIMOTHY 5:8

God has squarely placed the responsibility for provision in the home on the husband or father. It would be better for Cooper to stand before his God someday as a deserter who puts his family's needs as a priority, than a non-deserter who stayed with his troops and ignored the cries of his wife and children.

The Bible places serious consequences on the man who neglects his own family. As Christians, we need to reevaluate our priorities.

Grant's Optimism in the Face of Adversity

MUCH HAS been said about Robert E. Lee's leadership abilities and character in battle, but we must not overlook General Grant's leadership ability. One fine character trait he had was his uncanny optimism. This was exemplified when great odds were against him in East Tennessee. Grant had learned from experience it would do no good to get "rattled" in frustrating situations, which is well noted by author Wiley Sword:

> *For much of his life, adversity had been a familiar companion to the former Illinois store clerk Sam Grant. Through the early war years, his attitude had remained resolute and his purpose fixed. Yet the burden and responsibility had become increasingly heavy . . .*
>
> *Grant had long ago learned life's hard lesson about apprehension and despair: that it often was the consequence of fear and inertia. Initiative he believed was the engine of accomplishment . . . His bull-dog-like tenacity to face a challenge and persevere until the task was accomplished would be fully tested in Chattanooga. . . .*
>
> *Grant reflected on his dilemma . . . "The responsibility of guarding all, to a great extent, evolves upon me," he told his wife . . . "With all this I lose no sleep . . . and find no occasion to swear or fret. I am [still] very hopeful."* [241]

Grant's firm resolve in the face of uncertainties is evidence of his faith in a power outside of himself. From letters he wrote, we know he had a great respect for the power of God and Scripture. For Grant to sleep at night with all the responsibilities on his shoulders reveals that he had learned to place the heavy burdens of battle in God's hands.

> If you continue in your faith, established and firm, not moved from the hope held out in the gospel. This is the gospel that you heard and that has been proclaimed to every creature under heaven, and of which I, Paul, have become a servant.
> —COLOSSIANS 1:23

Permission for a Prayer Meeting

CHRISTIAN SOLDIER John H. Worsham was one of Stonewall Jackson's foot cavalry. He shared how the Lord led him and others to start a prayer service in camp. He also revealed how important the Bible was to these soldiers.

George W. Peterkin, Esq,

Dear Sir—We, the undersigned comrades in arms with yourself, have been struck with the propriety of evening prayer, and desire, if agreeable to you, that you, from this time, and so long as we may remain together, conduct that service . . .

Every man carried a Bible, given with her blessing by mother or sweetheart, and I suppose every man in the Confederate army carried one. This Bible was read as a book never was before. I read mine through the first year. They were a blessing to many, and life savers, too, as I heard of and saw many lives saved by bullets striking the Bible, carried in the breast pocket.

Worsham said of Peterkin's Christian character:

This gallant young soldier and truly good man conducted the service each night, and by his Christian example won the respect and affection of every member of the company; and when he left us in 1862, to take a staff appointment, it was like breaking up a household.

This is the same George W. Peterkin who has for a number of years been the honored and respected Bishop of West Virginia.[242]

> O LORD, hear my prayer, listen to my cry for mercy; in your faithfulness and righteousness come to my relief.
> —PSALM 143:1

All significant revivals began with prayer. When people pray, God puts a holy hunger in the hearts of believers for more of God's Word. The stress and uncertainties of the battles wore upon the minds of the young soldiers. Many found the relief they needed in battle through the powerful influence of God's Word and prayer.

A Company of Soldiers
Went to Church

A CONFEDERATE SOLDIER wrote in his diary concerning religion in his camp and said:

On Sundays many of the boys go to Church; and on last Sunday evening I was much gratified to see the majority of the company collected in one of our rooms and singing several beautiful hymns from memory. After the singing was over a proposition was made to close with prayer; which was unanimously agreed to, and Mr. Gibson led in a beautiful prayer. Afterwards it was agreed to hold meetings of a religious character every Sunday evening. There are several other church members in the other companies of the regiment, and if we all get together, we will no doubt have a very pleasant and profitable meeting. Pray for us. After our regiment is thoroughly organized, and we get our chaplain, we will feel more at home, as we will have, no doubt a good spiritual adviser.[243]

We must admire these soldiers in their efforts to organize a church service on Sunday evening. Without songbooks or a chaplain, they sang the beautiful hymns of the faith from memory. For many young men attending those meetings, their desire for worship was a reflection of their upbringing. Undoubtedly, godly moms, dads, and Sunday school teachers had a strong influence on them before the Civil War.

> Train a child in the way he should go, and when he is old he will not turn from it.
> —PROVERBS 22:6

While knocking on doors one day in Western Kentucky, I asked a couple if their children attended church.

"We don't try to influence our children's religious beliefs. We let them to make up their own minds about the Bible and religion."

My heart was saddened by this response, and I thought, *What chance do those children have? They do not have a mom and dad that take responsibility for their souls!* The Bible clearly commands parents to train their children in the way they should go.

A Definite Conversion
to Christianity

SOUTHERN SOLDIER Edward P. Walton wrote a letter of Christian sympathy to the wife of his friend, Colonel Baylor, who had recently been converted and then died in battle.

> *Another characteristic struck me* [about Colonel Baylor] *as very indicative of a saving change. I never knew a man addicted to swearing that could refrain from profanity when provoked, without Divine assistance: and yet I have seen Col. Baylor under the most harassing provocations, without yielding to the promptings of his old habit. He had completely mastered, at least, that habit.*
>
> *His conversation during the last day we were together (Tuesday before his death) furnished the strongest proof of his concern on the subject of religion and his faith the power of Prayer. He asked not less than half a dozen times, during the day, an interest in my prayers, in view of the impending conflict, and the last words that he spoke to me were "Walton, I do hope that Christians are praying for us, at home."*
>
> *He frequently conversed with Gen. Jackson on religious subjects. It is well known that the General indulged the warmest feeling of esteem and affection for your Husband. On one occasion, when he thought that Col. Baylor was absent from his command and a severe engagement was going on he expressed fears that the Brigade would not maintain its reputation; but when he was told that your Husband was at his post, he replied "all is right, they will prove worthy of their commander."*
>
> *Our whole Brigade mourns with you his irreparable loss . . .*
>
> *Yrs, warmly*
> *Edwd. P. Walton*[244]

> Thus, by their fruit you will recognize them.
> —MATTHEW 7:20

Jesus said that we would recognize the reality of a person's conversion by their fruit. Fruit grows on the outside of trees, not on the inside. Whatever is in the heart of a person will eventually show outwardly.

Lincoln's Farewell Address

LINCOLN WAS preparing to leave his beloved Springfield, Illinois, to assume his duties in Washington, D.C. Before he left, he gave the following farewell speech to supporters:

> *My friends, no one can appreciate the sadness I feel at this parting. To this people I owe all that I am. Here I have lived more than a quarter of a century. Here my children were born, and here one of them lies buried. I know not how soon I shall see you again. A duty devolves upon me which is perhaps greater than that which has devolved upon any other man since the days of Washington. He never would have succeeded, except for the aid of Divine Providence, upon which he at all times relied. I feel that I cannot succeed without the same divine aid which sustained him; and in the same Almighty Being I place my reliance for support; and I hope that you, my friends, will all pray that I may receive that divine assistance, without which I cannot succeed, but with which success is certain. Again, I bid you all an affectionate farewell.*[245]

Lincoln depended on God's help to lead our nation. Considering he had no formal education, we can imagine Lincoln lying near the huge fireplace in his log cabin home, where the flickering of the firelight reflected on the family Bible he was reading. He grew up in a home that did not own many books, so Lincoln borrowed from friends. But one book that was in almost every home in those days was a family Bible. Lincoln read it through and learned its precepts, which helped mold him into a man who depended on God.

> Do not let this Book of the Law depart from your mouth; meditate on it day and night, so that you may be careful to do everything written in it. Then you will be prosperous and successful.
>
> —JOSHUA 1:8

They Followed Me on to Their Death

GENERAL GEORGE PICKETT of the Confederate army wrote in his diary of the loyalty of his men toward his leadership:

> *Even now I can hear them cheering as I gave the order, "Forward!" I can feel the thrill of their joyous voices as they called out all along the line, "We'll follow you, Marse George. We'll follow you—we'll follow you." Oh, how faithfully they kept their word—following me on—on—to their death, and I, believing in the promised support, led them on—on—on—Oh, God!*
>
> *I can't write you a love-letter to-day, my Sally, for with my great love for you and my gratitude to God for sparing my life to devote to you, comes the overpowering thought of those whose lives were sacrificed—of the broken-hearted widows and mothers and orphans. The moans of my wounded boys, the sight of the dead, upturned faces, flood my soul with grief—and here am I whom they trusted, whom they followed, leaving them on that field of carnage—and guarding four thousand prisoners across the river back to Winchester. Such a duty for men who a few hours ago covered themselves with glory eternal!*[246]

> Then I acknowledged my sin to you and did not cover up my iniquity. I said, "I will confess my transgressions to the LORD," and you forgave the guilt of my sin.
>
> —PSALM 32:5

God had forgiven David's sins of adultery and murder, but he was still under a load of guilt. Even rest seemed impossible. Psalm 32 conveys his agony as he cries for forgiveness. Finally David received peace from the Lord.

General Pickett felt guilt over the loss of his men as they followed him into battle. At times we carry guilt over our sins, but we have a Redeemer who will forgive us and relieve us of our guilt. By turning to the cross, we can find peace.

Music and Morale

MUSIC HAS inspired people down through the ages. In the Civil War, music was used to increase morale.

A correspondent, writing from the army of the Potomac, in June, 1862, says: ". . . For months there has been a standing order against the playing of bands in camp . . . During the fight yesterday afternoon, an order came for Morell's division to repair to the hill near where the battle was going on, and set as a support for the reserve artillery . . . the weather was scorching hot, and they had been four days without rest or sleep."

A happy thought struck Captain Thomas J. Hoyt, of General Butterfield's staff, who saw that the men looked weary and exhausted. He immediately gathered all the regimental bands, placed them at the head of the brigade, and ordered them to play. They started the "Star spangled Banner;" and the first note had hardly been struck when the men caught the spirit, and cheer after cheer arose from regiment after regiment, and was borne away upon the bosom of the placid river. The band continued to play, and other regiments and other brigades caught the spirit, and the air resounded with tumultuous applause at the happy hit, until all the columns on that vast plain were vying with each other to do homage to the inspiriting strains of the band. After several tunes, Major Welch of the Sixteenth Michigan, in a brief speech, proposed three cheers for the hero of the command, General Daniel Butterfield, which were given in magnificent style. To add to the enthusiasm, General McClellan happened to ride through the field just then, and was received with an outburst that fairly astonished him. The scene was continued, the brigade moved off with the band playing, and had there been a fight in the next field, the men would have gone into action on the double-quick to the tune of "Yankee Doodle," if every one had known that death would be his fate.[247]

> When they had sung a hymn, they went out to the Mount of Olives.
> —MATTHEW 26:30

Jesus knew what was ahead. It was appropriate to sing a hymn before he went to the garden and finally to the cross. When you are faced with difficulties, try singing.

"Confiscate de Ole Man!"

IT WAS A TRAGIC situation for African-Americans held as slaves on plantations of the South. Some masters treated their slaves well, while others persecuted them. For the old black man in the following story, the prospect of gaining freedom through the help of the Northern armies was thrilling.

> One of the Pike County boys at Louisiana (Missouri) found an old negro in the woods who had heard that secession property was to be confiscated, and therefore commenced by executing the order upon himself. He surrendered to the invader, and gave a history of himself, concluding by saying: "Gorry, massa! I'll brack your boots, brush your close, bring you water—do anything you want me, if you'll only confiscate de ole man!" [248]

When we read stories of African-Americans like the one above, we are reminded of the shamefulness of slavery. Thank God for men like Martin Luther King, who in the spirit of nonviolence, let the world know the yearning of black people to be treated with equality. As we move closer to King's dream, let us vow that we, as Americans, will never become oppressors again, but help deliver all races.

> I have indeed seen the oppression of my people in Egypt. I have heard their groaning and have come down to set them free. Now come, I will send you back to Egypt.
> —ACTS 7:34

They Parted as Friends

THE FOLLOWING is a touching incident of a Northern and Southern soldier reconciling to one another before their deaths:

A wounded Federal soldier was hastily carried to a wood, and placed by the side of a dying Georgian. The Georgian, evidently a gentleman, said to him, as they lay bleeding side by side, "We came on the field enemies—let us part friends;" and extended to him his hand, which the other grasped with the reciprocal expression of friendly feeling. They were both Christian men, and they lay with clasped hands on that bloody field, until the hand of the noble Georgian was cold in death. How beautiful that scene, amid the horror of the battle-field! Who shall say, in view of it, that because of this strife between the North and South, they can never again clasp hands in mutual friendship and esteem? Who shall say that the time shall not come, when, on some well-fought field, they who met as enemies shall part as friends, and peace and restoration and mutual esteem ensue?[249]

To forgive those who forgive you is good, but to forgive those who hate you and try to kill you is divine. Jesus forgave those who crucified him because they didn't know what they were doing. He opened the way for us to have a relationship with God.

> Jesus said, "Father, forgive them, for they do not know what they are doing."
> —LUKE 23:34

Relationship problems can seem impossible to mend, but life is too short for us to be at odds with our neighbors. As these two Northern and Southern soldiers lay side by side, bleeding and dying, they realized they should forget the past and forgive one another.

The Awful Slave Trade of Natchez, Mississippi

WILLIAM J. ANDERSON was a slave for twenty-four years. He was sold eight times; in jail sixty times; and whipped three hundred times. Anderson revealed the dark times of slavery in America and gave an account of the slave trade in Natchez, Mississippi.

> *. . . for the sake of money, they are sold separately, sometimes two hundred miles apart, although their hopes would be to be sold together. Sometimes their little children are torn from them and sent far away to a distant country, never to see them again. O, such crying and weeping when parting from each other! For this demonstration of natural human affection the slaveholder would apply the lash or paddle upon the naked skin. The former was used less frequently than the latter, for fear of making scars or marks on their backs, which are closely looked for by the buyer. I saw one poor woman dragged off and sold from her tender child— which was nearly white—which the seller would not let go with its mother. Although the master of the mother importuned him a long time to let him have it with its mother, with oaths and curses he refused. It was too hard for the mother to bear; she fainted, and was whipped up. . . . I had an opportunity of seeing the distress of the poor slaves of Natchez; but in a few years afterwards God visited them with an awful overthrow. . . .*
>
> *When I arrived on the farm, and beheld the way they were fed, worked, clothed, whipped and driven, my poor heart faltered within me, to see men and women reduced to the hardships of cartelism. . . . The only money I possessed was one dollar. With this I purchased a Bible, but it was taken from me and torn up, and I was whipped for reading it. We had no preaching or meeting at all—nothing but whipping and driving both night and day—sometimes nearly all day Sunday.*[250]

> For the LORD had compassion on them as they groaned under those who oppressed and afflicted them.
> —JUDGES 2:18

Even though slavery was eradicated in the United States after the Civil War, it still lives on in third world countries. Pray for and support Christian missionaries who minister to oppressed peoples around the world.

Prayer for a Sick or Wounded Soldier

T HE FOLLOWING is a prayer out of an official Confederate prayer
book to be used by a sick or wounded soldier:

*O, Almighty God, Father of men and angels, in whose hands are the
keys of life and death, to whom it belongs justly to punish sinners, and
to be merciful to those who truly repent, look down in great mercy on
me, Thy unworthy servant, now suffering sickness and pain, which
Thou in Thy wise providence has sent upon me.*

*Thou hast commanded us to call upon Thee in our trouble, and
hast promised to deliver us. Give me grace to rely with unshaken confidence on Thy glorious promises . . . Give me patience and resigna-
tion, a perfect abandonment of my own will and a conformity to thine,
that I may be prepared to endure evil at Thy hand with fortitude, or to
receive good with thankfulness.*

*But yet, O Lord my God, give Thy servant
leave to pray unto Thee, that Thou wilt not cut
me off in the midst of my days, nor forsake me
when my strength faileth. Spare me, O God,
that I may live to serve Thee, to redeem my time
misspent in folly, to gain victory over my temptations, and perfect dominion over my passions.
O spare me a little, that I may recover my
strength before I go hence and be no more seen;*
*so shalt Thy servant rejoice in Thy mercies, and speak of Thy loving-
kindness in the church of the redeemed. Give me true repentance for
all my sins. Enable me steadfastly to believe in Jesus Christ the Lamb
of God, which taketh away the sins of the world . . .*[251]

> The salvation of the
> righteous comes
> from the LORD: he is
> their stronghold in
> time of trouble.
> —PSALM 37:39

We can imagine a soldier in his dying moments on the battlefield while
his buddy read this prayer. The Word of God is a great source of comfort in
time of need. It still has the power to comfort today.

Jackson, a Christian Hero

THE REV. JAMES B. RAMSEY was the pastor of the Lynchburg Presbyterian Church, Lynchburg, Virginia. The following is part of a sermon preached by Ramsey on May 24, 1863, after the death of his friend, Stonewall Jackson:

> *Thus walking with God in prayer and holy obedience, he reposed upon God's promises and Providence with a calm and unflinching reliance beyond any man I ever knew. I shall never forget the manner and tone of surprise and child-like confidence with which he once spoke to me on this subject. It was just after the election in November, 1860, when the country was beginning to heave with the agony and throes of dissolution We had just risen from morning prayers in his own house, where at the time I was a guest. Filled with gloom, I was lamenting in strong language the condition and prospects of our beloved country. "Why," said he, "should Christians be at all disturbed about the dissolution of the Union? It can only come by God's permission, and will only be permitted, if for his people's good, for does he not say that 'all things shall work together for good to them that love God?' I cannot see why we should be distressed about such things whatever be their consequences." Nothing seemed ever to shake that faith in God. It was in him a truly sublime and all controlling principle. In the beautiful language of this Psalm, he dwelt in the secret place of the Most High, he made the Most High his habituation, and was thus placed on high from the fear of evil. Together with that extreme fear of offending God in even the least thing, which was the only fear he ever knew . . . that made him the model soldier, the true Christian hero.*[252]

> Many are the plans in a man's heart, but it is the LORD's purpose that prevails.
>
> —PROVERBS 19:21

Jackson believed in the prevailing purposes of God, and for that reason he feared no circumstance of life. If we are sure that God is in control, we can live stress-free lives.

Chickamauga: High Tide of the Southern Confederacy

SURGEON JOHN ALLAN WYETH was a surgeon in the Fourth Alabama Cavalry at Chickamauga. His recollection of the battle and the horrible scenes he witnessed there testifies to the faith, courage, and patriotism of the brave men in blue and gray.

Right after the Chickamauga battle I was detailed to gather up guns and other wreckage on the field, and the dead Federals were scattered everywhere, in some places very thick. I counted seven who had fallen in one pile, and I recall but one that had not been stripped of all outer clothing; yet not one of all these dead men but had some covering left for the sake of modesty . . .

> Be self-controlled and alert. Your enemy the devil prowls around like a roaring lion looking for someone to devour.
> —1 PETER 5:8

As we began the advance our regiment was the extreme left of our line, and when we struck the Chickamauga we waded the stream just below the Lee & Gordon mill-dam. Hoping to get over dry, a number of us started to run across the dam; but an officer shouted: "Get off! They're going to rake you with grapeshot," and we leaped into the water like so many bullfrogs . . . I never saw such determination . . .

The battle of Chickamauga marked what history must record as the "High Tide of the Southern Confederacy," and ended one of the great campaigns of the Civil War. . . . The courage, the heroism, the self-sacrifice of the soldiers who made up his great army were in vain. Fully informed of every movement of his over-confident opponent, and with time to make his preparations either for battle or retreat, he hesitated with a vacillation which lost to him the confidence of his subordinates and finally the respect of his adversary . . .[253]

A lion can pounce on its prey suddenly without warning. The Southern commander hesitated and did not strike when opportunity availed itself. And today, we must be alert, for Satan is like a lion, ready to strike when we least expect it.

1

The Call of Duty

FOR MANY SOLDIERS to be shot in the leg would require immediate hospitalization, but for the brave soldier of the Maine Fifth Regiment, a musket ball in the leg only motivated him to business as usual.

As the Maine troops were leaving the field of battle, a soldier stepped up to one of the officers of the Fifth regiment, and requested him to lend him a knife. The officer took out a common pocketknife, and handed it to the soldier, who sat down at the side of the road, pulled up the leg of his trousers, and deliberately dug a musket-ball out of his leg, jumped up, and resumed his march.

When the news of the repulse reached the camp meeting at Desplaines, Ill., Rev. Henry Cox, who was preaching at the time the intelligence was received, remarked, on closing his sermon, "Brethren, we had better adjourn this camp meeting, and go home and drill."[254]

We will sometimes be wounded in the battles of life. Like the apostle Paul, we need to stand firm, never letting the enemy move us from our faith in Christ. If we give ourselves fully to God's work, we will find that our labor has not been in vain. Developing a "tough skin" while keeping a soft heart is essential for endurance in the Lord's service.

> Therefore, my dear brothers, stand firm. Let nothing move you. Always give yourselves fully to the work of the Lord, because you know that your labor in the Lord is not in vain.
> —1 CORINTHIANS 15:58

The Bible in Public Education

A BOOK ENTITLED, *Daily Life in Civil War America,* by James and Dorothy Volo, cites a report concerning public education in Pennsylvania. The Bible played an important role in the educational system in Civil War America.

> *The Bible is read in 140 schools; not read in 17 I trust that all our teachers may become so deeply impressed with a sense of their duty, in the moral education of their pupils, that we may soon report the Bible read in every school. . . .*
>
> *[The Bible] is calculated to improve the heart, and elevate and expand the youthful mind; accordingly, whenever the subject has admitted of it, such observations have been made as tend to illustrate the excellence of Christian religion, the advantages of correct moral principles, and the superiority of enlightened institutions.*[255]

Public school education in America, for the most part, has been secularized. In years past, education used to go hand in hand with the Bible. The Bible provided correct moral principles. Parents comprised the public school boards, hired, and fired teachers. They were responsible for their children's education.

God told the Israelites to teach their children diligently from the time they rose up in the morning until they went to bed at night. The Lord has always placed the responsibility of education and religion in the hands of parents.

> These commandments that I give you today are to be upon your hearts. Impress them on your children. Talk about them when you sit at home and when you walk along the road, when you lie down and when you get up. Tie them as symbols on your hands and bind them on your foreheads. Write them on the doorframes of your houses and on your gates.
> —DEUTERONOMY 6:6–9

A Dying Soldier
and His Children

A TOUCHING INCIDENT of the identification of a dead Union soldier is recorded in the book, *Daily Life in Civil War America.*

*Perhaps the most famous battlefield identification of a departed sol-
dier was that of Amos Humiston, a sergeant in the 154th New York
Volunteers. Humiston's body was found on the battlefield following
the battle of Gettysburg, clutching in his hand an ambrotype [a tintype
picture] of his three little children. His name remained a mystery
for months. Francis Bourns, a physician, obtained the picture, had it
copied on an engraving plate so that it could be circulated in the hope
of learning the identity of the fallen soldier, and set up a fund for the
orphaned children. Many newspapers across the country supported the
effort. Finally, it was learned that a woman in western New York had
read the account in the religious newspaper "American Presbyterian."
She had sent her husband a picture of their three small children and
had not heard from him since July. A copy of the picture was sent, and
her worst fears came to fruition. James G. Clark wrote a poem set to
music based on the story called, "The Children of the Battlefield." The
net proceeds of the sales of the music, which
contained an introductory sketch melodramati-
cally detailing the entire incident, were "reserved
for the support and education of the Orphan
Children," Frank, Frederick, and Alice.*[256]

> Sons are a heritage
> from the LORD,
> children a reward
> from him.
> —PSALM 127:3

What a touching scene of a soldier who loved
his children so much that he died with a picture of
them in his hands. As tragic as this story is, what
a beautiful memory must have been cherished in those children's minds as
they remembered a loving father whose last thoughts were for them.

How touching to know that Jesus' first and last thoughts on the cross
were for us.

Lee Helps an Enemy

IN A REVIEW of Robert E. Lee's exemplary life after the Civil War, one author recounts the general's humble kindness.

> *One day not long before his death, General Lee was seen standing at his gate talking pleasantly to an humbly-clad man, who seemed very much pleased at the cordial courtesy of the great chieftain, and turned off, evidently delighted, as a third person came up. After exchanging salutations, the General said, pointing to the retreating form, "That is one of our old soldiers, who is in necessitous circumstances." It was taken for granted that it was some veteran Confederate, when the noble-hearted chieftain quietly added, "He fought on the other side, but we must not think of that." It afterwards transpired—not from General Lee, for he never alluded to his charities—that he had not only spoken kindly to this "old soldier" who had "fought on the other side," but had sent him on his way rejoicing in a liberal contribution to his necessities.[257]*

Lee's kindness extended much further than his own circle. He humbly helped those who were once his enemies. If we limit our love to those who love us, we are no better off than the world in our philanthropy. But when we reach out to those who are against us, we are doing it in Christ's stead.

> In Joppa there was a disciple named Tabitha (which, when translated, is Dorcas), who was always doing good and helping the poor.
>
> —ACTS 9:36

Doing Our Best

PHOEBE YATES served as a nurse in a besieged Richmond, Virginia, hospital. In her diary, she told of the courage and faith of a young wounded soldier.

> *He had remained through all his trials stout, fresh and hearty, interesting in appearance, and so gentle-mannered and uncomplaining that we all loved him. Supported on his crutches, he had walked up and down his ward for the first time since he was wounded, and seemed almost restored. . . .*
>
> *Following the nurse to his bed, and turning down the covering, a small jet of blood spurted up. The sharp edge of the splintered bone must have severed an artery. I instantly put my finger on the little orifice and awaited the surgeon. He soon came—took a long look and shook his head. The explanation was easy: the artery was imbedded in the fleshy part of the thigh and could not be taken up. No earthly power could save him . . . The trial of my duty was laid upon me; the necessity of telling a man in the prime of life, and fullness of strength that there was no hope for him . . . Then he turned his questioning eyes upon my face. "How long can I live?" "Only as long as I keep my finger upon this artery." A pause ensued. God alone knew what thoughts hurried through that heart and brain, called so unexpectedly from all earthly hopes and ties. He broke his silence at last. "You can let go."—But I could not. Not if my own life had trembled in the balance. Hot tears rushed to my eyes, a surging sound to my ears, and a deathly coldness to my lips. . . . I fainted away.*[258]

> She did what she could. She poured perfume on my body beforehand to prepare for my burial.
> —MARK 14:88

When the nurse woke up from her fainting, the young soldier's pain and trials were over. She had done her best and that is all that the Lord required of her.

Before Jesus' death, a woman anointed Jesus' feet with precious, expensive perfume. He said that wherever the gospel was preached, what she did would be told in her memory.

Others

Mary Bethell wrote in her diary:

We are having some cold weather now. I often think of the soldiers, some of them in cloth tents. I hope and pray that God may bless them, and that we may soon have peace restored to our unhappy country, war is a dreadful calamity, but it will all work out for good to our country . . . I have commenced again to read the Bible regularly through. I read 4 chapters every day. I have set times for private prayer, it is a privilege which I enjoy, I believe that God has commenced to sanctify my soul. I feel that the glory of God shines in my soul and on my road.[259]

Mary Bethell took time to think about others. Jesus made it his business to look for needs in others. He went out of his way to go to a place called Samaria because he knew a needy woman would come to draw water from the well. While the disciples bought food, Jesus was feasting on the spiritual opportunity to lead this poor woman to know him as Savior (see John 4).

> Each of you should look not only to your own interests, but also to the interests of others.
> —PHILIPPIANS 2:4

People all around us are hurting. We need to develop spiritual radars, always attuned to the needs of others. Johnny Hunt of the First Baptist Church of Woodstock, Georgia, makes it a practice to pause before meals at a restaurant. He says to the waiter or waitress, "I am getting ready to pray over my meal. Do you have any needs you would like for me to pray about in your life?" Almost always these people will tell him about needs in their lives with tears in their eyes. Through those experiences come opportunities to share Christ.

Try reaching out to someone in need today.

A Musician's Amputation

AUTHOR FRANK MOORE wrote:

The morning following the battle of Yorktown, I had the curiosity to attend the wounded. Among others whose limbs were so much injured as to require amputation, was a musician, who had received a musket ball in his knee. As usual in such a case, preparations were made to prevent the possibility of his moving. Says the sufferer, "Now, what would you be at?" "My lad, I'm going to take off your leg, and it is necessary that you should be lashed down." "I'll consent to no such thing. You may pluck my heart from my bosom, but you'll not confine me. Is there a violin in the camp? If so, bring it to me." A violin was furnished, and tuning it, he said, "Now, Doctor, begin." And he continued to play until the operation, which lasted about forty minutes, was completed, without missing a note or moving a muscle.[260]

A joyful song can lift a troubled or burdened heart. When I was pastor of a small church in Kentucky, our building was a "Woodsman of the World" cabin in the middle of the woods. I carried a heavy burden as I helped that little church grow from its new beginning. One day I went to the cabin, walked down by the lake, and sang the old hymn, "He Keeps Me Singing." Before long my sadness turned to praise and I forgot about my troubles as I sensed the Holy Spirit's presence around me.

For the soldier who was about to lose his leg, music acted as an anesthetic to soothe his heart and take his thoughts away from the pain.

If you're burdened with a load of care, try singing.

> David told the leaders of the Levites to appoint their brothers as singers to sing joyful songs, accompanied by musical instruments: lyres, harps and cymbals.
>
> —1 CHRONICLES 15:16

Boots Finds a Friend

UNION SOLDIER E. N. BOOTS wrote the following to his mother:

Plymouth N.C., Sep 8th [1863]

Dear Mother,

We have been having preaching every night for some days by McGraves an agent of the Christian commission. He is a pretty good old fashioned preacher. It is a great pleasure to listen to an old fashioned sermon once more. We have a Bible class that meets every Sabbath. I have attended several times & have found it very pleasant. The teacher is a Sergeant of the Artillery. Last Sabbath a boy came into the class that I had never seen before. Last night he was at church, after service he came up to me & introduced himself saying that he wished to become acquainted with me. He said that he belonged to the cavalry & that they were such a wicked set that he had no pleasure with them. I told him who I was & asked him to call on me . . . His is a hard lot, for the cavalry are a terribly rough set. I begin to think that there is some possibility of the war ending after awhile & then I hope to see you all once more. . . . Many that I once knew have passed away from earth, to a better country let us hope. All these things say "Be ye also ready". Let us try to be ready so that when the summons comes we can say that we were "Only waiting . . . give my love to all."

> Oil and perfume make the heart glad, so a man's counsel is sweet to his friend.
>
> —PROVERBS 27:9

Your Son etc E N Boot, Q. M. Dept   101st Reg P. V.[261]

Among my friends, none was as faithful as my brother. I could count on his support in spite of failure and hard times. Jeff enjoyed having a multitude of friends. He did not wait for others to claim him as their friend, rather he met needs in their lives and won a friend. Jeff is with the Lord now, but his influence as a brother and friend lives on.

We need to live lives that will cause others to seek our friendship. The counsel of a friend can be sweet in times of battle.

An Effectual, Fervent Prayer

LIEUTENANT DAVID LOGAN of the Seventeenth South Carolina Volunteers wrote in his diary concerning the kindness shown him "in the darkest hour of disease."

> *Here I must record an act of kindness performed towards me, which I never wish my self or children to forget. In the darkest hours of disease, Mrs. Chapin gave me the most devoted attention and came in her carriage and conveyed me to her own house where ever thing that could minister to my welfare was performed . . . I must record . . . by their many kindnesses such as . . . Mr. G. M. Moore, whose voice I often heard in the evening devotions ascending to Heaven on my behalf . . .[262]*

Peter and John were preaching the gospel and this upset the priests and Sadducees who "were greatly disturbed because the apostles were teaching the people and proclaiming in Jesus the resurrection of the dead" (Acts 4:2). In fact these leaders were so distressed by Peter and John's preaching that they had both of them thrown in jail. Upon

> When they heard this, they raised their voices together in prayer to God.
> —ACTS 4:23

their release, they demanded that these two apostles stop preaching in Jesus' name. When Peter and John reported what happened to the believers, a prayer meeting was held for them, and voices were raised to God on their behalf.

It's important that God's people take time to pray for one another. We can only imagine how the prayers of G. M. Moore comforted this needy soldier.

Is there someone you should be praying for today?

A Consistent Profession

THOMAS JEWETT GOREE, aide to General James Longstreet, spent time and counsel with Lee's inner circle of Confederate generals. These men influenced Goree, but his mother influenced him more. In a letter written to her he confessed spiritual problems.

My Dearest Mother,

Since I commenced the practice of my profession, I am aware that I have not led a life consistent with my profession as a Christian, but for some time past I have been led to consider of my course, and I have deliberately come to the conclusion and have commenced to make my actions conform with my profession. Although I know that I have improved very much since the formation of my resolves, yet I feel and know that there is still room for improvement . . .[263]

The Holy Spirit convicted Goree and showed him that his actions did not match his testimony. Thankfully, he allowed the Lord to work in his life to bring about change. In Ezekiel's time, many professed to know God but denied him by their actions. Even today, people of the world are looking to find Christians whose profession and practice match.

> Indeed, to them you are nothing more than one who sings love songs with a beautiful voice and plays an instrument well, for they hear your words but do not put them into practice.
>
> —EZEKIEL 33:32

A Soldier's Bible

WILLIAM W. CRUMLY, while serving as chaplain at a hospital in Richmond, discovered a soldier's Bible among the bundles of clothes and knapsacks in one of the baggage rooms. The soldier's name was Albert Nearby. Nearby's prized possessions were his Bible and a daguerreotype (tin picture) of his sweetheart. When Crumly made the discovery, he remembered Nearby and related the following story:

> *The book had the appearance of being carefully read, there being many chapters and verses marked with pencil, as though they had strongly impressed themselves on the mind of the young reader . . . his [Albert's] first night in camp was a trying one . . . Albert felt that he must maintain his religious character . . . By the camp fire he read a chapter in his Bible and knelt on the ground and prayed . . .*

> As for God, his way is perfect; the word of the LORD is flawless. He is a shield for all who take refuge in him.
> —PSALM 18:30

> *He was thrown in the battle of Manassas, on the 21st July, 1861, with scarcely time to kneel by an apple tree in battle line, over which the shells were howling furiously. Here, in prayer, he hastily committed his soul and body to his faithful keeper, then rose calm and serene, with an assurance that no weapon of the enemy would harm him.*

> *When the battle was over . . . he had escaped unharmed, with a deep consciousness that God had been his shield and hiding place in the hour of danger . . .*[264]

The chaplain said that Albert, for a time, stopped reading his Bible and praying. Not long after, he lay wounded from a minie ball. When he regained consciousness, he asked for his Bible. Then as Albert slipped slowly into the valley of death, the faithful chaplain added:

> *"He then gently laid his hand on his Bible and the daguerreotype that lay near his side, and amid this profound stillness . . . the curtain dropped . . . [and] this noble youth fell asleep in Jesus . . ."* The precious treasure, the soldier's Bible, was returned to the family.[265]

A Desire to Grow

MARY BETHELL wrote in her diary about her own personal growth in Christ:

Sept. 12th 1861

Several days past my soul was in darkness, was cast down and tempted, I desired a deeper work of grace, I wanted to feel that God had sanctifyed me, throughout soul, spirit and body. I sought comfort in reading God's word and private prayer many times in the day. My soul hungered and thirsted after righteousness after many days of temptation, I at last found comfort. I awoke this morning one hour before day, I got up to pray. After spending nearly one hour in prayer, it was impressed on my mind to read the five chapters of 1st Peter, while reading them I was much comforted. I felt peace and love to Jesus Christ as my Saviour, I could praise God with joyful lips, light shone into my soul, I felt the witness of the Spirit. I want to grow in grace every day, and in the knowledge of my Lord and Saviour Jesus Christ.[266]

> You still the hunger of those you cherish; their sons have plenty, and they store up wealth for their children. And I—in righteousness I will see your face; when I awake, I will be satisfied with seeing your likeness.
>
> —PSALM 17:14, 15

As we develop a deeper walk with Christ, we become dissatisfied with our own mechanical attempts to grow in grace. Growing as a Christian necessitates that we make this number one priority our number one priority.

Is your personal relationship with Christ growing?

A Faithful Steward

DR. S. M. POTTER'S letters reveal an affectionate, God-fearing man who loved his family. Potter may have had a premonition that he would not make it back home. In the letters he wrote prior to his death, he seemed to be preparing his wife and family for the inevitable. After his death, J. R. Floyd of the Sixteenth Pennsylvania Cavalry wrote to Potter's widow.

Sept. 12 1864
Mrs. Potter,

> Each one should use whatever gift he has received to serve others, faithfully administering God's grace in its various forms.
> —1 PETER 4:10

I suppose you have already learned of the death of your husband. I have just been officially notified that Dr. S. M. Potter died at U.S. Gen'l Hosp, Pt Lookout, Ma., on the 6th at 1 A.M. of chronic Diarrhea . . . The Dr. was a faithful Steward. He stood high in the estimation of every officer & man in the Reg. We miss him very much. His loss we deeply lament not only as a member of the non-commissioned Staff of our regiment, holding the responsible position of Hospital Steward but as a man and friend. The Doctor too had all the elements of a good soldier. He shrank from no danger or hardship when duty called . . . Had he died here I should have had his body embalmed & sent to you. But I hoped by sending him to Pt. Lookout that he might be sent to Wash. from there & by a change of climate, diet etc. finally recover. But God's ways are not our ways nor his thoughts our thoughts. May His Grace temper this sad affliction to your stricken heart, and may we all be reminded of mortality & be prepared as the Dr. gave ample assurance that he was, for the great change that awaits us all, whether at home or abroad, whether surrounded by friends or among strangers at home or in the Army.

Yours resp.
J.R. Loyd 16 Pa. Cav.[267]

It was said of Dr. Potter that he was a faithful steward and a good soldier. He was loved by those around him and honored because he did not shrink from duty or danger.

Divine Protection

THE FOLLOWING letter was written by a member of a Christian family, the Kimberlys. During the battle for Nashville in the Civil War, the women mentioned were involved as spies or at least helped the Confederate cause which resulted in their imprisonment. George, a member of the Kimberly family, was presumed dead but came through the battle unscathed.

I wrote you that the Federals are encamped on our stable lot. Cousin Elizabeth Harding, Mrs. Barrow & Mrs. Nicholson are imprisoned in the Penitentiary. They will live in history, the first Nashville ladies who have been imprisoned. Frank is now in Atlanta. He is on his way to Chattanooga, George & Jim is at Knoxville on their way to Nashville. You know they were in the battles in Ky, George had his horse shot under him & the enemy seeing him going down concluded he was killed & had it thus published in their accounts of the battle, but he passed through the battles uninjured, but his old regiment the 1st Tenn. suffered severely . . .[268]

George, in passing through the battle uninjured, is a comforting reminder to us. The Lord has not promised we will not go through the floods and the fire, but has promised that he will go with us.

> When you pass through the waters, I will be with you; and when you pass through the rivers, they will not sweep over you. When you walk through the fire, you will not be burned; the flames will not set you ablaze.
> —ISAIAH 43:2

Testing and the Sweetness
of God's Mercy

SOUTHERN CHRISTIAN lady Sarah Wadley wrote in her diary at the beginning of the war:

September 15, 1861

I cannot help feeling sad this evening, Oh when we think what may be before us, how can any of us be aught but sad. Father, Mother and Major Bry have just walked over to Dr. Young's who returned from Virginia Thursday night. Young is in high spirits and expects that we will be victorious and that soon; but oh if we are, how many bleeding hearts will that victory cost! I sicken at the thought.

Father and Major Bry think that the war will continue through administration, but I pray that God in his mercy may avert this trial, I have never contemplated a long war, I have steeled myself to bear great and bloody battles and, many privations and even suffering for a little while . . . my heart sinks, my courage utterly fails; can I bear it? but why speak thus, I know I must bear it, and it only rests with me to decide whether I shall bear cheerfully or repiningly. I hope I may be enabled to be cheerful, and I sometimes think I can be so, but there are moments of darkness, in which I cannot think of the brightness which is often hid by clouds, and waits but for the stormy wind to scatter them and make its glory apparent. Oh, that I might have grace given me to wait on the Lord's good pleasure, I am too impatient, and I sometimes fear that God has wholly withdrawn his countenance from me, else I should not so rebel against his chastisements.

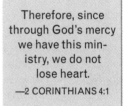

Therefore, since through God's mercy we have this ministry, we do not lose heart.

—2 CORINTHIANS 4:1

I think too much of my sorrows and too little of my blessings, truly God has been very kind to me, and though he has sent trials to me, yet how do I know but that if it had not been for them I should never have tested the sweetness of God's mercy.[269]

In times of testing, we are often tempted to lose heart. Yet we cannot fully understand God's mercy until we suffer hardships. Sarah Wadley struggled with seeing the light that was hidden behind the clouds. By allowing trials, God wanted her to taste the sweetness of his mercy.

Life's Deepest Sorrow

A SOLDIER wrote the following to his dear wife from Nashville, Tennessee, thankful his family had been spared from death. That was not true for many others.

How Nashville has suffered! Gen Zollicoffer, Gen. Rains, Henry Fogg, Col Patterson, Pretty Frank McNairy, young Orville Ewing, and some others I have forgotten, all killed. O Bettie how thankful I am that though tried in other ways, death the deepest sorrow has been spared us— and all four brothers in the service we have no right to expect all to pass safely through.[270]

The glories of war soon gave way despair for those who lost loved ones in battle. Wives became widows and childless almost overnight. To those who suffered such losses, their only sure foundation was the "Rock" of Christ.

David knew that the sorrows of life made a clear passageway to a deeper relationship with God. The prospect of death and the threats of ungodly enemies only heightened his need to cry unto the Lord. He could not have known the Lord as his rock, his fortress, and his deliverer had he not gone through tough times. If you are experiencing sorrow or despair, call to God for help. He will hear and answer.

> The LORD is my rock, my fortress and my deliverer; my God is my rock, in whom I take refuge. He is my shield and the horn of my salvation, my stronghold. I call to the LORD, who is worthy of praise, and I am saved from my enemies. The cords of death entangled me; the torrents of destruction overwhelmed me. The cords of the grave coiled around me; the snares of death confronted me. In my distress I called to the LORD; I cried to my God for help. From his temple he heard my voice; my cry came before him, into his ears.
>
> —PSALM 18:2–6

Chickamauga: A Day of Slaughter

COLONEL JOHN T. WILDER, of Indiana, who participated in the bat-tle of Chickamauga, Georgia, wrote the following account of that bloody battle:

There was a fearful slaughter of Longstreet's men at the time they were driving back the left wing of the nationals. This celebrated corps, as des-perated soldiers as ever lived, attacking two divisions, Van Cleve's and Davis', to the right and a little in front of Wilder, separated them and pushed on through the open space, yelping—the rebel shout is a yelp . . . A portion of them had to cross a small field, behind which in the bordering woods, Wilder lay, and through which ran a ditch, five or six feet deep, to carry off the water of an adjacent stream or swamp.

As the rebels entered this field in heavy masses, fully exposed, the mounted infantry, with their seven-shooting rifles, kept up a continu-ous blast of fire upon them, while Lilly, with his Indiana battery, hurled through them double-shotted canister from his ten-pounder rifles, at less than five hundred yards. The effect was awful. Every shot seemed to tell. The head of the column . . . appeared to melt away . . . for though continually moving it got no nearer.

It broke at last, and fell back in great disorder . . . and with desperate resolution pushed through the solid fire to the ditch. Here all who could get in took shelter. Instantly, Lilly wheeled two of his guns and poured right down the whole length of the ditch his horrible double canister. Hardly a man got out of it alive. "At this point." Said Wilder, "it actually seemed a pity to kill them so. They fell in heaps, and I had it in my heart to order the firing to cease, to end the awful sight. But the merciless seven-shooters and canister would not stop, and again the

> "The wolf and the lamb will feed together, and the lion will eat straw like the ox, they will neither harm nor destroy on all my holy mountain," says the LORD.
> —ISAIAH 65:25

boasted flower of Lee's army was crushed into a disorderly mob and driven off. When the firing ceased, one could have walked two hun-dred yards down the ditch on dead rebels, without ever touching the ground."[271]

Chickamauga:
The Night after the Battle

GENERAL JOHN B. GORDON described the night after the battle of Chickamauga in graphic detail and said:

> There will be no more night. They will not need the light of a lamp or the light of the sun, for the Lord God will give them light.
> —REVELATION 22:5

> *. . . Night after the battle! None but a soldier can realize the import of those four words. To have experienced it, felt it, endured it, and is to have witnessed a phase of war almost as trying to a sensitive nature as the battle itself. . . . To the two armies, whose blood was still flowing long after the sun went down on the 19th, neither of them victorious, but each so near the other as to hear the groans of the wounded and dying in the opposing ranks, the scene was indescribably oppressive. . . .*
>
> *The faint moonlight, almost wholly shut out by dense foliage, added to the weird spell of the somber scene. In every direction were dimly burning tapers, carried by nurses and relief corps searching for the wounded. All over the field lay the unburied dead, their pale faces made ghastlier by streaks of blood and clotted hair, and black stains of powder left upon their lips when they tore off with their teeth the ends of deadly cartridges. Such was the night between the battles of the 19th and 20th of September at Chickamauga.*
>
> *At nine o'clock on that Sabbath morning, September 20, as the church bells of Chattanooga summoned its children to Sunday-school, the signal-guns sounding through the forests at Chickamauga called the bleeding armies again to battle.*[272]

The night after the bloody battle of Chickamauga seemed most depressing. Still with the dawning of a new day came the call of the distant church bells to yet another battle.

Life's agonies invade our peace more in the shadows of night than in the sunshine of day. A sick child's fever worries an anxious mother more in the dark hours of the night than in the bright hours of the day. Christians have the promise of an eternal day when there will be no more night.

Voices from Chickamauga

BECAUSE OF THE DRAMA of movies, we get a wrong perception of virtual reality on the battlefield. B. F. Taylor's eyewitness account of the battlefield of Chickamauga gave an accurate picture of the sights and sounds one would hear:

> *"If anybody thinks," says B. F. Taylor, in his account of the battle of Chickamauga, "that when men are stricken upon the field they fill the air with cries and groans, till it shivers with such evidence of agony, he greatly errs. An arm is shattered, a leg carried away, a bullet pierces the breast, and the soldier sinks down silently upon the ground, or creeps away if he can, without a murmur or complaint; falls as the sparrow falls, speechlessly; and like that sparrow, I earnestly believe, not without a Father. The horse gives out his fearful utterance of almost human sufferings, but the mangled rider is dumb. The crash of musketry, the crack of rifles, the roar of guns, the shriek of shells, the rebel whoop, the Federal cheer, and that indescribable undertone of rumbling, grinding, splintering sound, make up the voices of the battle-field."*[273]

The description of the wounded men on the battlefield of Chickamauga reminds us of the suffering Savior on the cross of Calvary.

I once heard a missionary from Brazil describe buying meat at the local market. The area he lived had little means of refrigeration. If you asked for meat, the animal was often slaughtered in your presence. One day he observed the butcher preparing a lamb for slaughter. He hung the lamb from its hind feet on a rope which he had looped over the branch of a tree. The butcher then lifted the lamb's head and slit its throat. The missionary said, "Then the most amazing and heart-touching thing happened. The lamb stretched out his front legs in silence, hung there, and bled to death without even the slightest sound."

> He was oppressed and afflicted, yet he did not open his mouth; he was led like a lamb to the slaughter, and as a sheep before her shearers is silent, so he did not open his mouth.
>
> —ISAIAH 53:7

Bloody Chickamauga

GENERAL JOHN BROWN GORDON reflected on the battle of Chickamauga and said:

REARED from childhood to maturity in North Georgia, I have been for fifty years familiar with that historic locality traversed by the little river Chickamauga, which has given its name to one of the bloodiest battles of modern times . . . One of the most prominent features of the field was the old Ross House, built of hewn logs . . . In this old building I had often slept at night on my youthful journeyings with my father . . . Snodgrass Hill, Gordon's and Lee's Mills, around which the battle raged, the LaFayette road, across which the contending lines so often swayed, and the crystal Crawfish Spring, at which were gathered thousands of the wounded . . .

I am encouraged to attempt a brief description of the awful and inspiring events of those bloody September days in 1863 Words, however, cannot convey an adequate picture of such scenes; of the countless costly, daring assaults . . . always dauntless courage; of the grim, deadly grapple in hand-to-hand collisions; of the almost unparalleled slaughter and agony.

> And blood flowed out of the press, rising as high as the horses' bridles for a distance of 1,600 stadia [180 miles].
> —REVELATION 14:20

An American battle that surpassed in its ratio of carnage the bloodiest conflicts in history outside of this country ought to be better understood by the American people. Sharpsburg, or Antietam, I believe, had a larger proportion of killed and wounded than any other single day's battle of our war; and that means larger than any in the world's wars. Chickamauga, however, in its two days of heavy fighting, brought the ratio of losses to the high-water mark. At Chickamauga thousands fell on both sides fighting at close quarters, their faces at times burnt by the blazing powder at the very muzzles of the guns. The La Fayette road became the "bloody lane" of Chickamauga.[274]

As we read about the bloody battle at Chickamauga, consider an even bloodier battle that will take place in the future between the forces of righteousness and evil at the battle of Armageddon.

Major General Ambrose E. Burnside—
A Devout Christian

GENERAL AMBROSE E. BURNSIDE arrived in Knoxville to the cheers of people who lined the crowded streets to welcome the Union army. Almost immediately upon his arrival, he sent word to the Reverend Thomas Humes to resume services at St. John Episcopal Church. Burnside attended the services and the sermon was taken from Psalm 30 which said, "I will magnify thee, O Lord; for thou hast set me up, and not made my foes to triumph over me."

Further insight into Burnside's Christian character can be found in Gordon Seymour's book, *Divided Loyalties*:

> *General Burnside himself was a deeply devout Christian. At Camp Nelson on August 14, just before his invasion of East Tennessee, he issued the following order to the Army of the Ohio: "Whenever regimental evening dress parades are held, it shall be the duty of the commanding officer to see that the chaplain, or some proper person, in his absence, holds some short religious service, such as the reading of a portion of the Scripture, with appropriate prayer for the protection and assistance of divine protection."*[275]

Burnside believed that providing his men with religious services was his duty. His concern was that they have daily Scripture reading and prayer. It is refreshing that a general of the United States Army realized the value of spiritual warfare. Undoubtedly, Burnside believed that our greatest battle was not with "flesh and blood." The Word of God has been given to Christians to fight Satan and his demons (Eph. 6:17). Paul reminds us that prayer is a powerful way to invoke God's protection as he surrounds us with his angels in tough times.

> You are my hiding place; you will protect me from trouble and surround me with songs of deliverance.
>
> —PSALM 32:7

WILLIAM TECUMSEH SHERMAN
The National Archives

A Brave Drummer Boy
Who Impressed Sherman

A BRAVE DRUMMER BOY named Orion P. Howe served in the Fifty-fifth Illinois Volunteers. Orion soon was in the thick of the battle at Vicksburg, Mississippi. Major General William Sherman was so impressed by this young man that he wrote a letter to Secretary Edwin Stanton to tell of his great bravery, which undoubtedly secured him a promotion.

> *When the assault at Vicksburg was at its height on the 19th of May, and I was in front near the road, which formed my line of attack, this young lad came up to me wounded and bleeding, with a good, healthy boy's cry: "Gen. Sherman, send some cartridges to Col. Malmborg; the men are nearly all out." "What is the matter, my boy?" "They shot me in the leg, sir, but I can go to the hospital. Send the cartridges right away." Even where we stood, the shot fell thick, and I told him to go to the rear at once, I would attend to the cartridges, and off he limped. Just before he disappeared on the hill, he turned and called as loud as he could; "Caliber 54" I have not seen the lad since, and his Colonel, Malmborg, on inquiry, gives me his address as above, and says he is a bright, intelligent boy, with a fair preliminary education.*
>
> *What arrested my attention then was, and what renews my memory of the fact now is, that one so young, carrying a musket ball wound through his leg, should have found his way to me on that fatal spot, and delivered his message not forgetting the very important part even of the caliber of his musket, 54, which you know is an unusual one.*
>
> *I'll warrant that the boy has in him the elements of a man, and I commend him to the Government as one worthy the fostering care of some one of its national institutions.*[276]

> Have I not commanded you? Be strong and courageous. Do not be terrified; do not be discouraged, for the LORD your God will be with you wherever you go.
> —JOSHUA 1:9

Our God often calls upon us to take steps of faith that test our courage. The Lord will never lead us into areas where he has not prepared and equipped us for service.

The Effects of the
Sword on Our Lives

DR. T. DEWITT TALMAGE, pastor and biblical scholar during the Civil War, spoke about the effects of the sword:

The sword has developed the grandest natures that the world ever saw. It has developed courage—that sublime energy of the soul which defies the universe when it feels itself to be in the right. It has developed a self-sacrifice which repudiates the idea that our life is worth more than anything else, when for a principle it throws that life away as much as to say, "It is not necessary that I live, but it is necessary that righteousness triumph."

There are thousands among the Northern and Southern veterans of our Civil War who are ninety-five percent larger and mightier in soul than they would have been had they not, during the four years of national agony, turned their back on home and fortune, and at the front sacrificed all for a principle.[277]

Even though the sword is thought of as a destructive weapon in battle, we can readily see from the thirteenth chapter of Romans that the sword can be used constructively by God to bring about results in our lives, Talmage aptly taught this truth after the war in a sermon that described the character of such men as Jackson, Lee, and others. On both sides, the sword of battle revealed the true intent of the hearts of those who bravely fought for what they believed in. The Civil War was, as Lincoln put it, "a birth of a new nation." Because of convictions and loyalties to principles on both sides, our nation ultimately came together.

> For he is God's servant to do you good. But if you do wrong, be afraid, for he does not bear the sword for nothing. He is God's servant, an agent of wrath to bring punishment on the wrongdoer.
> —ROMANS 13:4

The sword of fiery trials we face as Christians can be used by God to strengthen our faith and solidify our character as men and women of God. The Bible tells us that God's Word is the "sword of the spirit." Using God's Word regularly can increase our faith and character.

Can His Word Fail?

A DAUGHTER of the Lenoir family wrote to her brother the following:

Crab Orchard Sept 27th 1863

Dear brother,

Allow me to suggest again that the best remedy . . . a simple non-hesitating affectionate reliance on the goodness and mercy of God. The worst now that can be taken of the war only shows that our arms of flesh may fail us; that man's wisdom and man's strength may fail to maintain us in the enjoyment of those temporal blessings which they have heretofore enabled us to call our own. But it does not appear in all that that God's favor is withdrawn or that his almighty arm will fail to support us. Our very disasters may be blessings sent from him in disguise; they most assuredly will prove so to those that love him and trust in him, and to their children and children's children. . . . It is God's mercy, through the atonement of Christ. He has said he will be a father to the fatherless; and do you fear that he will not provide as well as you? He has said, "Fear not them which kill the body but are not able to kill the soul." He has said, "Take no thought, saying what shall we eat? Or what shall we drink? Or wherewithal shall we be clothed? For your heavenly Father knoweth that you have need of all these things." He has said, "Blessed are ye when men shall revile you and persecute you." And can his words fail? [278]

> So is my word that goes out from my mouth: It will not return to me empty, but will accomplish what I desire and achieve the purpose for which I sent it.
> —ISAIAH 55:11

Many of the disappointments we experience in life happen because people let us down. We cannot depend on people to guide us through the problems we face. We must learn to lean on Jesus and his Word. Humans will fail us, but Jesus never fails.

Dealing with Suicide

THE CONTENT of the following letter to Sade Lenoir is in reference to the suicide of her husband, William Lenoir:

Fayetteville April 12th 1861

Dear Aunt Sade:

I know I can say but little, indeed, nothing to comfort you in your great sorrow, but I feel as if I must tell you that we have heard of your afflic-tion, and can feel for you for we have suffered—I never could feel for the distressed as I now can, I could always rejoice with the rejoicing; but now I can weep with the weeping—You have had a great shock, but I trust you will be sustained by God's grace, "it will be sufficient for you." We must "only believe" and our Heavenly Father will let us take comfort even when the sky seems entirely over-cast, "sorrow may endure for a night but joy cometh in the morning"—When bowed down with grief it seems hard, at times, to realize that it is God that deals thus with us, when the cup of sorrow seems full to overflowing, we can not understand why another drop is added? So often do we see Gods faith-ful children deprived of almost every joy and comfort, and if we did not believe the chastening was a token of love—what a dark world this would be! If we could feel always that we are but sojourning here to be fitted for another world . . . Oh! Aunt Sade it was the greatest comfort to me to feel that Jesus had suffered grief and had even wept on Lazarus' grave—I never felt the same way about it before—I never appreciated my Redeemer—I had to be laid in the depths of woe [sic], so that I might taste the greatest blessing of my life . . .

> The eternal God is your refuge, and underneath are the everlasting arms.
> —DEUTERONOMY 33:27

Your affectionate Cousin[279]

If you know someone who lost a loved one to suicide, being an atten-tive and understanding friend can make a big difference. Remind them the Lord has big arms and is able to handle any burden we place on him.

No One Knows the Day or Hour

S OLDIER SAMUEL POTTER wrote to his wife, Cynthia, in Virginia the
following letter:

> I have not heard of any stir in the front. The report here is that the rebs
> are falling back. I think their energies are turning to defeat Gen.
> Rosecrans so the army of the Potomac will have some rest from march-
> ing & fighting. We don't live here quite so well here as we did in the
> front. The army has been here all summer & the whole of this once
> beautiful country is a continuous scene of desola-
> tion. There are no cornfields nor potato patches,
> hogs or sheep munching over the fields. What
> few citizens remain here have nothing to sell or
> trade for our coffee or sugar but still we live well
> & I have as good health as ever. . . I suppose Mr.
> Burns death will be a lesson for all of us to be
> ready for we know not the day nor the day when
> the angel of death will take either of us from this
> earth. May we strive for a home in heaven. We
> know our time will come to die & so let us be prepared to meet the
> author of our existence to give an account of the deeds done here on
> earth & oh that we may hear that welcome sentence. "Well done good
> & faithful servant, enter thou in the joy of thy Lord." What will
> become of us when we die? Will we have time & opportunity?[280]

> No one knows about
> that day or hour, not
> even the angels in
> heaven, or the Son,
> but only the Father.
> —MATTHEW 24:36

Potter poses a good question to us: "What will become of us when we
die? Will we have time and opportunity?" The answer to Potter's question
is found in Jesus' words, "I must work the works of him that sent me, while
it is day: the night cometh, when no man can work" (John 9:4, KJV). Since
no one can know the day or the hour of our Lord's return, he tells us to be
ready. The time to grow close to Jesus is now. One more day may be one
day too late.

Victory Must Be Ours

GENERAL BRAXTON BRAGG, commander of the Army of Tennessee, was in the field at La Fayette, Georgia, on September 16, 1863. Realizing the grave importance of winning that battle, Bragg sent a motivational speech to his men to inspire them to victory.

> *Heretofore you have never failed to respond to your general when he has asked sacrifice at your hands. Relying on your gallantry and patriotism, he asks you to add the crowning glory to the wreath you wear . . . your generals' will lead you; you have but to respond to assure us a glorious triumph over the insolent foe. I know what your response will be. Trusting God and the justice of our cause, and nerved by the love of the dear ones at home, failure is impossible and victory must be ours.*

Braxton, Bragg,
General, Commanding[281]

Generals from both sides of the Civil War trusted in the providence of God. They put their confidence in God for victory. If the battle didn't end in victory, they accepted it as God's will.

Joab's call to the Israelites was a rallying call to fight the enemy leaving the ultimate results up to God. If we could believe that God had absolute control of every aspect of our battles, then even defeat would have a significant spiritual meaning.

> Be strong and let us fight bravely for our people and the cities of our God. The LORD will do what is good in his sight.
> —2 SAMUEL 10:12

A Reluctant Chaplain

THE FOLLOWING anecdote is told by General Jubal Early:

During the recent fight on the Rappahannock, he saw a man rushing past him.

"Where are you going?" cried the General.

"To the rear," replied the man. "I am a non-combatant."

"Who are you?" demanded the General.

"I am a chaplain," replied the runner.

"Well," said the General, "here is consistency! For twenty years you have been wanting to get to heaven, and now that there is a chance, you run away from it."[282]

Even though the story of the reluctant chaplain above is humorous, we wonder what might have occurred for the chaplain had he gone with his men into battle. He might have won the respect and had opportunities to minister in a way he had never experienced before. God could have done great things through him if had the courage to go forward.

God had a plan for Jonah, but Jonah was blinded by his own prejudice and refused to carry out the mission God had given him—to preach to the people of Nineveh. So Jonah ran from God, but the enormous fish that God provided brought about a sudden change of plans.

> But Jonah ran away from the LORD and headed for Tarshish. He went down to Joppa, where he found a ship bound for that port. After paying the fare, he went aboard and sailed for Tarshish to flee from the LORD.
>
> —JONAH 1:3

The Annoying Pestilence

CONFEDERATE SOLDIER Arthur Ford wrote of frustrating conditions while on picket duty near Charleston, South Carolina, in the summer of 1864,

We spent the summer of 1864 doing picket duty at Combahee Point, and along the Ashepoo River (Charleston, S.C.) . . . The camp was located on the edge of the abandoned rice field . . . The old rice fields were more or less overflowed, the banks having been broken for two years or more, and in them were numerous alligators, some of considerable size. . . . , but were annoying to us. But the most serious disturbers of our peace were the mosquitoes. These were of such size and venom and in such numbers as to cause real suffering, and necessitate the use of unusual schemes to protect ourselves against their attacks.

> I will say of the LORD, "He is my refuge and my fortress, my God, in whom I trust" Surely he will save you from . . . the deadly pestilence . . . You will not fear the terror of night, nor the pestilence that stalks in the darkness.
> —PSALM 91:2, 3

Accounts of these mosquitoes must seem incredible to any one who has never spent a midsummer's night in the rice fields . . . During the day [there were] comparatively few . . . but when night fell, and the myriads came up from the fields and marsh, then the situation became serious. When we were on sentry duty, walking post, many of us wore thick woolen gloves to protect our hands; and over our heads and necks frames made of thin hoops covered with mosquito netting. And when we wanted to retire to our small "A" tents, we had to make smudge fires in them first, and then crawl in on our hands and knees, and keep our faces near the ground to breathe, until finally we got asleep. . . . we dared not let our faces or hands touch the sides of the tent, for immediately the mighty insects would thrust their proboscis through the canvas and get us . . .[283]

Sometimes in life, the little things frustrate us the most, but God promises to be with us in times of frustration and insecurity. If we will put our trust in him, he will deliver us from the "pestilences" of life.

When Heroes Die

THOMAS HUGHES who was the son of a controversial writer had unusual access to the Confederate capitol where he viewed the body of General Stonewall Jackson. He wrote of his observations:

Free access to the Capitol gave me the opportunity to observe minutely the funeral arrangements for General Thomas J. Jackson. Stonewall Jackson's remains were brought to Richmond to lie in state in the Capitol preparatory to his funeral. And they arrived late one evening and were first deposited in a little room on the left of the entrance to the Capitol on the side next to the Governor's house. The burial casket was placed on a bier, uncovered, and the custodian of the Capitol permitted a favored few including myself to view the remains. The coffin had evergreen heavily intertwined around it. There were no flowers. His face was exactly as appears in his photographs, except it was thinner, the features were perfectly placid, not evidencing that he had suffered pain, his whiskers and mustache were of unusual thickness, his forehead high and his hair coal black. I brought a small portion of the evergreen on the casket away with me. After lying in state when his funeral took place the cortege was preceded by a brass band that played a funeral dirge; the horse that General Jackson rode with General Jackson's boots hanging down one on each side of his saddle came next to the hearse and was led by his body servant. The funeral was impressive as only such a one could be.[284]

> For Moses said, "The Lord your God will raise up for you a prophet like me from among your own people; you must listen to everything he tells you."
>
> —ACTS 3:22

Moses' life was nearly over. He had accomplished what the Lord had sent him to do. People could not imagine anyone else in leadership but Moses, yet for every Moses, there came a Joshua to do an equal or greater job for the Lord. God has men and women for every generation and every task. Are you one of them?

A Handkerchief Full of Tears

M ICHAEL REID HANGER was born in Staunton, Virginia, on May 10, 1840. While working as a carpenter in Lexington, he enlisted in the "Rockbridge Rifles" on April 18, 1861, in response to Governor John Letcher's call for volunteers to defend Virginia. A reporter for the *Lexington Gazette* described the ceremony:

> *When all was ready, after bidding adieu to friends and relatives, the Rifles were formed in front of the Court House, where Rev. Mr. Tebbs and the venerable Dr. McFarland stood prepared to call upon the Lords of Hosts for his protecting care under the trying circumstances in which they were soon to be placed . . . All hearts were softened; all eyes were moistened by the tear of sorrow for the necessitation of the case. Every soldier was determined, if need be, to stand to the last, and die in a cause so just and a service so honorable. His [Elisha F. Paxton's] young wife with sad forebodings, wept until her handkerchief was wet with tears. In their last fond embrace he took this from her hand and as a reminder of her love carried it on many a bloody battlefield.[285]*

> Thou tellest my wanderings: put thou my tears into thy bottle: are they not in thy book?
> —PSALM 56:8 (KJV)

In ancient Roman times, those who were grieving the losses of loved ones collected their tears in a lachrymatory, a type of bottle as a memorial to the one deceased. Tombs have been opened in ancient Rome that reveal grieving family members who placed those tear-filled bottles in the grave with their deceased loved ones.

We are reminded in Scripture that our Lord collects our tears for the day of judgment when our sorrows will be turned to joy.

Rejoicing in Present Victories

LIEUTENANT WILBUR F. HINMAN of the Sixty-fifth Ohio Infantry (Harker's Brigade) became a brigade historian after the war and gave the following account of the taking of Lookout Mountain in Chattanooga, Tennessee:

> *We neared Lookout, but not a shot was heard. As we rounded the point of the mountain, far below the frowning cliffs, our eyes discerned, through the clouds of dust that filled the air, the spires and buildings of Chattanooga. A wave of prodigious cheers swept along the column, and this was repeated again and again. The blood, which was the price paid for Chattanooga, was to be shed a few days later. But the soldiers knew not, reconed not, of the future. They thought only of the present, and rejoiced with exceeding great joy in the possession, so easily gained, of the Confederate stronghold . . .*[286]

> And when the LORD sent you out from Kadesh Barnea, he said, "Go up and take possession of the land I have given you."
>
> —DEUTERONOMY 9:23

Moses led the Hebrews out of Pharaoh's bondage and brought them toward a wonderful land which God promised. As they looked across the borders of Kadesh Barnea, God said, "Go up and take possession of the land I have given you."

Spies brought back the report that giants inhabited the land. The people in fear complained about what lay ahead. Because of their unbelief, God sent them back to the wilderness for forty years. There is a parallel here with some Christians in our day. Some can step out by faith as long as life runs smoothly, but when trouble arises, they head back to unbelief. We do not know what lies ahead, but if God has led us safe this far, he is able to lead us the rest of the way.

The Federal soldiers cheered when they saw Chattanooga, but little did they know that bloody Chickamauga was just ahead.

The Compassion of a Confederate Chaplain

A LEXANDER BETTS was a Confederate chaplain who commanded great respect as a man of God with his soldiers. His love and compassion was felt by his fellow soldiers as well as the enemy.

CHAPLAIN
ALEXANDER BETTS
Courtesy
University of
North Carolina,
Chapel Hill

I found a wounded Federal sitting on the field—a broken thigh, a rifle ball through his arm and a bruised shoulder made him right helpless. His undressed wounds were sore. He asked me if I thought our surgeons would care for him. I assured him they would. He said he had a wife and two little children in his northern home. His parents were pious and had raised him piously, but he had neglected his own soul. I said: "Brother, Jesus loves you. You came down here to kill my brothers, but I love you." He broke down and sobbed aloud: "You don't talk like one man that came here." He upbraided me. He told me our men had been very good to him during the three or four days he had been there.

. . . They had just taken the last Confederate wounded from that part of the field. He was on the surgeon's table a few yards away. I trust this Federal was soon taken to that table. . . . As I took him by the hand and commended him to God, I think my heart was as tender as it ever was. His bones may be in that field now. I hope to meet his soul in Heaven in a few years . . .[287]

Most likely, someone will cross your path today who needs prayer, compassion, and understanding.

> Because of the LORD's great love we are not consumed, for his compassions never fail. They are new every morning; great is your faithfulness.
>
> —LAMENTATIONS 3:22–23

Guardian Angel of
the Battlefield

NURSE CLARA BARTON became known by both the North and South as the "guardian angel of the battlefield." Her compassion for friend and enemy alike stand as a testimony to the love and compassion of Christ. In a very rare book by L. P. Brockett (1820–1893), the following statement of gratitude was written about Barton:

> *Among those who have sacrificed all the comforts of life, the pleasures of society, and the delights of intellectual culture and association for the still higher and holier joy of ministering to those, who, on our great battlefields, have fallen in defense of their country, there is none more deserving of the nations gratitude and enduring remembrance than Miss Clara H. Barton.*[288]

Clara Barton's reputation was established on the battlefield of Antietam. Over a thousand soldiers fell wounded in that battle and the work of the surgeons was not nearly finished when darkness began to descend on the hospital camp. The medical staff feared that many would die in the hospital tents in total darkness. The surgeons had

> You are the light of the world. A city on a hill cannot be hidden.
> —MATTHEW 5:14

little prospect of light in the camp that night. Yet, because of Clara Barton's experience, she arranged ahead of time for mules and wagons to bring lanterns to the hospital camps.

Clara Barton brought light to a place of darkness. Jesus reminds us of our mission when he says, "You are the light of the world." He has called us to carry his light into sin-darkened places throughout the world. Barton had a sense of mission and courage that far surpassed many men of her day.

Ask the Lord to increase your light within your neighborhood and community.

Yankee Revival in Chattanooga

R EVIVAL among the troops not only drew the soldiers into a closer walk with Christ, but also inspired them to be more determined to fight on to victory which is evidenced by the following:

In the Fall and Winter of 1863, the Union army in Chattanooga, Tennessee had been besieged by a strong Confederate force, strongly entrenched in the mountains around the city. The Union soldiers were deeply affected by the revival, and many attributed their surprising victory over the Confederates as "a visible interposition of God." Soon after their victory at Chattanooga, the Union troops were pursuing their enemy as they retreated towards Atlanta. The fires of revival continued for the Union troops in Ringgold, Georgia, where hundreds of men were baptized in Chickamauga Creek.[289]

The Israelites often needed renewal from the Spirit of God. Because we live in a busy world, we are apt to get caught in the rush. We busy ourselves with many things that have no eternal significance until we are drained of spiritual strength. We cannot live apart from the Lord's influence without it affecting our lives negatively. In those times, we need to humble ourselves in the presence of the "high and lofty One." To repent of our sins is the key to experiencing heaven-sent revival. When we experience a spiritual revival, we cease running from the enemy—rather we put him on the run.

> For this is what the high and lofty One says— he who lives forever, whose name is holy: "I live in a high and holy place, but also with him who is contrite and lowly in spirit, to revive the spirit of the lowly and to revive the heart of the contrite."
> —ISAIAH 57:15

Doubting God's Existence?

I SAAC WHITE was appointed an assistant surgeon in the Confederate army on September 2, 1861, and served with the Virginia Active Volunteer Forces.

On Picket near New Hope Va
October 6th/64

My Dear Jinnie

I have not received a letter from Mother for a long time only one since the death of my poor dear brother. I would like so much to know whether or not my dear brother thought he would die + if so had he a hope in heaven it would be consoling to me above all things in this world to know that he is now in heaven for heaven would have more charms for me if I knew my dear brother was there. I feel that I have a hope in Gods wand though I am tempted often to doubt the exis-tence of such a being. Is it not strange that one should ever doubt his existence? Common scorn should teach us better. I am . . . a corrupt man fond of the pleasures of this world . . . Our stay in this world is very short. At last I feel this memory that I can say "Thy will oh God not mine be done."

> The fool hath said in his heart, there is no God.
>
> —PSALM 14:1

Your devoted Isaac[290]

Isaac White's struggle with the existence of God could be linked to the horrors of war and the suffering it brings. To subject one's self to suffering, agony, and despair on a daily basis weakens the mind and raises questions that cannot be fully answered. Job wrestled with such questions and in the end declared through great tribulation that he knew his Redeemer lived. How could Job come to such a conclusion? He looked through the eyes of faith.

A Sweet Christian Farewell

ANNIE SEHON'S husband came home from the war to be with his wife when he learned she was dying from a hemorrhage. Following is the record of his sweet farewell to Annie:

> When we returned, my father met me at the gate, and told me that Annie was extremely prostrate . . . Hurrying to her room, I found her with her pulse very low, prostrated by what I was satisfied was a hemorrhage from the bowels. I did not think she could survive during the night . . . Consulting the physician . . . I found that my worst fears were correct. Placing myself on the side of the bed beside her, I was compelled to tell her, my angel, my darling, my wife, Oh, my God, how can I write it, that she was about to be taken home to heaven. She answered me, "My husband I am not afraid to die, but I would not think I am dying, surely, God will give me some sign, some feeling that I am to die, I have no such feeling yet." I then told her that, of which she was still ignorant, that the discharges from her bowels were of blood, in the nature of hemorrhages, and that the physicians thought she could not live long. Turning them full on me her heavenly eyes, she asked, "And now my husband lie down by me, and put your arms around me, let my head lie on your shoulder as it has done every night" folding her in my arms, she said, "Oh! Husband we have been so happy, so happy, and I have loved you so much more than you could ever know" . . . After night fall her delirium became violent . . . [but] she became quiet and so remained until her last breath, which, oh, my sister, bore to heaven the gentlest spirit, the truest soul that ever made man happy.[291]

> Who shall separate us from the love of Christ? Shall trouble or hardship or persecution or famine or nakedness or danger or sword?
> —ROMANS 7:35

There is no hardship so hard that God's love is not present. There is no danger so dangerous that God's love is missing. God's love is present in the middle of terminal illness. When my father learned he had terminal cancer, the whole family was devastated. After the initial shock, we became concerned about making my dad comfortable. We found that dad's main need was being touched and loved by us.

Wielding the Sword

WHEN IT COMES to wielding the sword of the Spirit, the Christian can make a difference that will last for eternity.

As Bishop Rosecrans (brother of the General) was at dinner, the conversation reverted to the war. "It would seem to me, Bishop, that you and your brother, the General, are engaged in very different callings," remarked a gentleman. "Yes, it appears so," returned the Bishop. "And yet," he continued, "we are both fighting men. While the General is wielding the sword of the flesh, I trust that I am using the sword of the Spirit. He is fighting the rebels, and I am fighting the spirits of darkness . . ."[292]

The surgeon can wield his knife and prolong a life, but his patient will eventually die. When we wield the sword of the Spirit, we can see spiritual life take place that will last for eternity. We are waging warfare in the unseen world against satanic forces. Our greatest offensive weapon is the "two-edged sword," the Word of God.

Satan cannot stand up to the authority of Scripture. Jesus proved the power and authority of the Word when Satan tempted him in the wilderness.

Have you wielded your sword lately?

Therefore put on the full armor of God, so that when the day of evil comes, you may be able to stand your ground, and after you have done everything, to stand. Stand firm then, with the belt of truth buckled around your waist, with the breastplate of righteousness in place, and with your feet fitted with the readiness that comes from the gospel of peace. In addition to all this, take up the shield of faith, with which you can extinguish all the flaming arrows of the evil one. Take the helmet of salvation and the sword of the Spirit, which is the word of God . . .

—EPHESIANS 6:13–18

My Life Is in Your Hands

LAMAR FONTAINE, a dispatch bearer for the Southern forces around Vicksburg, Mississippi, had a father and mother who prayed for his safe return and believed in the overruling providence of God. His father wrote the following account about Fontaine in 1863:

> *Lamar is almost continually in the saddle, and employed in very hazardous enterprises. His last feat of arms was the most daring he has yet performed. He left my house, under orders from Gen Johnston, to bear a verbal dispatch to Gen. Pemberton, in Vicksburg, and to carry a supply of percussion caps to our troops in that besieged city . . . the family were called together for prayers, and we prayed fervently that the God of our fathers would shield him from all danger, and enable him to fulfill his mission to* Vicksburg *successfully, and give him a safe return to us all. I then exhorted him to remember that, it was the will of God for him to live and serve his country, all the Yankees owned by* LINCOLN *could not kill him; but if it was the divine will that he should die, he would be in as much danger at home as in Vicksburg, and death would certainly find him, not matter where he might be . . .*[293]

> They all joined together constantly in prayer, along with the women and Mary the mother of Jesus, and with his brothers.
> —ACTS 1:14

Fontaine's family believed in the power of prayer. Like the New Testament believers, they brought their burdens to the Lord. For many families in the Civil War era, prayer was their only means of comfort. Information did not travel quickly in the 1800s. For that reason, Christian families had a choice when it came to the fate of their husbands and sons in battle—they could worry or they could pray. The Fontaine family decided to do the latter. They fervently prayed, released their anxieties to the Lord, and continued to trust in God to answer their prayers in accordance with his will.

A Firsthand Account of Battle

ONE OF THE MOST graphic accounts of what it was like to be a Civil War soldier in the heat of battle was written by a Union soldier who fought in the battle of Piketon, Kentucky.

I was riding along, somewhat carelessly, when crack! crack! crack! went their rifles, and down fell our men. Crack! crack! crack! they came. Off I jumped from my horse, when along came the Major, and gave me his horse to hold; but I soon hitched them both to a tree down by the river, and sprung again up the bank, when whiz! Went a bullet past my face, about three inches from it, and made me draw back in a hurry . . . Here comes another—buzz, buzz—(you can hear their whiz for fully a hundred yards as they come)—get out of the way. But where is it to go to? Whew! That was close. But, great God! It has gone through a man's shoulder within a few yards of me! He falls! Some of his comrades pick him up.

Now a horseman comes past in a hurry. He is right opposite me—when whiz, crack! a ball strikes his horse in the fore-shoulder. Off tumbles the man; down falls the horse, stiffened out and dead. If the bullet had gone through the animal, it would doubtless have struck me.[294]

> The noise of battle is in the land, the noise of great destruction!
> . . . I set a trap for you, O Babylon, and you were caught before you knew it.
> —JEREMIAH 50:22, 24

The people of God had a long captivity under the rule of the Babylonians, but the Lord in mercy did not forget them. Their captivity was coming to a close and the Lord was now ready to take vengeance on the Babylonians and set his people free. We will go through tough times in our life that we cannot understand. But one thing we must not misunderstand—God has not forgotten us. He is full of mercy and compassion and is able to put our feet back on a solid foundation as he did for Israel.

A Hunger for the Word

CONFEDERATE CHAPLAIN J. William Jones was author of one of the best documentaries of the Great Revival. Nearly every Confederate brigade was affected during this revival. Approximately 10 percent of the soldiers in the Army of Northern Virginia accepted Christ. Night after night, troops participated in prayer meetings, worship, and listened to ministers proclaim the good news of the gospel of Christ. Every gathering ended with soldiers coming forward to accept Christ or to receive prayer. If a pond or river was in the vicinity, soldiers were baptized no matter how cold the weather. During the revival, Jones told how Confederate soldiers formed "reading clubs," where soldiers passed around a well-worn Bible. Always hungry for scarce Testaments and religious tracts, the soldiers would see Jones approaching camp and cry, "Yonder comes the Bible and tract man!" They would run up to him and beg for Bibles and Testaments like they were treasures of gold. Jones would quickly exhaust his supply of reading material and sadly have to turn away most of the men. "I have never seen more diligent Bible-readers than we had in the Army of Northern Virginia," he said.[295]

> Blessed are those who hunger and thirst for righteousness, for they will be filled.
> —MATTHEW 5:6

The uncertainty of life and the keen awareness of mortality inspired a hunger for God's Word during the Civil War that could not be quenched. People always seem to read the Bible and more so during a crisis or a war. If we could only learn to be more disciplined in our reading of Scripture in times of ease, we may be more fitted to bear up in times of trouble.

Tomorrow may bring a crisis. Have you read your Bible today?

A Child's First Letter

THE SWEET LETTER that Mr. Hope wrote to his little girl should remind us of the love of our heavenly Father toward his children.

Camp Cummings near Mobile, Ala.
Apr. 25, 1864

Dear Child,

It is with pleasure and delight that I write you a few lines, which will be the first letter you ever received and one too which I hope you will preserve until you can read it.

By the misfortunes of war, I have been separated from your Momma, but by the blessings of God, I hope to soon return to you, never more to leave you, until death shall separate us. My dear and only child, be a good girl, ever love and obey your affectionate Momma, and don't forget your first letter writer, who has not nor never will forget you, who daily prays to God, in his infinite mercy, to spare, bless and protect you amid the troubles of this world, and should you live to become old, may God bless you and prepare your soul in this life to go to that happy world after death.

Your Father,
P. M. Hope[296]

The apostle John used the terminology, "My dear children." He admonishes us to stay close to Jesus Christ so we will be confident at his second coming.

Soldier P. M. Hope looked forward with anticipation to heaven. In case he did not make it back home, he was anxious for his daughter to be prepared to go there. He wanted to meet her there some happy day. A good parent prepares his or her children for eternity.

> And now, dear children, continue in him, so that, when he appears, we may be confident, and unashamed before him at his coming.
> —1 JOHN 2:28

The Wildest Boy in the Regiment

CHAPLAIN ALEXANDER BETTS of the Southern army wrote in his diary concerning the death of a young man in his regiment who came to know Jesus before he died.

C. H. Ruffin, of Nash Co., wounded yesterday. Dies in my arms—in perfect peace. Charlie enlisted at 17, and perhaps, was the wildest boy in his Regiment. He was very respectful to me, but showed no signs of any care for his soul till April last. About the time I was disappointed in my hopes to go home, he began to seek my company and give good attention to preaching. He became deeply convicted and was happily converted and I took him into the Missionary Baptist Church, and sent his name to the home church the day I started home If I had gone home at the time I first proposed, he might not have been converted. Just before he breathed his last I asked him about his case. He sweetly smiled and said: "Bro. Betts as soon as I die I shall go straight to my blessed Jesus." That was a happy moment to me. As I write about it in October 1896 the joy I feel pays me a thousand times for all the nights I ever slept on frozen ground, snow or mud.[297]

For Chaplain Betts, sleeping on frozen ground, snow, or mud was a small price to pay for the salvation of the many souls he led into the kingdom of Christ. Young Ruffin seemed to have no doubt about his departure nor his destination. He had settled the account and he was ready to meet Jesus face-to-face. All the things that used to be important to Betts faded away in light of the battle, and his purpose came into full view. For Betts, no amount of comfort could take the place of the joy of seeing men converted and prepared to meet Jesus!

> But whatever was to my profit I now consider loss for the sake of Christ.
> —PHILIPPIANS 3:7

Like Betts, we have a duty and mission to perform. It may mean hardship, discomfort, or even persecution. Whatever we must endure we can be sure that Christ has already been there before us.

A Civil War "Joan of Arc" at Chickamauga

In 1863 a young nineteen year old lady from New York felt as though she was destined by providence to lead the Union armies to victory. It was first thought by her parents that her mind had become weak through reading accounts of the war and so they treated her as though she were a sick child. This only heightened her determination to fight in the war. She was soon taken to Ann Arbor, Michigan for a few weeks where she was watched closely by her aunt and confined to the house. One day she mysteriously disappeared. In April 1863 she was finally given up for dead after detectives searched far and wide for her whereabouts.

The girl was not dead, but had secretly disguised herself as a drummer boy and entered the Michigan regiment at Detroit. She finally succeeded in going with her regiment to the Army of the Cumberland. While many of the strong men in the campaign fell in battle, the girl somehow survived. Finally during the battle of Chickamauga on a bloody Sunday battle, the girl fell, pierced in the left side by a Minnie ball; and when borne to the surgeon's tent, her sex was discovered. When she was told by the surgeon that she would not live she asked if she could write a letter to her father:

> Honor your father and mother—that it may go well with you and that you may enjoy long life on the earth.
> —EPHESIANS 6:2, 3

"Forgive your dying daughter. I have but a few moments to live. My native soil drinks my blood. I expected to deliver my country, but the fates would not have it so. I am content to die. Pray, pa, forgive me."[298]

Undoubtedly, the aspiring young lady left her aunt's home without her parent's approval. The desire for adventure and love of country motivated her to leave all. Yet, her absence must have grieved her praying mother and father. Her final request was for forgiveness. If only she had obeyed her parents, she might have lived a long life. With the command to honor our parents comes God's promise: "That you may enjoy long life on the earth."

Reminiscences from the "Stonewall Brigade"

A SOLDIER who rode with General Stonewall Jackson in his "Stonewall Brigade" tells of the religious and moral character of Jackson both on and off the battlefield:

> *Of this muscular Christian his admiring foes competed in phraseologies of generous praise, "forgetting his fatal error to applaud the greatness of his soul." They recounted with genial iteration the separate virtues of the man—his courage, his patience, his sincerity, his devotion, his singleness of purpose, his self-abnegation, his just obedience, and his faith in God; of the Christian, the simplicity of his every word and action, his perfect truthfulness, his mildness and his mercy, his religious enthusiasm, his continual prayerfulness, his almost superstitious observance of the Sabbath, his iron rule of duty, and "first and last and all the time," his faith in God . . .*
>
> *Stonewall Jackson, in his last hours, was careful to explain to some members of his staff who hung upon his parting words, that the honorable title belonged to his men, not to him . . .*[299]

> Be kindly affection-
> ate one to another
> with brotherly love;
> in honor preferring
> one another.
> —ROMANS 12:10

Notice Jackson's response in his dying moments. He gave the credit to his men and not to himself. One of the secrets to Jackson's great leadership was his ability to prefer others above himself.

It is amazing what we can accomplish for the Lord when it does not matter who gets the credit.

"I've Got the Blues!"

FOR A CIVIL WAR SOLDIER in Georgia, the sound of rain on his tent reminded him of how good he had it back home. The little things we take for granted at home become a magnified luxury when separated from it. The more a homesick soldier thought of home, the more melancholy he became. In his diary, one soldier poured out his frustration as follows:

> It has commenced raining this evening like fury. It is not necessary to say anything about having the blues. I heard today we will winter here. If they attempt that, I will leave sure as fate. The weather is most disagreeable here—damp and cold all the time. Couldn't I enjoy the luxuries of home now! How I would like to go to bed at home on such a rainy evening as this, knowing that I could sleep soundly and be perfectly dry until morning. The most disagreeable thing I can now think of is to be rained upon at night, when you are very tired and sleepy. I have heard of swearing as being characteristic of a soldier—and he would very apt to do it then.[300]

> Praise the LORD, O my soul, and forget not all his benefits.
> —PSALM 103:2

Here is a soldier who got the "blues" for the comforts of home. We seldom realize how good we have it until we leave home and experience the discomforts of the world. Whatever the circumstances, we can rejoice that our heavenly Father has given us an open invitation to his heavenly home. The discomforts of this life are only temporary. The glories of heaven will make the discomforts we experienced here seem a small price to pay. Thank the Lord for a dry spot to sleep and a peaceful place to rest at home.

General Jackson:
A Testimony That Pleased God

A BRAHAM FULKERSON, a childhood friend of Stonewall Jackson, wrote his wife to express sorrow at the death of the great leader. From this letter we can see that a Christian may have a more powerful testimony after death than he had in life.

Abram Fulkerson to his wife, Selina
1863 May 18

The intelligence of the death of Gen. Jackson came upon us like a shock. We feel that his death is a national calamity. The poorest soldiers among us appreciated his worth—loved the man, and mourn his loss. I knew him well. He was my preceptor for more than four years and whilst during that time I did not appreciate the man, as school [mates] are not like to do, yet I always had great reverence for the man on account of his piety & uprightness of character. Among the many heroes of this revolution, none have lived so much adored, none have died so much deplored, and none have left a character as spotless as that of Stonewall Jackson. Could his life have been spared till the close of this cruel war, the unanimous voice of a grateful people would have proclaimed him chief ruler of the nation? But God has seen proper to take him from us, and what He does is right and for the best. It is [illegible] therefore that we make the sacrifice cheerfully, th'o we cannot see why our country should be deprived of his services at her hour of greatest need.[301]

> By faith Enoch was taken from this life, so that he did not experience death; he could not be found, because God had taken him away. For before he was taken, he was commended as one who pleased God.
> —HEBREWS 11:5

The greatest epitaph that could ever be placed on a Christian's tombstone is one that reads, HE PLEASED GOD.

Revival in Dalton

REVIEWING THE DISPLAYS of God's power during the Civil War should convict us to pray for revival in America. The following revival among Confederate soldiers at Dalton, Georgia, is an example of what the Holy Spirit can do when people seek after Christ in repentance and contrition.

> As revival began to spread west from the Appalachians, it reached its pinnacle in Dalton, Georgia. Chaplain A. D. McVoy said he had never seen a better field for preaching the gospel, and Evangelist John B. McFerrin reported that in all his life, he had never witnessed more "displays of God's power in the awakening and conversion of sinners." Results at Dalton were "glorious." Thousands were "happily converted" and "prepared for the future that awaited them." Dalton revivals touched officers and enlisted men alike. One chaplain said work there had no parallel. "In the coldest and darkest nights of the winter," he reported, "the crude chapels were crowded, and at the call for penitents, hundreds would come down in sorrow and tears." He said that Dalton "was the spiritual birthplace of thousands."[302]

> This is the one I esteem: he who is humble and contrite in spirit, and trembles at my Word.
> —ISAIAH 66:2

The word "repentance" is used seldom among Christians today. Nonetheless, the Bible makes it plain that we can have no revival without repentance. Until people become contrite and humble over sinning against a holy God, the nation will never experience revival like the hundreds of soldiers did at Dalton, Georgia. As we pray for revival, we should pray with the psalmist who so humbly asked, "Will you not revive us again, that your people may rejoice in you?" (Ps. 85:6).

A Baptism in Blood

T HE TERM "baptism in blood," was used symbolically by those who
fought in the Civil War and wrote of its horrors. The following quote
gives more insight into the origins of the term and its deeper meaning among
the soldiers of both the North and South:

> For the Civil War to achieve its messianic destiny and inculcate an
> ongoing civil religion, it required a blood sacrifice that appeared total.
> While the term "baptism in blood" did not originate in the Civil War,
> it enjoyed a prominence in the war rhetoric of both the Union and the
> Confederacy that had no precedent. Speakers and readers came to
> accept the term literally as the lists of war dead continued to lengthen
> and civilians watched their lives and properties being destroyed by
> invading armies. The Civil War was indeed the crimson baptism of our
> nationalism . . . For the unbeliever, both blood sacrifices seem irra-
> tional. But for the true believer, blood saved. Just as Christians believe
> that, "without the shedding of blood there can be no remission for
> sins," so Americans in the North and the South came to believe that
> their blood letting contained a profound religious meaning for the col-
> lective life as nations.[303]

No other subject has been so neglected in Christian teaching than the blood of Christ. The blood of Christ and the resurrection are the identification marks of the Christian faith. Without Christ's shed blood, there would be no hope for a lost world.

The book of Hebrews speaks loud and clear about the importance of Christ's shed blood.

> In fact, the law requires that nearly everything be cleansed with blood, and without the shedding of blood there is no forgiveness.
>
> —HEBREWS 9:22

Faith, a Much Better Shield

JAMES I. ROBERTSON in his book, *Soldiers, Blue and Gray,* wrote about the important role of religion in both the Northern and Southern armies. The war for many had similarities to a personal crusade for Jesus Christ. By joining the army, the biblical principles learned at home were put into action in war. Robertson comments:

> *Faith in God became the single greatest institution in the maintenance of morale in the armies. To the devout soldier, religion "was the connecting link between camp life and home. As he prayed and sang hymns of praise, his thoughts could not help but wander to his home church wherein he felt a mother, a father, a wife, or a child might be united with him in asking for his speedy return." Furthermore, many soldiers, North and South, agreed with Louisiana sergeant Edwin Fay, who did not believe "a bullet can go through a prayer" because faith was a "much better shield than . . . steel armor."*[304]

> The LORD is with me; he is my helper. I will look in triumph on my enemies.
> —PSALM 118:7

Faith is a powerful defensive weapon. The apostle Paul spoke of its power to deflect the "fiery arrows" of Satan and his demons. For a vast majority of soldiers on both sides of the conflict, faith meant that one could totally place one's life in the hands of God's providential care. No bullet could enter a soldier unless God allowed it. For that reason, faith was always predicated by "Yet, not my will, but yours be done" (Luke 22:42).

God will not conform to our every desire. When we come to him in faith, we are to believe that we shall receive. But we must also ask according to his will. Consequently, we must pray more often, "Lord, help my will to be conformed to your will. Help me not to desire anything that will not please you."

Just in the Nick of Time!

CHAPLAIN C. T. QUINTARD of a Tennessee regiment was told to minister comfort to a condemned deserter:

A grave had been dug. The coffin was placed beside the grave, the prisoner was seated on it, and I took my place by his side . . . The prisoner was then informed that if he wished to make any remarks, he had now an opportunity. He requested me to cut off a lock of his hair and preserve it for his wife. He then stood up and said; "I am about to die. I hope I am going to a better world. I trust that one and all of my companions will take warning by my fate."

He seated himself on his coffin again and I began the Psalm: "Out of the deep I called unto Thee, O Lord," and after that the "comfortable words." We then knelt down together, and I said the confession from the Communion Office. Then I turned to the office for the Visitation of Prisoners, and used the prayer beginning, "O Father of Mercies and God of all Comfort," and on down to the benediction, "Unto God's gracious mercy and protection I commit you." I shook hands with him and said: "Be a man! It will soon be over!"

After the command of "ready", "aim" a major rode forward on his horse and read a full pardon for the condemned man and restored him to duty![305]

God's grace often comes just in the nick of time. Someone called it "nick-a-time grace." The world was lost and on a collision course with eternity, then God appeared incarnate through his Son, Jesus Christ. His grace is sufficient to save the lost and sustain the Christian.

> For it is by grace you have been saved, through faith—and this not from yourselves, it is the gift of God.
> —EPHESIANS 2:8

Taking Time to Pray

POSED FOR BATTLE on the brow of a hill about two miles from Chattanooga road, Tennessee, Chaplain William W. Lyle of the Eleventh Ohio rode up to Colonel P. P. Lane and asked for five minutes to pray with the men before the battle of Chickamauga in September 1863. Lane, recognizing the encouraging effect of Lyle on his men, suggested that Lyle could take time for a brief service with them. A correspondent writes of that touching day:

> ... The chaplain rode up in the front of the line, and the colonel gave the order which, on being executed, formed the regiment, in two divisions, with the chaplain in the center. Without dismounting, he addressed the troops in a clear, loud voice that sounded strangely amid the loud explosions of the artillery and rattle of musketry.
>
> "It is but little I can do for you," said he, "in the hour of battle, but there is one thing I will do—I will pray for you. And there are thousands all over the land praying for you this morning, and God will hear them. You must now pray, too; for God is a hearer of prayer. And if this is the last time I shall ever speak to you, or if these are the last words of Christian comfort you shall ever hear, I want to tell you, dear comrades, that God loves you. I pray God to cover your heads in the battle storm. I pray that he may give you brave hearts and strong hands today. Be brave, be manly!" ...
>
> With uncovered head the General rode up to the regiment and remained until the conclusion of the brief services. At the moment they were concluded he uttered a hearty Amen, which had a thrilling effect. Grasping the chaplain's hand and shaking it warmly, while a tear glistened on his cheek, he was heard to exclaim, "Sir, I am glad I was here to join with you!" And instantly rode off, followed by his staff.[306]

> My prayer is not that you take them out of the world but that you protect them from the evil one.
> —JOHN 17:15

Five minutes later the troops moved forward and engaged the enemy in battle. Prayer gave them the courage to face the enemy.

Prayer covers your head in the battle storms. God hears prayer, for he listens for the cries of his children.

Lee's Philosophy of Life

GENERAL ROBERT E. LEE said,

You can have anything you want—if you want it badly enough. You can be anything you want to be, have anything you desire, accomplish anything you set out to accomplish—if you will hold to that desire with singleness of purpose.[307]

Lee said we can do anything we set out to accomplish if we "will hold on to that desire with singleness of purpose."

The apostle Paul refused to let past failures hinder him from accomplishing God's mission for his life. Referring to a Greek marathon runner, Paul said that a person who is running for the prize cannot afford to look behind him. Looking back can only slow down the runner. He must keep his eyes fixed resolutely on the goal, the finish line. He must stay focused on the task at hand.

Satan uses the tactic of distraction. His plan is to get us to take our eyes off Jesus. But we must continue to press forward. Our race will not be completed until the Lord calls us home. Until that time, we must carry on running with our eye on the prize. Remember, with God, "all things are possible."

> Not that I have already obtained all this, or have already been made perfect, but I press on to take hold of that for which Christ Jesus took hold of me. Brothers, I do not consider myself yet to have taken hold of it. But one thing I do: Forgetting what is behind and straining toward what is ahead, I press on toward the goal to win the prize for which God has called me heavenward in Christ Jesus.
> —PHILIPPIANS 3:12–14

A Slave Auction Storefront in Atlanta, Georgia
The Library of Congress

Religious Pride and Prejudice

MAINLINE denominational churches in the 1800s did not allow slaves to use their buildings for fear of soiling the furniture. But a children's Sunday school song reminds us, "Red and yellow, black and white, all are precious in his sight."

> *After the alarm caused by Nat Turner's insurrection had subsided, the slaveholders came to the conclusion that it would be well to give the slaves enough of religious instruction to keep them from murdering their masters. The Episcopal clergyman offered to hold a separate service on Sundays for their benefit. His colored members were very few and also very respectable—a fact which I presume had some weight with him. The difficulty was to decide on a suitable place for them to worship. The Methodist and Baptist churches admitted them in the afternoon; but their carpets and cushions were not so costly as those at the Episcopal Church. It was at last decided that they should meet at the house of a free colored man, who was a member.*[308]

Christians should reach out to the oppressed of society and offer compassion and mercy. Jesus condemned the self-righteous Pharisees who rejected the outcasts of society, calling them "unclean." We cannot allow ourselves to be consumed by such pride and prejudice, for in doing so we are no better than the slave masters.

> Whenever the LORD raised up a judge for them, he was with the judge and saved them out of the hands of their enemies as long as the judge lived; for the LORD had compassion on them as they groaned under those who oppressed and afflicted them.
> —JUDGES 2:18

Lincoln Settles His Salvation

CHRISTIAN THEOLOGIANS have debated the subject of Abraham Lincoln's salvation experience. Lincoln has always been viewed as a man who depended on the providence of God. He spoke much of God's intervention in the affairs of men, yet there seemed to be no concrete evidence that he had a personal relationship with Jesus Christ. Was Lincoln a born-again Christian? The following puts the argument to rest:

1865

> *A gentleman, having recently visited Washington on business with the President, was, on leaving home, requested by a friend to ask Mr. Lincoln whether he loved Jesus. The business being completed the question was kindly asked. The President buried his face in his handkerchief, turned away and wept. He then turned and said: "When I left home to take this chair of State I requested my countrymen to pray for me; I was not then a Christian. When my son died, the severest trial of my life, I was not then a Christian. But when I went to Gettysburg, and looked upon the graves of our dead heroes, who had fallen in defense of their country, I then and there consecrated myself to Christ. Yes, indeed, I do love Jesus."*[309]

> Therefore, my dear friends, as you have always obeyed . . . continue to work out your salvation with fear and trembling.
> —PHILIPPIANS 2:12

We all will stand before God someday and give account of ourselves. We must search our hearts to make sure we have a personal relationship with Christ. Like Lincoln, we need to settle this matter. Lincoln had always made reference to God and respected providence, but it was not until he personally made a decision to consecrate himself to Christ that peace flooded his heart and mind.

The Nature of the Human Heart

AS A YOUNG Confederate soldier, James Hall witnessed many scenes of death and despair on the battlefield. He joined the war effort, not realizing the harsh realities and terrible conditions of camp, and the inclement weather he would face. Many times he had "the blues." Hall mentioned in his diary that he had joined the army as a healthy young man, but after one year of service, he could tell that his health was beginning to be affected. The following is one of his experiences on the battlefield as he witnessed the death of a friend:

Dec. 15 . . . Affairs are tolerably quiet. Some of our wounded men are dying occasionally. This is the Sabbath. On this day twelve months ago I arrived home from Morgantown. How little did I think my condition would be so changed—I have seen enough of war. O my God, how forcibly it illustrates the folly and depravity of the human heart. Many of our men died. Many were groaning from extreme pain, with the cold, clammy sweat of death upon their brows. I hope never to witness such scenes again. I was particularly distressed with the sad fate of my esteemed friend John Nutter, 1st Sgt. in Co. C. Early in the battle I saw him raise his hands and fall. I hurried to his side, but saw he must soon die. I spoke to him, but he could only raise his eyes and smile a faint recognition. He asked very faintly for water, but I could not tarry longer with him. We hurried over here in the wild excitement of the hour, and left him there to die alone. When I saw him again he was dead. The vital current had ceased to flow, and a hitherto warm and faithful heart was forever cold and still.[310]

> There is no one righteous, not even one; there is no one who understands, no one who seeks God. All have turned away; they have together become worthless; there is no one who does well, not even one.
>
> —ROMANS 3:10–12

Hall said that war "illustrated the folly and depravity of the human heart." When Christ comes into the heart, a change takes place. All things are new.

A New York Soldier and the Resurrection

POET WALT WHITMAN wrote of his experiences visiting Northern soldiers in hospitals:

This afternoon, July 22, I have spent a long time with Oscar F. Wilber, Company G, One Hundred and Fifty-fourth New York, low with chronic diarrhea and a bad wound also. He ask'd me to read to him a chapter in the New Testament. I complied, and ask'd him what I should read. He said: "Make your own choice." I open'd at the close of one of the first books of the Evangelists, and read the chapters describing the latter hours of Christ, and the scenes at the crucifixion. The poor, wasted young man ask'd me to read the following chapter also, how Christ rose again. I read very slowly, for Oscar was feeble. It pleas'd him very much, yet the tears were in his eyes. He ask'd me if I enjoy'd religion. I said: "Perhaps not, my dear, in the way you mean, and yet, may-be, it is the same thing." He said: "It is my chief reliance." He talk'd of death, and said he did not fear it. I said: "Why, Oscar, don't you think you will get well?" He said: "I may, but it is not probable." He spoke calmly of his condition. The wound was very bad; discharg'd much. Then the diarrhea had prostrated him, and I felt that he was even then the same as dying. He behaved very manly and affectionate. The kiss I gave him as I was about leaving he return'd fourfold. He gave me his mother's address, Mrs. Sally D. Wilber, Alleghany Post-office, Cattaraugus County, N. Y. I had several such interviews with him. He died a few days after the one just described.[311]

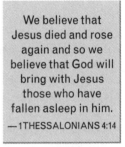

We believe that Jesus died and rose again and so we believe that God will bring with Jesus those who have fallen asleep in him.
—1 THESSALONIANS 4:14

Whitman's experience with Oscar Wilber reveals something about the death of Christ. Without the resurrection, we would have no hope, and the gospel would be incomplete. Wilber was not satisfied until Whitman read the chapter about the resurrection. The resurrection brings hope!

The Trials of Lincoln

$\mathcal{S}$ PEAKING OF THE TRIALS of President Abraham Lincoln, Mrs. P. A. Hanaford said,

Whatever is highest and holiest is tinged with Melancholy. . . . A prophet is sadder than other men; and he who was greater than all prophets was "a man of sorrows, and acquainted with grief." . . . Sorrow is the great birth-agony of immortal powers; sorrow is the great searcher and revealer of hearts, the great test of truth; . . . sorrow reveals forces in ourselves of which we never dreamed; . . . sorrow is divine . . . sorrow to the human soul is one which elevates, strengthens, purifies. It is among the "all things that work together for good" to the child of God. Abraham Lincoln was among those favored ones for whom the "light afflictions" of this world were to "work the far more exceeding and eternal weight of glory." . . . By the very greatness of Lincoln's character, we may measure the discipline of trial and sorrow through which he had pass . . .

A personal friend of Lincoln's, Colonel Deming said in essence that the weight of responsibility was sad and solemn for the president:

> These are they that came up out of great tribulation, and have washed their robes, and made them white in the blood of the Lamb.
> —REVELATION 7:14

Lincoln above and beyond all other men loved peace, and hated war; because sieges, battles, strife, swords, bayonets, rifles, cannon, all the paraphernalia and instruments of brute force, were abhorrent to his enlightened and benevolent nature . . .

During his presidential term, he lost his second son Willie . . . Even that trial was a blessing to his spirit. Heaven seemed nearer, doubtless, because Willie had passed through the gate. And, most assuredly, all the trials which our President was called to endure, though they were "not joyous, but grievous," yet they wrought in him "the peaceable fruits of righteousness," and day by day he was ripening for the immortality into which he was soon to enter.[312]

Lincoln's Short Sermon

LINCOLN HAD a short sermon that he preached occasionally to his children:

> *Don't drink, don't smoke, don't chew, don't swear, don't gamble, don't lie, don't cheat; love your fellow-men as well as God; love truth, love virtue, and be happy!*[313]

Character and virtue in America are in short supply. Simple biblical virtues like honesty, integrity, and justice are fading away in light of humanistic, postmodern philosophy based on situation ethics. So many gray areas of morality have been manufactured by unenlightened thinking that our youth have difficulty discerning between truth and error.

Our nation needs to get back to the basics of the Bible and the Ten Commandments. Lincoln taught his children moral principles of virtue. He wisely warned them against vices that so often enslave society. The basics in our day include paying bills on time, not cheating on income taxes, denying ourselves of alcohol and substance abuse, and a host of other vices.

> This is what the LORD Almighty says: 'Administer true justice; show mercy and compassion to one another."
> —ZECHARIAH 7:9

Our Lord has given parents the responsibility of training children in the virtues and morals taught in the Bible. When parents take seriously their roles as spiritual leaders, we will begin to see a difference in the attitude of our youth. Dr. Lee Roberson, former pastor of the Highland Park Baptist Church, Chattanooga, Tennessee, said, "Everything rises and falls on leadership." We can make a difference in our children's lives, but it will take discipline and work.

Lincoln's Love for the Bible

AUTHOR P. A. HANAFORD wrote the following shortly after President Lincoln's death:

As long as he lived, the President valued the best of Books. One who knew him intimately says, "The Bible was a very familiar study with the President; whole chapters of Isaiah, the New Testament, and the Psalms being fixed in his memory: and he would sometimes correct a misquotation of Scripture, giving generally the chapter and verse where it could be found. He liked the Old Testament best, and dwelt on the simple beauty of the historical books. Once, speaking of his own age and strength, he quoted with admiration that passage, "His eye was not dim, nor his natural force abated." I do not know what he thought then, how, like that Moses of old, he was to stand on Pisgah, and see a peaceful land which we was not to enter.

It has been said that the President was in the habit of rising early, and spending an hour in the reading of the Scriptures, and prayer. It would be well if all in authority would imitate an example so good and salutary: then might we hope that our nation would speedily become "one who's God is the Lord . . ."[314]

It is humbling to realize that a great president like Abraham Lincoln felt the necessity of reading his Bible and having a quiet time each day. How much confusion and pain could be avoided if we would only follow Lincoln's example. The Word of God gives light to the darkened path of life.

> Your word is a lamp to my feet and a light for my path.
> —PSALM 119:105

Tears over a Missed Battle

WHILE THERE were many deserters in the Civil War, others wanted to fight for their country and were disappointed when not given an opportunity. Such is the story of Private Joseph Gann.

I once saw a man shed tears because he had missed being in a battle. The man was Joseph Gann of our company. When we received orders . . . to strike tents and start we knew not where, Joe was down sick and could not go with us. But when the news reached him that a battle was actually going on at Manassas, he got up and set out to join the company. He reached us two or three days after the battle and, standing in a group of the boys who were telling incidents of the day, he listened as eagerly as a child to a fairy tale. As he drank in the stories, his eyes filled with tears that flowed over and coursed down his cheeks. "Excuse me, boys; I can't help it; the one battle that I came out here to be in has been fought and I have missed it;" I was at his side when we went into the next battle . . . and I am sure he was glad when the order to charge was given; and when the Vermonters took to their heels at our first volley, accompanied by the stirring "rebel yell," and we stopped from our pursuit of them and dropped into the ditch at the water's edge, I could hardly keep him from hugging me. He was so overjoyed. He was in a number of other engagements, but after awhile he left us to take a lieutenant's place in a company of the Fifty-fourth Georgia, in the western army, and in the battle in Atlanta. July 22, 1864, he was killed—three years to a day, almost exactly, from the day he shed tears because he had missed the battle of Manassas.[315]

> David said to Saul, "Let no one lose heart on account of this Philistine; your servant will go and fight him."
> —1 SAMUEL 17:32

Joseph Gann had the same eagerness David had when he answered the challenge of Goliath with a slingshot. What made the difference for David was his utter dependency on God.

No Cloud between God and Me

CHRISTIANS NEED to evaluate their lives to see if there is anything that would hinder one's relationship with Christ.

A Floridian by the name of Major P. B. Bird, when mortally wounded in the trenches of Richmond near the end of the war, considered his relationship with the Lord and said, "But for leaving my wife and children, I should not feel sad at the prospect of dying. There is no cloud between God and me now."[316]

The old hymn, "Nothing Between My Soul and the Savior," by Charles A. Tindley sums up the words of the dying soldier, Major P. B. Bird:

> Nothing between my soul and my Savior,
> Naught of this world's delusive dream;
> I have renounced all sinful pleasure;
> Jesus is mine, there's nothing between.[317]

David had sinned against God and confessed his sin and asked for forgiveness. The Lord heard his prayer, but David wanted to make sure there was nothing between him and his God.

Is there anything between you and the Lord that needs to go?

> Create in me a pure heart, O God, and renew a steadfast spirit within me. Do not cast me from your presence or take your Holy Spirit from me. Restore to me the joy of your salvation and grant me a willing spirit, to sustain me.
> —PSALM 51:10–12

Standing at the Post of Duty

A LADY OF CLARKE COUNTY, Virginia, whose husband had been imprisoned two years in a Yankee prison, wrote her husband the following letter:

> *If it were possible, I should like you to be at home; but I do not want you . . . ever to give up the struggle for liberty and our rights . . . I would love to be with you; but do not expect it now, in these times . . . I would rather [my husband] . . . be held as a prisoner for the war, than have him at home dodging his duty, as some do. I am proud to think every man in my little family is in the army. If I have but two, they are at their post of duty.*[318]

One of the most important characteristics of a Christian is steadfastness. Job exemplified the art of being steadfast even in difficult circumstances. God allowed the Devil to take away everything Job owned, including his own children, and yet Job did not turn from his steadfastness. The Lord knew he could trust Job even in the midst of trial and adversity.

If God has chosen you for trials, rejoice because God only chooses his best servants to go through the fires. How you react through your circumstances will make all the difference in your testimony with others. Is the Lord trusting you with adversity? Could it be that he knows your faithful character, and he wants to display it before others?

> Then the LORD said to Satan, "Have you considered my servant Job? There is no one on earth like him; he is blameless and upright, a man who fears God and shuns evil. And he still maintains his integrity, though you incited me against him to ruin him without any reason."
>
> —JOB 2:3

Fulfilling Our Destiny

(General J. E. B. Stuart's Parting Words)

CONFEDERATE GENERAL J. E. B. Stuart lay mortally wounded having been struck down by a Union bullet. In the closing hours before death, pastors, comrades, and President Davis gathered around his bed as he spoke his last words.

> *About noon Thursday, President Davis visited his bedside, and spent some fifteen minutes in the dying chamber of his favorite chieftain. The President, taking his hand, said, "General, how you feel?" He replied, "Easy, but willing to die, if God and my country think I have fulfilled my destiny and done my duty."* [319]

We all have destinies to fulfill in God's service. The apostle Paul knew he had a race to finish.

Are you fulfilling God's purpose for your life? If you are not doing what God means for you to do, you will have a void, an emptiness, and dissatisfaction that will gnaw at you until you get on the course God has laid out for your life.

> I have fought the good fight, I have finished the race, and I have kept the faith.
> —2 TIMOTHY 4:7

Our Main Bulwark

SERGEANT HENRY W. TISDALE of the Thirty-Fifth Massachusetts wrote the following letter expressing concerns about his relationship with the Lord.

Find I need to cultivate my perceptive faculties also hard work to keep awake nights when on guard duty. This being obliged to be on the watch nights when nature craves sleep is one of a soldier's duties which I must learn to bear and discharge faithfully. Notice I am drifting to a neglect and loss of love for prayer. Feel that the duty and privilege of prayer and morning and evening study of God's word are to be my main bulwark against forgetfulness and neglect of the service of God and of eternal things . . . Have had some ammunition given to us and one were ordered to sleep with our equipment on and be ready to turn out at a moment's notice. Some are quite elated at these prospects of actual fighting.

> Keep yourselves in God's love as you wait for the mercy of our Lord Jesus Christ to bring you to eternal life.
>
> —JUDE 21

Sergeant Tisdale said that he noticed he was neglecting his prayer life. He felt that prayer and Bible study was his "main bulwark" against neglecting God's service. A strong Christian relationship is not automatic. As we work on our relationship with our spouse to create a strong marriage, we must also work on our relationship with God.

How do we accomplish drawing closer to God in our modern age? I suggest the following practical guidelines:

1. Set aside a quiet time with the Lord every day for Scripture reading and prayer.
2. Keep gospel CDs and sermon tapes in your vehicle to listen to regularly.
3. Attend church regularly and take notes from your pastor's sermons.
4. Take the whole family to an outreach ministry of your church.
5. Hang out with friends that you feel are spiritually mature.
6. Go to a Christian retreat.
7. Keep good Christian literature near your bed to read regularly.

Letting Trials Make Us Wiser

THE FOLLOWING was found in a diary that had been stored in an attic where Union sympathizer Virginia Miller stayed for a time during the Civil War:

Wednesday night, January 1st, 1862 The first evening of another year! How little I dreamed one year ago, how frightened with startling and fearful events, the New Year would be! How little we can foresee the future and how thankful we should be to an All Wise God that such is the case. New Year '61 has closed, its opening was dark and gloomy to me, but oh! how completely private grief's have been swallowed up, the utter terror and amazement, at the complete destruction of our once glorious Union, and in sympathy for the hundreds—I might almost say thousands—of hearts and homes, made desolate by devastating war. Oh God! When will these things cease, and peace once more reign supreme throughout our unhappy country. Oh, Father grant that this terrible scourge may make us a wiser and better people, and in particular, I would implore Thy blessing upon me, in this New Year, prosper me in all my undertakings and make me Thy humble servant, for Jesus' sake.[320]

Virginia prayed that the Lord, through the terrible scourge of the Civil War, would make our country wiser. We would never gain wisdom, experience, or perseverance if the Lord did not allow us to go through some tough times. James admonishes us to let perseverance finish its work in our lives so we can become mature in Christ.

> Consider it pure joy, my brothers, whenever you face trials of many kinds, because you know that the testing of your faith develops perseverance. Perseverance must finish its work so that you may be mature and complete, not lacking anything. If any of you lacks wisdom, he should ask God, who gives generously to all without finding fault, and it will be given to him.
> —JAMES 1:2–5

On Eagles' Wings

JOSEPH WADDELL writes of a day that Confederate President Jefferson Davis set aside for prayer and fasting:

Wednesday night, Nov. 16, 1861

This day was observed as a day of prayer, by recommendation of President Davis. The service this morning in our church was informal, and a prayer-meeting, remarkably well attended, was held in the afternoon. I feel revived and encouraged . . . We read in the Bible again and again of His interfering in behalf of those who sought His assistance and He is the same God, still mighty in power and full of mercy. We are utterly undeserving of His favor, it is true; but they were sinful men who prevailed with Him of old—"Elias was a man subject to like passions as we are"—And we have a great High Priest who has made our atonement and intercedes for us. God may not answer as exactly as we now desire, but if he blesses us we shall be satisfied. Notwithstanding all we have suffered, and all we apprehend in the future, we have great cause for thankfulness— We thank Him for turning so many of our people to Himself, and giving us so many God-fearing rulers and soldiers. He said to the children of Israel: "I bare you on eagles' wings, and brought you unto myself." . . . Show us wherefore Thou contendest with us!—If for any special sin, reveal it to us, and cause us to repent of it and forsake it! [321]

> Then Moses went up to God, and the LORD called to him from the mountain and said, "This is what you are to say to the house of Jacob and what you are to tell the people of Israel: 'You yourselves have seen what I did to Egypt, and how I carried you on eagles' wings and brought you to myself. Now if you obey me fully and keep my covenant, then out of all nations you will be my treasured possession."
>
> —EXODUS 19:3–5

With the many discouragements that he experienced, Waddell was encouraged that the Lord would lift him up on "eagles' wings." The eagle symbolizes freedom. When we are bound by the chains of depression, we can be encouraged in the Lord and soar to the heights of his blessings.

A Fountain Opened

DURING THE CIVIL WAR Joseph Waddell considered his own personal relationship with Christ and wrote:

*Of how little account am I in the world! How little do I accomplish for the cause of God! Why do I live at such a distance from Him? It is hard to give even the necessary attention to worldly business and not have a worldly spirit. But the Christian life is compared to warfare. "Sure I must fight if I would win." The gifts of Christ and the Holy Spirit include everything necessary for our triumph over the world, and it is my sin that I live so far from God and that my affec-*tions *toward him are so cold. I have sinned this day in thought and feeling grievously. But the glorious truth still remains that there's "a fountain opened for sin and uncleanness." I can only look to the cross. That God may cause me to love and serve Him more is my earnest prayer.*[322]

> On that day a fountain will be opened to the house of David and the inhabitants of Jerusalem, to cleanse them from sin and impurity.
>
> —ZECHARIAH 13:1

William Cowper's hymn best expresses the need of Joseph Waddell as he searched his own heart regarding his relationship with Christ. Written in 1772, this hymn became popular in camp meetings and has inspired millions down through the centuries.

> There is a fountain filled with blood drawn from Emmanuel's veins;
> And sinners, plunged beneath that flood, lose all their guilty stains.
> Lose all their guilty stains, lose all their guilty stains;
> And sinners, plunged beneath that flood, lose all their guilty stains.
> The dying thief rejoiced to see that fountain in his day;
> And there may I, though vile as he, wash all my sins away.
> Washed all my sins away, washed all my sins away;
> And there may I, though vile as he, wash all my sins away.[323]

A House Not Made with Hands

ANNA MELLINGER felt blessed to be able to move into a new house after the war. She was so thankful that she took her blessing and adapted it to a spiritual meditation in her diary:

May 1866

We moved in our new house. O Lord, preserve us that we can move in thy house made without hands. This is my prayer for in this Earthly house or Tabernacle is a great many temptations and trials and Short comings. O Lord preserve us to the end of our pilgrimage that we can lead a quiet and a upright life before thee and all men and to Establish thy truth.[324]

I have fond memories of my childhood home near Boonville, Indiana. The folks who lived on either side of us became more like family than neighbors. We thought those wonderful times would last forever, but like all temporary things, the years sped into decades, and inevitable changes took their natural course. My father was diagnosed with cancer and soon traveled to his heavenly home. Mom sold the house, and the state bought the property to make way for a new highway. Knowing the impending fate of the old home, my son and I returned for one last visit.

> Now we know that if the earthly tent we live in is destroyed, we have a building from God, an eternal house in heaven, not built by human hands.
> —2 CORINTHIANS 5:1

Near the end of our trip down memory lane, we discovered a homemade cross someone had propped on the mantel over the fireplace. I took the cross as a token and bid farewell to our old home. As I stepped out of the garage door one last time, I thanked the Lord for "a house in heaven, not built by human hands, which will never fade away."

Tools in the Hands of the Lord

I N THE FOLLOWING letter to her children, Catherine and Amos Miller, Eliza Stouffer describes the physical state of those at home and the importance of maintaining religious faith.

Chambersburg, Pa.

Nov 26th 1862
Dear Children

. . . Will close but yet say a few words more concerning our eternal welfare which is of far more value than all these passing events, Yet when I look to myself I have very little to say, and feel that I need to be admonished myself, rather than to admonish others, and all the encouragement, I have for myself & others is to be given up rightly, and to be humble and nothing in our own estimation, So that Gods Spirit may work and dictate for us poor short sighted creatures, Oh that we might be given up as tools in the Lords hands, and not choose for ourselves, For we must so often see that our ways are not his ways, and we must acknowledge, when all goes according to the desires of the flesh that the Inner man is weakened and the soul suffers loss, Oh when we look at the reality of our being here and the uncertainty of things belonging to this life should we not be willing to forsake our all, and alone cling to him who is mighty & powerful, to save to the uttermost if we put our trust in him, and why should we not, when there is no other to save from utter destruction.
No more at present, ever remaining your Mother[325]

> And when they had brought their ships to land, they forsook all, and followed him.
> —LUKE 5:11

When Jesus called Peter, James, and John, they gave up everything to follow him. They understood that this meant never turning back to their old way of living.

The Handwriting on the Wall

JOHN QUINCY ADAMS CAMPBELL, of the Fifth Iowa Volunteer Infantry, believed that God's handwriting was on the wall. If the South wanted freedom, she must be willing to grant others the same opportunities for freedom.

Thursday, November 12, 1863

Started at 7 o'clock A.M., marched 3 miles towards Winchester and camped. I have employed myself today to writing letters. We will probably start for Chattanooga tomorrow. General Grant is evidently gathering a large army at Chattanooga, and a big battle will doubtless be fought in Northern Georgia within 30 days. It is useless to speculate as the result. While I believe that it will result in a great victory for our army, I cannot tell what the result will be, if even we should be victorious. Every day my conviction becomes firmer that the hand of God is in this and that in spite of victories and advantages he will deny us peace unless we grant to others the liberties we ask for ourselves—"break every yoke and let the oppressed go free. The difficulties of this war have proved knotty questions to our Belshazzars and our "wise men" but in a generation from this time, every child will so be a Daniel—able to interpret the handwriting of God, telling us that we have not been faithful to the charge he committed to our trust. My earnest prayer to God is that we may have mercy and not judgment. I believe that our Nation will yet emerge from the conflict, entire and triumphant but it will only be after she has been purged with fire . . .[326]

> Through love and faithfulness sin is atoned for: through the fear of the LORD, a man avoids evil.
>
> —PROVERBS 16:6

For Campbell, the outcome of the Civil War hinged on "breaking the yoke" of the oppressor. Although the war did not begin over the issue of slavery, it soon became the rallying cry for Union sentiment. Campbell prayed that the nation would emerge unified and purified by God's righteous fire and the absence of slavery.

A Meeting in Heaven

A BRAHAM ESSICK, a Lutheran minister, shared his thoughts and challenges of preaching in wartime. The follow-up letter he wrote to his sister revealed that he was still grieving over the loss of his wife, Elizabeth.

Saturday evening.
Mrs. Anna M. Reynolds
My Dearest Sister:

I have just returned from Gettysburg, and found your letter on my desk. I read it with a sorrowful heart, as I have read all the letters received from my friends since the death of my dear Elizabeth. I have no words to convey the utter desolation of my heart at this lone hour of night, as I have just put our dear little John into the bed where his mother slept and died and seated myself in our chamber with all its furniture, just as she left it, every article recalling the memory of her sweet presence, and then leaving me to the sad consciousness that her presence will never cheer me again in this world . . .

There are delightful thoughts in the midst of our deep gloom and as I hear the children repeat them so often, I think how true it is that "Out of the mouths of babes and sucklings He has ordained strength." . . . I have every reason to believe that Elizabeth was a Christian. While she made no parade of her religion I may say with truth (as far as one may judge, who knew her secret life best) she lived the life of the righteous. She taught the children (John especially) a great deal of scripture-hymns-prayers, etc., and by her great conversations with them about heaven and their meeting their little brother there—showed that she understood its language— and was laying up treasures there . . . She continually expected to meet in heaven that she was so anxious to have trained for heaven.[327]

> But store up for yourselves treasures in heaven, where moth and rust do not destroy, and where thieves do not break in and steal.
> —MATTHEW 6:20

According to her husband Abraham, Elizabeth took the training of her children seriously. She taught them Scripture hoping that one day they would be converted.

Be a Shooter

LIEUTENANT GENERAL Daniel H. Hill, corps commander of the Army of Tennessee had a good sense of humor. One example of his wit and humor is found in the response of a request made by one of his soldiers who wanted to play in the army band.

> Hill rejected a soldier's request to be transferred to the band, noting: "Respectfully forwarded, disapproved. Shooters are more needed then tooters!"[328]

As the old saying goes, "Actions speak louder than words."

Many Christians talk about their Christian faith, but bear little fruit in the kingdom of God. We can tell the whole world that we're Christians, but if our actions do not reinforce our words, we are nothing more than "sounding brass and tinkling cymbals." We need shooters, not tooters, in the Lord's service.

> My dear brothers, take note of this: Everyone should be quick to listen, slow to speak and slow to become angry, for man's anger does not bring about the righteous life that God desires. Therefore, get rid of all moral filth and the evil that is so prevalent and humbly accept the word planted in you, which can save you. Do not merely listen to the word, and so deceive yourselves. Do what it says.
> —JAMES 1:19–22

The Benefits of War

W ITH ALL the cries for peace, the question may be asked, "Is God for war?" Passivity often challenges this question. An excerpt from a sermon preached by the Rev. T. V. Moore, on November 16, 1861, seeks to provide an answer:

> *That war is an evil, and often, a sore and terrible evil, and a thing at variance with the spirit of the Gospel, is what no Christian can for a moment doubt. But these facts do not place it beyond the employment of God, as a means of working out His purposes on earth. Sickness, suffering, famine and pestilence, are also evils, yet God employs them in this way, and having declared that "the wrath of man shall praise Him," He may also use war to affect His designs among nations. Had there been no sin, there would have been no war, as there would have been no suffering of any other kind . . . Indeed, our Lord expressly declares that wars and rumors of wars shall be among the signs that shall herald the end, so that our fond dreams of a universal peace, when in millennial blessedness, men shall "beat their swords into ploughshares, and their spears into pruning-hooks," may be realized only in those final scenes that lie beyond the great day, and not on this side of it, "in the new heavens and new earth, wherein dwelleth righteousness." But war is not an unmitigated evil, terrible as its ravages . . . yet accomplishing ends in the physical world that can be accomplished by no other agencies . . .*[329]

My grandmother talked about another trying time in our nation's history, World War II. This war affected our small town of Boonville, Indiana. When President Roosevelt called the nation to prayer, people would stop what they were doing and literally fall on their knees on the courthouse square to pray for our troops. War tends to bring a Christian nation to its knees. No one likes war, but war does have a way of drawing us closer to God.

> Devote yourselves to prayer, being watchful and thankful.
> —COLOSSIANS 4:2

The Way to Feel Safe

AUTHOR JAMES I. ROBERTSON in his book, *Soldiers, Blue and Gray,* told about the devotional habits of some soldiers:

> *An untold number of soldiers performed devotionals by reading the Bible alone . . . or praying in the seclusion of a tent or nearby woods. One Confederate wrote his brother in 1862: "The greatest pleasure I have is when I am reading my Bible and praying to my Creator and Heavenly Father for in his care a lone do I feel safe. I some time take my Bible on the Sabbath and go to some grove where I have no one in my way."* [330]

The importance of finding a quiet time and place for meditation with the Lord cannot be overemphasized in the Christian experience. When I was in my twenties in western Kentucky, I met a country preacher who took his quiet time seriously. One day while visiting him, he said, "Come on, preacher, go with me. I want to show you something." We drove in his truck to a farm on a large tract of land surrounded by hills. He parked the truck, and we walked about a half mile to a clearing on top of a hill by a huge rock. There the preacher showed me the secret of having a quiet time. There on that Kentucky hillside we were ushered into God's presence. I then realized the importance of getting alone with God. The absence of distractions freed our hearts and minds of everyday cares and enabled us to pray without interruption.

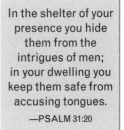

In the shelter of your presence you hide them from the intrigues of men; in your dwelling you keep them safe from accusing tongues.
—PSALM 31:20

Set aside time today to get alone with God. You'll find blessing in his presence.

Love God Supremely

MRS. STONEWALL JACKSON provided extracts of letters that her husband wrote during their engagement. She said he expressed a tenderness of heart, a love for nature, and "a boundless love and gratitude to him who was the giver of all." She said in one letter:

> *I do not believe that an attachment ever is or can be, absolutely too strong for any object of our affections; but our love to God may not be strong enough. We may not love Him so intensely as to have no will but His . . . Is there not a comfort in prayer which is nowhere else to be found?*[331]

May we not become so worldly that we confuse people as to the genuineness of our profession in Christ. Our Lord commanded us not to "love the world or the things of this world." When we love the world church attendance drops, Bibles begin to collect dust, prayer life suffers, and fellowship with God diminishes.

Jackson made the statement that "our love to God may not be strong enough." The love that the apostle John talked about desired only God's will for our lives.

> Do not love the world or anything in the world. If anyone loves the world, the love of the Father is not in him.
> —1 JOHN 2:15

Our Political Duty

T HE FOLLOWING was written by Sergeant Henry W. Tisdale of the Thirty-fifth Regiment of the Massachusetts Volunteers:

July 30, 1862

The past 22 days have been busy and eventful ones to me. Thursday, July 10th, enlisted as a volunteer in the service of the U.S. Soon after the President's call for the 300,000 volunteers felt it my duty to be one of them, feel it as much a Christian as a political duty, and feel that every citizen ought to feel it so. And certainly have never felt more peace of mind as flowing from a sense of duty done, as in this matter of enlistment into the service of our country. In most of the towns of our state volunteering goes on rapidly. In others, however, there seems to be but little true patriotism. All towns are offering liberal bounties, varying from one to three hundred dollars. I fear that some of our volunteers go more from motives founded in dollars and cents than from those drawn from true patriotism. May God bless our land and help us as a people to have that true patriotism which is founded in true Christian and political principles . . . May Thy blessing, My Heavenly father, be with me, and aid me to have thy love and service first and foremost upon the affections of my heart, and be the foundation motives of each thought, word and act, for Christ's sake.[332]

Sergeant Tisdale felt a great responsibility to God and his country. There was no separation of church and state with him. His allegiance to his country was his Christian duty. While other men enlisted in the army for the sake of money, Tisdale enlisted in the name of God and patriotism "founded in true Christian and political principles."

Christians must continue to play an active role in the government of our land. We must elect officials to serve whose convictions are founded on the fundamental principles of the Bible.

> For there is no authority except that which God has established.
> —ROMANS 13:1

Revival Better Than Peace

SOLDIER JOSEPH WADDELL wrote in his diary of the impending news of the movement of Lee's army and the religious state of affairs within the Army of the Rappahannock.

June 6, 1863

No Railroad train from Richmond this evening—Reason not given, but it is presumed that Gen. Lee's army is moving. This is indicated by various other facts. It is believed that Lee is advancing North of the Rappahannock by way of Culpeper. For some time past our cavalry have been assembling at Culpeper C. H. [courthouse] and a grand review was to have taken place yesterday. Yesterday and day before persons in different and remote parts of this county heard cannonading. A rumor to-day that it was the shelling out of a party of deserters who for some time past have occupied "Shiflet's Hollow," in Rockingham. Gen. Trimble is coming to the Valley to take command. News from Vicksburg very unsatisfactory—often unintelligible as given by Telegraph, but there is now a general feeling of security in reference to affairs at that point. I, however, never feel that all is safe till we have heard the end of the matter. Religion seems to be prospering in our army of the Rappahannock—quite a revival. At prayer meeting this evening Mr. Baker read extracts from letters received from Chaplains and from two young men of this place who have lately professed conversion. I have felt this evening that if God would grant to us a universal awakening and revival, it would be better than the peace we desire so much. Five of our town youths belonging to the army have lately united with the church.[333]

> Revive us, and we will call on your name.
> —PSALM 80:18

The Civil War heightened a spiritual awareness as young men contemplated their own mortality. As a result, revival took place as soldiers felt their need to get right with God before they went into battle. Hardships and trials helped to facilitate revival. Our trials end in great blessing when we submit ourselves to God and his will.

A Wonderful Work of Grace

NANCY EMERSON wrote about the wonderful grace of God in her assessment of Confederate soldier losses.

It is estimated that 142,000 Confederate soldiers have been converted as convicts since the war began. If human testimony can establish any thing it establishes this, that there has been a most wonderful work of grace in our army. How could a broader seal have been set upon the righteousness of our cause? The [Lord] has looked upon our affliction & our pain, & forgiven our sins, to a certain extent at least. I have gradually arrived at the firm persuasion that multitudes of our dying soldiers have been met by redeeming [grace]. Mrs. Gilbert one of our neighbors died a few months since, & when dying, she exclaimed [with delight] "O there's Jimmy & Johnny." They had come for their departing mother. They were two of [their] our young soldiers who had died not very long before from wounds received in battle. No one knew the state of their minds, but does not this circumstance support the hope that their pious mother's prayers had been answered for them?[334]

> From the fullness of his grace we have all received one blessing after another.
> —JOHN 1:16

The conversion of this large number of Confederate soldiers was stated as a "wonderful work of grace." Just think of it, all 142,000 who accepted Christ had God's grace working in their hearts.

We often look for miracles to confirm the power of God. Yet, if we've been saved, we do not have to look too far because the greatest miracle of all took place in our hearts and minds upon our conversions.

The Origin of "The Battle Hymn of the Republic"

T HE FOLLOWING was written by Julia Belle Howe, at Willard's Hotel in Washington, D.C., on November 19, 1861:

I distinctly remember that a feeling of discouragement came over me as I drew near the city of Washington . . . I thought of the women of my acquaintance whose sons or husbands were fighting our great battle; the women themselves serving in the hospitals, or busying themselves with the work of the Sanitary Commission . . .

> They will sing before the LORD, for he comes, he comes to judge the earth. He will judge the world in righteousness and the peoples in his truth.
>
> —PSALM 96:13

I went to bed that night as usual, and slept, according to my wont, quite soundly. I awoke in the gray of the morning twilight; and as I lay waiting for the dawn, the long lines of the desired poem began to twine themselves in my mind. Having thought out all the stanzas, I said to myself, "I must get up and write these verses down, lest I fall asleep again and forget them." So, with a sudden effort, I sprang out of bed, and found in the dimness an old stump of a pen which I remembered to have used the day before. I scrawled the verses almost without looking at the paper. . . . At this time, having completed the writing, I returned to bed and fell asleep, saying to myself, "I like this better than most things that I have written."[335]

Mine eyes have seen the glory of the coming of the Lord;
He is trampling out the vintage where the grapes of wrath are stored;
He hath loosed the fateful lightning of His terrible swift sword;
His truth is marching on.
I have seen him in the watch fires of a hundred circling camps;
They have builded him an altar in the evening dews and damps;
I can read his righteous sentence by the dim and flaring lamps;
His day is marching on. . . .
Glory! glory! Hallelujah! Our God is marching on.[336]

Being Loosed from a Clay Prison

H ANNAH ROPES, a nurse in a Union hospital in Washington, D.C., ministered to young soldiers and wrote the following in her diary:

November 20, 1862

The nurse came and asked me to go in and see Powers; he lay sleeping quietly, under cover of which the angels were loosing him from the clay prison, the hospital life so painfully distasteful to him, and making ready for him a home for which he pined in silence, for which he was so eminently fitted. I was glad he was unconscious, for he had a wife and two pretty children; their likeness lay under the pillow where his head rested, with the death damp dripping like tears onto the case so precious to him! Above his head was his Bible, presented by his wife, with her name on the flyleaf. Everything about him betokened respectability of soul and life.[337]

> I said, "Oh, that I had the wings of a dove! I would fly away and be at rest."
> —PSALM 55:6

Last year I was called to the bedside of a long-time friend named Joe. I had built many wonderful memories with Joe and his family as a young teenager in southern Indiana. Not long after I graduated from high school, Joe had a tragic automobile accident and was slowed down mentally. Years later a troubled young man shot Joe and the wound left him almost totally paralyzed. When I traveled to Louisville, Kentucky, to visit my longtime friend, I was disheartened to see him imprisoned in his own body. I had a wonderful time reminiscing with Joe, realizing it may be the last time I would see him on this side of eternity. I confirmed that he knew Jesus, which was a great comfort.

A couple of months later, I got the news that the Lord released Joe's spirit from his "fleshly prison," and he took his flight to his eternal home.

Many things happen to good people that we can't understand, but we know that life is temporary. When our mission is accomplished for Christ, we shall wing our way heavenward where there will be no more suffering, pain, or mysteries.

Abraham Lincoln's First Speech

A BRAHAM LINCOLN was twenty-two years old when he became a candidate for the state legislature in 1832. The following is his speech in its entirety:

> *Gentlemen, Fellow-citizens: I presume you all know who I am. I am humble Abraham Lincoln. I have been solicited by many friends to become a candidate for the legislature. My politics are short and sweet, like an old woman's dance. I am in favor of a National Bank. I am in favor of the internal improvement system, and a high protective tariff. These are my sentiments and political principles. If elected, I shall be thankful; if not, it will be all the same.*[338]

> I am not saying this because I am in need, for I have learned to be content whatever the circumstances.
>
> —PHILIPPIANS 4:11

From humble beginnings, Abraham Lincoln had learned to be content and thankful for the simple things of life. His sincerity, honesty, and kindness won the love and respect of people.

The apostle Paul learned the secret of true contentment: One cannot depend on outward circumstances to bring happiness and joy. They come from the indwelling presence of the Lord.

Are you looking for contentment? It only comes from the presence of the Lord within.

The Balance of My Days

SOLDIER N. HOOVER was thankful that the Lord had preserved him from the fate of so many of his comrades.

I must feel very thankful that the Lord is so very merciful that he has spared my life to this present time. While many of my fellow soldiers and comrades, are every day hurried to a long and unending eternity I had to feel so in particular when those two men were struck with lightening near my tent. I had to feel that easily it might have been my lot, and what would have been the consequence. I would have received a fatal and irrevocable doom, Friend Jacob. I must often reflect of times past, How Satan led me from the narrow path to the broad and sinful [way] one again and how happy and contented I was when I embraced religion, and now how miserable and wretched I often now feel If it ever should be my luck to get home again I will give myself up to the Lord and try and serve him [the remainder] faithfully the balance of my days.

N. Hoover[339]

> There is a time for everything, and a season for every activity under heaven: a time to be born and a time to die . . .
>
> —ECCLESIASTES 3:1, 2

Hoover's description of lightning striking two soldiers in his camp is a reminder to us that there is "a time to live and a time to die." God has told us to "number our days." Therefore, we should seek to be more time conscious when it comes to the work of God in our lives. We waste too much time on things that will not matter.

Ask the Lord to help you balance your days so that you can use them wisely.

Prayer and Persistence

M ARY JEFFREYS BETHELL, feeling troubled, wrote the following in her diary:

> *I was annoyed by vain and unprofitable thoughts for several days. I prayed to God to rid me of them The Battle for our minds he has answered my prayer, I feel peace, I am encouraged to ask God for more grace, and that he may make my husband, children and servants Christians. I offer them all up to God, and beg him to bless them, that I may rejoice with them in Heaven.*[340]

Prayer is the key to fighting and winning the battle for the mind. When Mary Bethell prayed, she found the peace she needed to continue in prayer, and the longer she prayed, the more confident she became that the Lord had answered her requests. She prayed for her family, offered them up to God, and begged him to bless them.

On this date many years ago our first daughter Ashley was born. As I witnessed her delivery, tears flowed down my face at the overwhelming feeling of fatherhood. I rejoiced, felt blessed by God, and was convicted all at the same time. I rejoice today that all three of my children are serving the Lord. Prayer and loving discipline in the home still works, even in a post-modern world.

Lift up the names of each of your children to God, and then expect good things to happen in their lives.

> And pray in the Spirit on all occasions with all kinds of prayers and requests. With this in mind, be alert and always keep on praying for all the saints.
> —EPHESIANS 6:18

In the Hollow of His Hand

SOLDIER and surgeon's assistant S. M. Potter wrote his dear wife, Cynthia, the following letter from a field hospital:

Dear Cynthia

My duties in the hospital are to give out the medicine the Surgeon prescribed. The sick call is at eight o'clock in the morning when all the sick in the companies come up to the hospital with their sore toes, sore shins, sore heads, bad colds, rheumatisms about 30 or 40 every morning come to get medicine & it takes the Dr. about 2 or 3 hours examining their ailments & prescribing the medicine for them which I have to put up for each one. Some are sick in their tent. The doctor visits & prescribes for them so they are coming in all through the day for medicine & some of us have to be on hand to give it out . . .

> My sheep hear my voice, and I know them, and they follow me: And I give unto them eternal life; and they shall never perish, neither shall any man pluck them out of my hand. My Father, which gave them me, is greater than all; and no man is able to pluck them out of my Father's hand.
> —JOHN 10:25–27 (KJV)

Well Cynthia I would very much like to have been there with you. I have felt uneasy for some time but now since it is over & you are doing well that care has been lightened & I pray God that he may continue your health that you may train up those children in the fear of the Lord & I would pray that . . . we may meet again & enjoy each others society . . .

Well Cynthia let us all still put our trust in that Almighty power that has kept us all in the hollow of his hand & we will be happy. No more at present but remain.

Your affectionate husband
S.M. Potter[341]

Being in God's hand is to live in complete security. Jesus said, "no one" or "no power" (according to the Greek language) can take us from Jesus' hand. Abiding in Christ means that we are locked firmly in the grip of God's grace.

God's Word and a Yankee Bullet

A SOLDIER of Cook's Brigade and a correspondent of a Southern newspaper reported the following remarkable incident:

There was a man of Company A. Twenty-seventh North Carolina troops, named George P. Piner, who went into the fight, with a small Testament in his breast pocket. A ball struck the book, and penetrated as far as the fifth chapter of Matthew, twenty-first and twenty-second verses. It merely blackened that passage, glanced off, and left the man uninjured. The verses read; "Ye have heard that it was said by them of old time, Thou shalt not kill, and whosoever shall kill, shall be in danger of the judgment, and whosoever is angry with his brother, without cause shall be in danger of judgment." The man said that Yankee ball was like the devil—it had to turn its course when met by scriptural opposition.[342]

As the New Testament in the pocket deflected a Yankee bullet for the Confederate soldier, so the Scripture has power to deflect the fiery darts of Satan. Jesus showed the power of God's Word on the Mount of Temptation when he responded to satanic opposition with the words, "It is written." If Jesus used God's Word against Satan's attacks, how much more should we wield the "sword" of the Word against the enemy's bullets.

> Again, the devil took him to a very high mountain and showed him all the kingdoms of the world and their splendor. "All this I will give you," he said, "if you will bow down and worship me." Jesus said to him, "Away from me, Satan! For it is written: 'Worship the Lord your God, and serve him only.'" Then the devil left him, and angels came and attended him.
> —MATTHEW 4:8–11

In the Bosom of My Family

Your letters carry my mind back home & what you write of yourself Mary & the children doing, I think I see you & hear you do. I think I can see the children carrying their walnuts down to the house & Bell laughing & talking when they come in with them & then looking for the mail to come in the last of the week & feel sure of a letter from you is a pleasure which keeps the time from being long & lonesome on my hands. Tomorrow is the Sabbath & I would like to keep it with you in the peace & quiet of our home instructing the children in the ways of holiness but this duty comes to you & my prayer is that God will give you grace for the performance of it.

The vows rest on us both & I hope to be spared to return to assist you & uphold you in the performance of all duties & to enjoy myself again in the bosom of my family. I must go on here in the performance of my duty & leave the issue to the Disposer of all events.

No more at present but I remain your loving & affectionate husband S. M. Potter[343]

POTTER HAD an intimate relationship with his family. Even on the fields of battle, he felt responsible for them. Our Lord has given Christian men the responsibility of loving leadership in the home. Notice Potter's concern that his children be instructed in the ways of holiness. He longed to attend worship with his family. A loving husband and father has his heart and mind continually turned toward home.

> If anyone does not provide for his relatives and especially for his immediate family, he has denied the faith and is worse than an unbeliever.
>
> —1 TIMOTHY 5:8

A Cry of Thirst

H ENRY C. CARPENTER served as a corporal in Company H, Forty-fifth Virginia Infantry, during the Civil War. He fought in the battle of Clod's Farm in May 1864. The following is a letter he wrote to his sister, Elizabeth, from his camp in West Virginia.

> . . . the Enemy had over three thousand all Cavalry they made several Charges on us but were repulsed every time. Our loss was 36 killed dead on the field 60 wounded and some prisoners the Enemy's loss is estimated at about 500 but I will give you their loss as far as I know. They left 50 dead on the field and 60 prisoners and 75 wounded. They only left such wounded with us as could not be moved. One of the Charges they made on us was led by a Major. The Major himself succeeded in getting through our lines he ran and squatted down behind a stump then jumped up and drew his sword on one of our men and demanded him to surrender which the fellow did. The Major took him by the Collar and started back to the Yankee lines when some of our men noticed him going back and shot him down and wounded the prisoner. He had taken, I noticed, another Yankee Captain who fell wondering about 30 yards of where I was standing. He lay there nearly all day calling for water and in the evening some of our men went and took him up he said he was Born and raised in Wheeling Va and he was a Southern man at heart and ought to be in the southern Army and if he ever gotten well he would not take up arms against us anymore he gave sergeant Beamer that took Care of him his pistols and a fine gold watch and then expired.[344]

> I was thirsty and you gave me something to drink . . .
> —MATTHEW 25:35

To give your enemy a drink of water is demonstrating the unconditional love that Christ demonstrated on the cross. According to Jesus, when one ministers a cup of water in his name, he will not lose his reward.

A Night on the Battlefield

IT HAD BEEN nighttime for Israel while in the captivity of the Babylonians, but the morning was coming when God would deliver them with a mighty hand. During the night seasons of our lives, we often grow weary and depressed. But let us not give up hope. After every night comes the dawning of a new day.

I have slept in many strange places during my three years of Army life . . . but, alas; the night that left the most lasting impression on my mind was a night on the battlefield. After the battle was over and the darkness had spread over the face of the earth, exhausted, on account of the mental as well as the physical strain, I spread my blanket down upon the ground and with my knapsack for a pillow I lay down to rest, and while my nostrils were being filled with the stench from off the field my ears were greeted with the cries of the wounded and the groans of the dying round about me. To the right of me lay the husband and father mortally wounded, and as he lay there weltering in his own blood I heard him praying for the wife who would soon be a widow and for the children who would soon be fatherless. On the left lay a young man, the pride of his mother, whose head had been pierced by a bullet, and as he pushed the blood stained locks back from his once-fair brow I heard him cry out in great agony; "My mother; God have mercy on me." Then when I heard the sullen roar of the enemy's guns as they were retreating in the distance I thanked God that the harvest of death for that day at least, was over. . . . I was about to close my eyes in sleep when suddenly I saw a glimmer of light in the east; I looked for a moment; it was the pale-faced moon just pushing up her modest face above the horizon. . . . I looked again at the moon through those clouds of smoke; her face was a crimson, which made me think that even pale Luna was made to blush when she looked down upon a field of blood and carnage like that.

> Watchman, what is
> left of the night?
> Watchman, what is
> left of the night?
> —ISAIAH 21:11

M. L. Roof, Co. A., 114th Ohio, Ashville, O.[345]

In the Presence of Death

BERRIEN ZETTLER was a soldier in the Eighth Georgia Regiment of Anderson's Brigade and Longstreet's Corps in the Army of Northern Virginia. He wrote the following in his book of stories about his war experiences regarding the battle of Bull Run in Manassas, Virginia:

> *Colonel Gardner remarked, "I see a battery taking position over yonder; they will need orders in a few minutes." A battery means an artillery company with four cannons . . . He had scarcely uttered the words when I heard a cannon, and a moment after I heard the shrieking ball—a conical shell, I afterward learned it was—and it seemed coming straight for me . . . I felt that I was in the presence of death. My first thought was, "This is unfair; somebody is to blame for getting us all killed. I didn't come out here to fight this way; I wish the earth would crack open and let me drop in." Now that cannon was only about a half mile away, and that ball was only two or three seconds reaching us, but all those thoughts passed through my mind in those brief moments. Then with a shrieking, unearthly sound—woo-oo-oo—p-o-w! It passed and exploded. To say I was frightened is tame. The truth is, there is no word in Webster's Unabridged that describes my feelings. I had never been in the very presence of death before, and if my hair at that moment had turned as white as cotton it would not have surprised me.*[346]

> For you, O LORD, have delivered my soul from death, my eyes from tears, and my feet from stumbling.
>
> —PSALM 116:8

Zettler's near brush with death was a wake-up call to his own mortality. God's servant, David, also lived with the constant threat of death. In those times of uncertainty, David lifted his voice in prayer and the Lord preserved his life and vindicated him.

Do you need deliverance from a problem or affliction? Tell the Lord about it today and find the peace that David experienced.

A Visit from Sherman's Army

IN BERRIEN ZETTLER'S book of Civil War stories for children, his sister was asked to recount the following:

Dear Brother:

You ask me to give you for your book an account of the visit to our home of Sherman's army on its march to Savannah.

. . . it was the 6th of December (1864) that the army reached our place . . . "Four cavalrymen came first. They rode through the front gate right up to the veranda. At the sight of their blue clothes I was terribly wrought up and frightened. They jumped off their horses and demanded money and firearms. They went into the house and through all the rooms, looking into closets, bureau drawers, and trunks . . .

About two hours later the infantry seem to have arrived, and they swarmed through the yard and the house, shooting turkeys, chickens, and pigs. Several of them put a rope around our dog's neck and swung him up. He was soon dead. We wondered why they did not shoot him as they were shooting everything else. . . . There were a few who acted very gentlemanly and seemed ashamed of the way the men generally were acting . . . Several were chasing a pig and shooting at it, and mother ran out and got between them and the pig, and one of the men aimed his gun at her, but the cap popped. She ran back into the house . . .

> Then he said to them, "Watch out! Be on your guard against all kinds of greed; a man's life does not consist in the abundance of his possessions."
> —LUKE 12:15

The soldiers killed, it seems to me, over a hundred cattle in our horse lot. They made a butcher's pen of it . . . father said he had in all about a hundred . . .

Oh, it was dreadful to see everything that our dear old parents had accumulated in a lifetime swept away in a day! But as I look back at it all, I am filled with thankfulness that not a soldier offered any violence to us or even used any insulting language . . .[347]

Jackson's Parting Words

DR. HUNTER McGUIRE was director of surgeons in Stonewall Jackson's army. General Stonewall Jackson was wounded, he was taken to a small farmhouse where McGuire and Mrs. Jackson cared for him.

December-January 1886

About daylight on Sunday morning Mrs. Jackson informed him that his recovery was very doubtful, and that it was better that he should be prepared for the worst. He was silent for a moment, and then said: "It will be infinite gain to be translated to Heaven." . . . at 11 o'clock Mrs. Jackson knelt by his bed and told him that before the sun went down he would be with his Savior . . . [Jackson said] "Doctor, Anna informs me that you have told her that I am to die to-day; is it so?" When he was answered, he turned his eyes toward the ceiling and gazed for a moment or two as it in intense thought, then replied: "Very good, very good, it is all right . . . It is the Lord's Day; my wish is fulfilled. I have always desired to die on Sunday." A few moments before he died he cried out in his delirium, "Order A. P. Hill to prepare for action! Pass the infantry to the front rapidly! Tell Major Hawks," then stopped, leaving the sentence unfinished. Presently a smile of ineffable sweetness spread itself over his pale face, and he cried quietly and with an expression as if of relief, "Let us cross over the river and rest under the shade of the trees . . ."[348]

> So there remains a Sabbath rest for the people of God.
> —HEBREWS 4:1

General Stonewall Jackson was firmly grounded in the sovereign grace of God. He was convinced of God's providence and purpose in all areas of life: as a result, Jackson had unprecedented courage on the battlefield. For him the reward of a life lived in the will of God was to cross over the river and "rest under the shade of the trees."

A day is coming for all of us when we too will fight our final battles, cross over the river, and arrive on heaven's shores to rest under the shade of the tree of life.

A Disappointing Christmas

SOUTHERN LADY Dolly Hunt wrote the following sad story in her diary:

December 24, 1864
A laugh from our boys is heard. Christmas Eve, which has ever been gaily celebrated here, which has witnessed the popping of fire-crackers [the Southern custom of celebrating Christmas with fireworks] and the hanging up of stockings, is an occasion now of sadness and gloom. I have nothing even to put in Sadai's stocking, which hangs so invitingly for Santa Claus. How disappointed she will be in the morning, though I have explained to her why he cannot come. Poor children! Why must the innocent suffer with the guilty?

December 25, 1864
Sadai jumped out of bed very early this morning to feel in her stocking. She could not believe but that there would be something in it. Finding nothing, she crept back into bed, pulled the cover over her face, and I soon heard her sobbing. The little negroes all came in: "Christmas gift, mistress! Christmas gift, mist'ess!" I pulled the cover over my face and was soon mingling my tears with Sadai's.[349]

Christmas can be a joyful and wonderful time of the year, yet for some it can be the worst time of the year. Working as a correctional officer at Indiana State Prison, I was shaken by this reality. I had been chosen to work the day shift on Christmas Eve. The inmates were given a sack of candy and a steak in the mess hall. As I neared the end of my shift, an eerie silence descended upon the prison. There were no parties, no Christmas music, no celebrations, just a sad, eerie, and troublesome silence. I was stirred in my heart, envisioning the men who would bed down behind bars that night with visions of family and home in their dreams.

This Christmas season may we find someone alone and forgotten and show them the true reason for the season.

> He will reply, "I tell you the truth, whatever you did not do for one of the least of these, you did not do for me."
> —MATTHEW 25:45

Sherman's Christmas Gift to Lincoln

THE MOST famous Christmas gift of the Civil War was sent by telegram from General William Sherman to President Abraham Lincoln on December 22, 1864.

> *"I beg to present you as a Christmas gift, the city of Savannah, with 100 and 50 guns and plenty of ammunition, also about 25,000 bales of cotton." The gift, of course, wasn't the guns, the ammunition or the cotton, but the beginning of the end of the Civil War.*[350]

History teaches us that extreme measures often must be taken in ending wars. In most cases, an enemy will not stop until forced to do so. A war coming in the future will be the war to end all wars. Our enemy Satan is frantically carrying out his desperate work on the earth at this moment for "he is filled with fury, because he knows that his time is short" (Rev. 12:12).

One great and glorious day, Jesus himself will cast Satan and his demons into their rightful place, the lake of fire! Until then, let us continue to fight the good fight of faith, realizing that our labor in the Lord is not in vain.

When the thousand years are over, Satan will be released from his prison and will go out to deceive the nations in the four corners of the earth—Gog and Magog—to gather them for battle. In number they are like the sand on the seashore. They marched across the breadth of the earth and surrounded the camp of God's people, the city he loves. But fire came down from heaven and devoured them. And the devil, which deceived them, was thrown into the lake of burning sulfur, where the beast and the false prophet had been thrown. They will be tormented day and night for ever and ever.

—REVELATION 20:7–10

The Power of Godly Influence

MANY ACCOUNTS can be given of the powerful influence that Christian officers often displayed to their men in battle, yet the influence of General Stonewall Jackson seems to rise above all the rest. One of his soldiers wrote about an incident that showed Jackson at his best.

> I saw something to-day which affected me more than anything I ever saw or read on religion. While the battle was raging and the bullets were flying, Jackson rode by, calm as if he were at home, but his head was raised toward heaven, and his lips were moving evidently in prayer . . .[351]

One of Jackson's staff writes concerning Jackson's influence and says,

> General Jackson never enters a battle without invoking God's blessing and protection. The dependence of this strange man upon the Deity seems never to be absent from his mind, and whatever he says or does, it is always prefaced "by God's blessing," "By God's blessing we have defeated the enemy," is his laconic and pious announcement of a victory . . .
>
> After a battle has been fought the same rigid remembrance of divine power is observed. The army is drawn up in line, the General dismounts his horse, and then, in the presence of his rough, bronzed-faced troops, with heads uncovered and bent awe-stricken to the ground, the voice of the good man, which but a few hours before was ringing out in quick and fiery intonations, is now heard subdued and calm, as if overcome by the presence of the Supreme Being, in holy appeal to the "sapphire throne."[352]

> Follow my example, as I follow the example of Christ.
> —1 CORINTHIANS 11:1

May we live the kind of life that will make an eternal impression on those around us. Paul so lived for Christ that he could present himself as a godly example for others. Do you live the kind of life that will give people a desire to follow Christ?

O Little Town of Bethlehem

SOME of the Christmas carols cherished and beloved by the modern world were born out of the Civil War period from 1861–1865. One such carol was written in 1862 by the beloved Pastor Phillip Brooks of Philadelphia.

> "But you Bethlehem Ephrathah, though you are small among the clans of Judah, out of you will come for me one who will be ruler over Israel, whose origins are from of old, from ancient times."
> —MICAH 5:2

I remember standing in the old church in Bethlehem, close to the spot where Jesus was born, when the whole church was ringing hour after hour with splendid hymns of praise to God, how again and again it seemed as if I could hear voices I knew well, telling each other of the Wonderful Night of the Savior's birth.[353]

As you read and sing this song once more at Christmas this year, pay particular attention to the depth of its scriptural meaning.

O little town of Bethlehem, how still we see thee lie!
Above thy deep and dreamless sleep the silent stars go by.
Yet in thy dark streets shineth the everlasting Light;
The hopes and fears of all the years are met in thee tonight.

For Christ is born of Mary, and gathered all above,
while mortals sleep, the angels keep their watch of wondering love.
O morning stars together, proclaim the holy birth,
and praises sing to God the King, and peace to men on earth![354]

No Good-Byes in Heaven

A. P. ADAMSON wrote a diary while a prisoner of war in Rock Island, Illinois (1864–1865). On Christmas of 1864 he wrote:

By the goodness of God, I have been spared to see another Christmas—which reminds me forcibly of the rapid flight of time. It seems but a short time since last Christmas, although the greater part of that time has been spent in trouble and wretchedness.

The return of this day recalls to my mind many vivid recollections of the past and of the manner in which I spent the time one year ago at home with my parents, brothers and sisters, from whom I am now far away from, separated perhaps forever. But I trust that I may be preserved to meet those dear ones again. But if the Almighty wills to the contrary, I hope to meet them in a better world where there will be no more wars, no separations, no imprisonment, but where eternal happiness reigns, the wicked cease to trouble, and the weary are at rest.[355]

> He will wipe every tear from their eyes. There will be no more death or mourning or crying or pain, for the old order of things has passed away.
> —REVELATION 21:4

For many of the Christian soldiers during this war, the prospect of a heavenly rest someday brought comfort and hope. They had faced battle, heat, cold, rain, and near starvation. To experience death was to receive a heavenly reward— what a glorious thought.

While working at Indiana State Prison as a correctional officer, I had an inmate threaten to kill me. I responded calmly, "Hey, man, you can't scare me with heaven awaiting!" The inmate then declared to the whole cell block that I was crazy.

All believers have a great future awaiting them in heaven; for that reason we need not fear death. For Christians, death is just the beginning.

Thoughts of Home at Christmas

ONFEDERATE SURGEON Dr. William McPheeters wrote the following in his diary:

December 24, 1863

Received an invitation through General Drayton to take Christmas dinner tomorrow at Parson Moore's. Dr. Haden, Med. Director of the Department arrived this evening and will spend the night with me. Christmas eve—would God that I was at home with my family tonight. The return of this anniversary brings sad reflections—Death has entered the home circle since last Christmas and my first born is no more; God bless his mother and the remaining children. May they be happy though we are separated and I a wanderer and a refugee living in a tent, but I repine not—our cause is just and I have no regrets for my course though it may cost me the loss of all my earthly possessions.[356]

Paul, like these soldiers, was separated from his Christian family and desired to see them but could not.

The Christmas season in modern times is a demanding time for families. We busy ourselves with so many activities that we scarcely have time to enjoy all the memorable times that we have had in the past.

> God can testify how I long for all of you with the affection of Christ Jesus.
> —PHILIPPIANS 1:8

Try making family time this Christmas a matter of priority. Togetherness is the key to making memories. One Christmas season our family went to see the movie *It's a Wonderful Life* which was playing at a nostalgic old theater in Knoxville, Tennessee. The movie put us in the "Christmas spirit," and our time together built some wonderful memories.

Schedule experiences with your family now, and keep your commitments. You will find added blessings this Christmas season.

An Old Soldier Walked with God

UPON THE DEATH of Dr. Eugene Goodwin, who was in the Soldier's Home in Marshalltown, Iowa, in 1905, his wife Hazel wrote:

Eugene Goodwin, of the 99th New York Infantry Regiment, kept a remarkable diary during his Civil War enlistment. He was a 28 year old schoolteacher when he entered the army and was an interesting and articulate writer . . . He witnessed important historical events, including the inauguration of President Lincoln on March 4, 1861, and the battle of the ironclads, the Monitor and Merrimac on March 9, 1862. . . .

> Noah was a righteous man, blameless among the people of his time, and he walked with God.
> —GENESIS 6:9

Dr. Goodwin was not only a well-educated man, but was patriotic—a good citizen, neighbor and friend—a man of high moral worth: strictly speaking, a true Christian gentleman. This little poem found in his possession tells the story of his devotional life:

> *Dear Saviour, help me every day*
> *To live more nearly as I pray;*
> *I would walk daily by thy side*
> *And trust in Thee whatever betide.*
>
> *Help me to live so near to Thee*
> *Thy likeness may be seen in me.*
> *Make me so kind, gentle, and true,*
> *that I would do as Thou wouldst do.*
>
> *To win some precious souls to Thee*
> *My errand here on earth would be*
> *And every day till Thou shalt come*
> *To do some good, to help some one . . .*

—Hazel Goodwin[357]

Eugene Goodwin had a testimony that caused his family to write about him with affection upon his death because he walked with God. Both Noah and Goodwin made a determined, conscious choice to live for God.

Spending and Being Spent

THE FOLLOWING was written in a diary of a soldier in the Eighty-ninth Ohio Volunteer Infantry during the Civil War in 1862:

> *My 21st birthday. I am a man now. God grant that my future life may be spent more to His honor and glory than my past has been. In fact that it may be spent wholly in His service. That I may devote myself earnestly to the sober realities of life. May He give me wisdom so that I may know how to live right; to enable me to distinguish right from wrong; good from evil. So that when I am called to my long home to enter into life in reality. I may look back on a life well-spent on a good preparation for the eternal life to come.*[358]

The soldier in the diary gave himself completely to God. He longed to look back on his life one day and be satisfied that it was well spent.

A Christian should always want his life to count for more than mere existence. God has given us opportunities to find purpose and meaning, not in temporary things, but in things eternal. The Bible says: "The world and its desires pass away" (1 John 2:17). Investing in God's eternal Kingdom will pay dividends long after we are gone.

> So I will very gladly spend for you everything I have and expend myself as well.
> —2 CORINTHIANS 12:15

Making the Best of a Bad Situation

THE IRISH BRIGADE of the Union army had a special fondness for the Christmas season. They made the best of harsh conditions during the Civil War while apart from family and loved ones as seen in this account:

On December 24, 1861, the Irish Brigade was in camp near Washington, D.C. Brigade historian D. P. Conyngham wrote of this first Christmas Eve of the war, "The soldier's thoughts fled back to his home, his loved wife, to the kisses of his darling child, to the fond Christmas greetings of his parents, brothers, sisters, friends, until his eyes were dimmed with the dews of the heart. However, to drive away these feelings of homesickness, the men gathered together at the head of each company street to tell stories, play instruments, sing Christmas songs and Irish airs, and dance jigs, reels, and doubles around the fire."

Religion was not neglected on this Christmas . . . One man remembered, "The attentive audience crowded the small chapel, and were kneeling outside on the damp ground under the cold night air." Father Dillon read the beautiful Gospel from Saint Luke, giving an account of the journeying of Joseph and Mary, and the birth of the infant Savior in the manger in Bethlehem; after which the hearers quietly retired to their tents.[359]

The Irish Brigade learned to make something good and meaningful out of a bad situation.

We all have times when we must face undesirable circumstances. As Christians we must learn to be unconquerable in our attitudes. We cannot allow the difficulties of life to rob us of the joy we have in Christ at Christmas or any other time of the year.

> Finally, brothers, whatever is true, whatever is noble, whatever is right, whatever is pure, whatever is lovely, whatever is admirable—if anything is excellent or praiseworthy—think about such things.
>
> —PHILIPPIANS 4:8

A Heart Yearns Toward Home

CONFEDERATE SURGEON Dr. William McPheeters wrote in his diary on Christmas 1863 to express his yearning for home. We can only imagine the suffering McPheeters witnessed as an army surgeon. The sounds of wounded soldiers groaning in agony must have had a depressing effect on him. Now it was Christmas and the doctor could not bear the thought of going to a Christmas party without his family, and so he writes the following:

December 25, 1863

There is a party at Gen. Tappan's quarters tonight to which, however, I did not go, preferring to remain at home. A merry Christmas to my dear wife and children—God bless them. How my heart yearns towards them tonight and how I long to be with them, but I know not when that happy day will arrive—not until this cruel war is over. God speed its end and grant us an honorable peace and our independence with all the blessings of home and peace.[360]

There is little doubt that Dr. McPheeters experienced loneliness that Christmas. Part of the cruelty of war is that it separates one from family. Without any modern means of communication, all Dr. McPheeters could do was write letters to his family and keep them in his thoughts and prayers.

In our age of high-tech communication, it's hard to imagine not being able to make contact with our loved ones for days. How did McPheeters and others deal with these frustrating times of loneliness? They learned to commune with God regularly.

> You have made known to me the path of life; you will fill me with joy in your presence, with eternal pleasures at your right hand.
> —PSALM 16:11

Hardened Veterans on Their Knees

H ERMAN NORTON in his book, *Rebel Religion*, gave the following
description:

*Between December 18, 1862 and May 1863 after the victory of the
Confederates at Fredericksburg, the southern chaplains took advantage of inactivity to promote the cause of Jesus Christ. William B.
Owen, chaplain of the 17the Mississippi Regiment began to sponsor
revival in Fredericksburg. A Baptist chaplain who helped Owen said
that on the thirty-first day of their revival meetings, those 75 penitent
men confessed their sins. It was reported there had been 112 public
professions of faith during the first 30 days of the revival and at least
100 others were seeking "the way of life." "It was a touching scene,"
wrote the Baptist chaplain. "to see the stern vet-
erans of many a hard-fought field, who would
not hesitate to enter the deadly breach or charge
the heaviest battery, trembling under the power
of divine truth, and weeping tears of bitter pen-
itence over a misspent life."* [361]

The gospel has the power to bring the toughest men to their knees. No life is hopeless with
God. The jailor was a rough sort by Roman standards, but the Lord specializes in hard cases.
There is no life beyond the reach of the trans-
forming power of God.

Do you know someone today who is a hard
case? The Lord can still break the hardest of hearts.

> The jailer woke up, and when he saw the prison doors open, he drew his sword and was about to kill himself because he thought the prisoners had escaped. But Paul shouted, "Don't harm yourself! We are all here!" The jailer called for lights, rushed in and fell trembling before Paul and Silas. He then brought them out and asked, "Sirs, what must I do to be saved?"
>
> —ACTS 17:27–29

Catching Last Words

JOHN McCANDISH KING JR. became a Union soldier in the Ninety-second Illinois Volunteer Infantry when President Lincoln called for volunteers. His diary entries are earnest, frank, and reveal unique details of war's horrors.

December 19, 1863
Chickamauga Battlefield, Georgia

In the morning when the fighting began it was like the sprinkle of heavy drops that precedes the shower, but as the lines were closed up and they settled together in a deadly conflict the roar of artillery and roll of infantry pouring their deadly rolls of musketry into each other's ranks was like the low muttering of distant thunder. The constant and rapid discharge of artillery from every knoll and hillock with the corresponding bursting of shells in mid air was like one constant peal of thunder that shook the earth beneath our feet. The eastern slope of Lookout Mountain echoed and re-echoed every explosion from every crevice, canyon, and cave. The fighting was dreadful in the extreme and the death rate was enormous. Wounded men came pouring to the rear in great numbers . . . The doctors were fairly jumping with work; sleeves up binding up ghastly wounds, sawing off mangled and shattered limbs, and giving chloroform to ease the dying pain of those mortally wounded. Every patriotic chaplain was at the hospital tents noting down the deaths and catching the dying words of expiring soldiers and getting their dying requests in shape to send them to the loved ones at home . . .[362]

> Jesus called out with a loud voice, "Father, into your hands I commit my spirit."
> —LUKE 24:36

Notice the main job of the chaplain was "catching the dying's last words." When Jesus hung on the cross his last words were "into your hands, I commit my spirit."

If we place ourselves in God's hands, we can save ourselves from many frustrations in life. The Lord wants us to lay this foundation for peace and contentment by depending on him.

Christmas without You

WILLIAM SAMUEL CRAIG was born in Nicholas County, Kentucky on January 8, 1832. His family moved to McLean County, Illinois, when he was around fifteen years old. He eventually joined the Union army. He writes an affectionate letter from his camp in Clerling, Tennessee, to his wife back home in Illinois.

December the 24, 1854
Clerling, Tennessee

My dear I wish I could enjoy Christmas with you all but can't this year but if I and you should live to see next Christmas we will be together I trust. My dear I often think of the happy hours and days that we used to spend together and Oh to God that day may come again. I often think when we was once so happy and free but now I am banished from the presence of a kind and loving companion. It grieves me still I must be contented and live in hopes if I die in despair I want to see all of my friends and relatives. I want to see my sweet little babies but above all I want to see you my dear beloved Levica the best and goodness. I love you better than the things of this world. I would sacrifice every-thing in this war for your comfort and happiness and if it was your request I would sacrifice my life if it would make you happy.[363]

> May your fountain be blessed, and may you rejoice in the wife of your youth.
> —PROVERBS 5:18

One can only imagine the pain of separation that took place between a homesick soldier and his dear wife back home, especially during the Christmas season. Truly there was an affectionate and loving bond between Union soldier Craig and his wife.

The Scripture tells the husband to rejoice in the wife of his youth. Almost twenty-seven years ago from this writing, I met my beloved wife, Jill. Satan has thrown his fiery ammunition at us continually over the years and we have walked through many trials together, yet we have found that all the forces of hell cannot separate two individuals who have firmly grounded their love and lives on Christ.

A Much-Needed Christmas Meal

URING THE WAR food became scarce because farmlands were neglected when husbands and sons marched off to battle. Combined with the pillaging of the enemy, many families were left with hunger throughout the year. Only on rare occasions could they enjoy delicacies once common in the land of plenty. The following was written about Christmas 1864 by Julia Fisher:

> *On Christmas day we fared sumptuously. Mrs. Lynn dined with us and furnished the turkey. We had some chickens and a piece of fresh pork. Gussie had been off ten miles and brought oysters—so we had an oyster stew and chicken salad, minus the greens, potatoes and rice. The turkey was dressed with corn bread. Our dessert was a corn meal pudding wet with water, enriched with bottled huckleberries and pork fat; sauce made of borrowed syrup and flour— it was excellent, how we did relish it! But we talked of the good pies and bread and cakes that linger in remembrance, and the nuts and apples that pass around so freely in that land of plenty. It is hard to be so entirely deprived of them but we try to console our-selves with the fact that we enjoy better health and appetites. We are always hungry—hungry the year round, but do not grow fat.*[364]

> I was young and now I am old, yet I have never seen the righ-teous forsaken or their children beg-ging bread.
> —PSALM 37:25

Lean times give us a profound appreciation for plenteous ones. David proclaimed in his old age that the Lord had never forsaken him. Notice the promise is for the righteous. For that reason, Paul could say to believers, "My God will meet all your needs" (Phil. 4:19).

God does not always provide elaborate delicacies, designer clothing, or beautiful homes, but he will provide the basic needs to those who place their trust in him.

"Ought Not It to Be a Merry Christmas?"

SEVERAL YEARS ago a movie about the Civil War entitled *Glory* played in theaters across America. It told about the first company of African-American soldiers of the Fifty-fourth Massachusetts Infantry led by Commander Robert Shaw. Shaw and a great number of these brave soldiers gave their lives fighting for the Union cause. The following is a brief quote given by Shaw at Christmastime in 1861. Shaw's statement reflects the down-hearted mood of young men spending Christmas away from home for the first time.

> *It is Christmas morning and I hope a happy and merry one for you all, though it looks so stormy for our poor country, one can hardly be in merry humor.*[365]

Every December many in our world desire to find the true spirit of Christmas. Robert Shaw was down in the dumps because a brutal war had taken him from all the outward circumstances that brought him joy at Christmas. He missed his home, his family, and his friends.

One of the most famous newspapers of the Civil War period was *The Harper's Weekly.* A soldier wrote an article after marching on Christmas Day in 1863. He said, "Ought not it to be a Merry Christmas? Even with all the sorrow that hangs, and will forever hang, over so many households while war still rages; even while there are serious questions yet to be settled—ought not it to be, and is it not, a merry Christmas?"[366]

> "For God so loved the world that he gave his one and only Son, that whoever believes in him shall not perish but have eternal life."
> —JOHN 3:16

Christmas North and South

For a nation torn by civil war, Christmas in the 1860s was observed with conflicting emotions. Nineteenth-century Americans embraced Christmas with all the Victorian trappings that had moved the holiday from the private and religious realm to a public celebration. Christmas cards were in vogue, carol singing was common in public venues, and greenery festooned communities north and south. Christmas trees stood in places of honor in many homes, and a mirthful poem about the jolly old elf who delivered toys to well-behaved children captivated Americans on both sides of the Mason-Dixon line.

> And she gave birth to her firstborn, a son. She wrapped him in cloths and placed him in a manger.
> —LUKE 2:7

But Christmas also made the heartache for lost loved ones more acute. As the Civil War dragged on, deprivation replaced bounteous repasts and familiar faces were missing from the family dinner table. Soldiers used to "bringing in the tree" and caroling in church were instead scavenging for firewood and singing drinking songs around the campfire. And so the holiday celebration most associated with family and home was a contradiction. It was a joyful, sad, religious, boisterous, and subdued event.[367]

Each of us may have an opinion of what constitutes a "perfect Christmas," yet, when we look at the first Christmas in Bethlehem, we see that circumstances were far from perfect. In fact, the world was not "believer friendly" at the announcement of the coming Messiah.

We all have certain traditions we hold dear at Christmas, but what if war separated us from enjoying our traditions and celebrations at Christmas? What would be left? Could we still give honor to Jesus regardless of the circumstances?

There were no Christmas trees and no Christmas feasts, just an animal stable, Mary, Joseph, and a child in a manger. As lowly shepherds made their way to Bethlehem, angels were singing, but the rest of the world knew nothing about the birth of Christ. Pondering the circumstances surrounding the first Christmas leads us to a less than romantic conclusion of the ideal Christmas. But Jesus did not come to this world to bring idealism; he came to save sinners.

The Battle of Little Round Top

AFTER THE WAR, General Joshua Chamberlain made his way back to the great battlefield where he fought on top of "Little Round Top" at Gettysburg. There he sat and meditated until the setting of the sun on the events of that heroic day:

> *I went, it is not long ago, to stand again on that crest whose one day's crown of fire has passed into the blazoned coronet of fame . . . I sat there alone, on the storied crest, till the sun went down as it did before over the misty hills, and the darkness crept up the slopes, till from all earthly sight I was buried as with those before. But oh, what radiant companionship rose around, what steadfast ranks of power, what bearing of heroic souls. Oh, the glory that beamed through those nights and days . . . The proud young valor that rose above the mortal, and then at last was mortal after all.*[368]

This December as you prepare for the Christmas season, set aside some time for quiet meditation on life's battle losses and victories of the previous year. As you think on the previous year's experiences, hopefully, you will realize that the Lord was there with you through victory and defeat. The Lord keeps his promises, even as he told Israel that he would remember his promises to them.

I recall my hard-working dad anxiously awaiting my homecoming from college. When we drove into the driveway of the old home place, Dad would greet me with a huge "bear hug," tearfully proclaiming, "Welcome home son!"

As the years pass by and the sunset of life comes near, may we be able to say with Joshua Chamberlain that "our crown of fire may one day turn into a blazoned coronet of fame."

> But for their sake I will remember the covenant with their ancestors whom I brought out of Egypt in the sight of the nations to be their God. I am the LORD.
> —LEVITICUS 26:45

Prepared by Prayer

GENERAL STONEWALL JACKSON had an African-American servant on his staff who had become so accustomed to his ways that he was able to discern whenever the general was about to start on an expedition. Someone asked him how he knew the general was about to depart without telling him.

"Oh, that's easy," answered the man. "The general prays every night and morning. But when he is on the eve of an expedition he prays two or three times during the night. I pack his baggage, for I know he is going out."[369]

Jackson knew the secret to winning battles. He got on his knees beforehand and prayed earnestly. Notice he did not wait until he was in the midst of the fight. Jackson knew he would need a great deal of wisdom and strength for the battle ahead, so he prayed twice as hard before he went into battle. It would be a step forward in our Christian growth if we would learn to pray beforehand.

In Ephesians 6, Paul used the analogy of a Roman soldier's armor to our spiritual armor to fight against Satan's attack. Before a Roman soldier went into battle, he put on each piece of armor with care so he could deflect any of the enemy's arrows. One way in which we can put Satan and his demons on the defensive is with the weapon of prayer. The weapon of attack against Satan in today's verse is prayer. According to Paul, we need to pray and keep on praying. God blesses persistent prayers.

> And pray in the Spirit on all occasions with all kinds of prayers and requests. With this in mind, be alert and always keep on praying for all the saints.
> —EPHESIANS 6:18

The Christmas Story
Saved a Soldier's Life

A LADY NAMED Ann Keegan tells a remarkable story about a young soldier and love:

So she made me six warm shirts, so she did: and over my left breast she fashioned a pocket in each one. Then she gave me a little Bible that just fitted in the pocket. And Bess, she told me to wear one of her shirts every day, and always to wear the Bible in the special pocket . . . One cold December night on the banks of a stream not far from Harpers Ferry, I was supposed to go on picket duty. Just before going I said to myself, "Do you know, it's close to Christmas, and I never have taken out that little Bible Bess gave me to read. I believe I'll just carry it in my shirt pocket tonight . . . I believe there's enough light from the moon for me to read about the angels and the shepherds and the little Baby Jesus." . . . I didn't know it but across that river, in a grove of big sycamores, some crack sharpshooters were posted. . . . I leaned my gun agin a tree . . . [then] Some thing like a sledge hammer hit me in my breast, and down and out I went . . . Next morning, when I woke up, our old regimental Doctor was sittin' on the side of my cot. He was holding the Bible that Bess gave me, and he was chuckling. "Young man." he said to me "You have a sweetheart who loves you very much. . . . Now take this little Bible here, See where the bullet meant for your heart tore through the first cover but stopped by the second?

Your girl had taken one of her corsets apart, got these stays . . . and sewed them inside the cover, front and back. . . . This Bible that I found in your shirt pocket was right over your heart.". . . We been married now nigh 49 years and I believe we care about each other more than we ever did.[370]

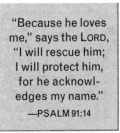

"Because he loves me," says the LORD, "I will rescue him; I will protect him, for he acknowledges my name."
—PSALM 91:14

Bess believed in the power of God's Word. Her gift of the Bible to her boyfriend literally saved his life. Fifteen years ago today we welcomed a sweet baby girl named Cortney into our home. Christian parents need to be praying for the consecration of their daughters to Christ's service.

A Fine Young Soldier with a Good Upbringing

UNION SOLDIER GEORGE DUNBAR wrote his godly aunt and uncle from camp in Maryland and said,

Dear Aunt and Uncle

It is with the Greatest Sense of pleasure that I seat myself in my crowded tent among my mischievous comrades to inform you where and how I am. Our regiment is encamped near Cumberland, Maryland in Alleghany County on the headwaters of the Potomac River the Potomac River is you know the scene of some of the Bloodiest Battles which you have read about I suppose dear aunt you know several of the boys with us but still I must inform you that We have a remarkable civil and Religious company There is scarcely any wicked or profane persons among us. We can go to church every Sunday for our chaplain always preaches two sermons on that day we have also prayer meeting every night in our tents I attend them regular and I think that they tend to keep a young man from falling into bad company. And I think it is a providential circumstance that I enlisted in this company for I hear that there is a desperate sight of wickedness in the very regiments that I came so near enlisting in. I have heard of the death of several of my acquaintances who belonged to the army and it always makes me feel like trying to do the duty of a Christian for I am no better than my young friends who have fell on the field of battle and the solemn thought arises in my mind although I am now well and healthy how soon might I be numbered with them.[371]

> A wise son brings joy to his father, but a foolish son grief to his mother.
> —PROVERBS 10:1

George Dunbar's character is a reflection of his godly aunt and uncle who were diligent in raising him in the instructions of the Lord. It's possible today to raise godly children successfully, but it takes diligence on the part of parents.

If you have obedient children, tell them how blessed and proud you are of them this Christmas. It may be their best Christmas gift.

Christmas Hardships

TALLY SIMPSON of the Third South Carolina Volunteers wrote the following letter on Christmas Day to his sister, Anna, from the trenches at Fredericksburg:

My dear Sister

This is Christmas Day. The sun shines feebly through a thin cloud, the air is mild and pleasant, [and] a gentle breeze is making music through the leaves of the lofty pines . . . All is quiet and still, and that very stillness recalls some sad and painful thoughts. . . .

> When King Herod heard this he was disturbed, and all Jerusalem with him . . . he asked them where the Christ was to be born.
>
> —MATTHEW 2:3, 4

If all the dead (those killed since the war began) could be heaped in one pile and all the wounded be gathered together in one group, the pale faces of the dead and the groans of the wounded would send such a thrill of horror through the hearts of the originators of this war that their very souls would rack with such pain that they would prefer being dead and in torment than to stand before God with such terrible crimes blackening their characters. Add to this the cries and wailings of the mourners— mothers and fathers weeping for their sons, sisters for their brothers, wives for their husbands, and daughters for their fathers—[and] how deep would be the convictions of their consciences. . . .

When will this war end? Will another Christmas roll around and find us all wintering in camp? Oh! That peace may soon be restored to our young but dearly beloved country and that we may all meet again in happiness.[372]

In our modern-day celebration of Christmas, we forget that the birth of Christ was a time of hardship for Joseph and Mary. King Herod was jealous that another king of Israel had been born, and he tried to locate Jesus so he could kill him. Satan continued to try to kill Jesus throughout his ministry. We cannot imagine what life would be like if Jesus had not been born. But he was born, he died, and he rose again. Hallelujah for the birth of the Savior!

A Longing for Peace

THE FOLLOWING is a portion of a poem written during the Civil War. The poem expresses the sentiment of the South toward the young men who camped in the Virginia snows.

> Glory to God in the highest, and on earth peace to men on whom his favor rests.
>
> —LUKE 2:15

Our Christmas Hymn
"Good-will, and peace! Peace and good-will!"
The burden of the Advent song,
What time the love-charmed waves grew still
To hearken to the shining throng;
The wondering shepherds heard the strain
Who watched by night the slumbering fleece,
The deep skies echoed the refrain,
"Peace and good-will, good-will and peace!"

And pledge the gallant friend who keeps
His Christmas-Eve on Malvern's height,
And him, our fair-haired boy, who sleeps
Beneath Virginian snows to-night;
While, by the fire, she, musing, broods
On all that was and might have been,
If Shiloh's dank and oozing woods
Had never drunk that crimson stain . . .

Somewhere, at last, will surely find
His rest, if through dark ways they keep
The child-like faith, the prayerful mind:
And some far Christmas morn shall bring
From human ills a sweet release
To loving hearts, while angels sing
"Peace and good-will, good-will and peace."

—J. Dickson Bruns, M.D., of Charleston S.C.[373]

A Good Christmas in Spite of Difficulties

FOR THE 116th Pennsylvania regiment, the Christmas season brought a somber tone because of the recent loss of its chaplain, Edward McKee. McKee left the camp on Christmas Eve because of poor health. The historian of the regiment wrote,

> *Christmas Day [1862] was celebrated in the camp; many boxes of good things from home were received, and shared by the recipients with comrades less fortunate. Some of the boys were a little homesick, to be sure, but enough were sufficiently light of heart to drive dull care away. A large Christmas tree was erected in the centre of the camp, and peals of laughter and much merriment greeted the unique decorations, tin cups, hardtack, pieces of pork, and other, odd articles being hung on the branches. At night the camp fire roared and blazed, the stars shone above the tall pines, and the canteen passed around, and care banished for the hour.*[374]

> If you continue in your faith, established and firm, not moved from the hope held out in the gospel. This is the gospel that you heard and that has been proclaimed to every creature under heaven, and of which I, Paul, have become a servant.
> —COLOSSIANS 1:23

Some Christians have the ability to make something good out of bad situations. The determination of these soldiers to have a good Christmas in spite of separation from family and home is the kind of spirit that characterizes the true Christian hero. To continue to serve in the face of less than desirable circumstances is a mark of Christian maturity.

So we ask: if all the decorations, gifts, and yuletide celebrations were stripped away from us at Christmas, could we still celebrate the birth of Christ with joy?

Christmas Bells

HENRY WADSWORTH LONGFELLOW (1807–1882) was one of America's best-loved poets. One day while his wife, Fanny, was using hot sealing wax to preserve the curls of her daughter's hair she had trimmed, the wax dripped on her delicate dress. As the sea breeze blew through the window, the hot wax ignited upon her dress. Henry wrapped himself around her, burning his own arms and face, but Fanny died as a result of her burns. The Christmas after Fanny's death, Longfellow wrote, "How inexpressibly sad are all the holidays. Perhaps someday God will give me peace." Longfellow's journal entry for December 25, 1862, reads: "A merry Christmas say the children, but that is no more for me."[375]

Almost a year later, Longfellow received word that his oldest son Charles, a lieutenant in the Army of the Potomac, had been severely wounded with a bullet passing under his shoulder blades, injuring his spine. On Christmas Day of 1864, Longfellow regained his strength and faith in God and was inspired to write the poem, "I Heard the Bells on Christmas Day."

The original poem had seven stanzas and is given in complete form as follows:

I heard the bells on Christmas Day,
Their old familiar carols play,
And wild and sweet, the words repeat
Of peace on earth, good-will to men!
And thought how as the day had come,
The belfries of all Christendom
Had rolled along, the unbroken song
of peace on earth, good-will to men!
And in despair I bowed my head;
"There is no peace on earth," I said
"For hate is strong, and mocks the song
Of peace on earth, good-will to men!"
Then pealed the bells more loud and deep:
"God is not dead; nor doth he sleep!
The wrong shall fail, the right prevail,
With peace on earth, good-will to men!"
Till, ringing, singing on its way,
The world revolved from night to day,

A voice, a chime, a chant sublime
Of peace on earth, good-will to men!
Then from each black accursed mouth
The cannon thundered in the South,
And with the sound, the carols drowned
Of peace on earth, good-will to men!
It was as if an earthquake rent
The hearth-stones of a continent,
And made forlorn the households born
Of peace on earth, good-will to men![376]

Be Thankful for Leftover
Christmas Blessings

THE FOLLOWING is from the Civil War diary of General Josiah Gorgas in 1864:

December 26th a despondent Christmas has just passed, yet people contrived to eat hearty and good Christmas dinners. The soldiers unfortunately have not even meat, and have had none for several days. The Commissary General has . . . failed in his duties; while there is plenty of food in Georgia there is none here. There is no sufficient excuse for this. The food must be brought here, and the means to do so provided and organized . . .[377]

December 26 is a weary time for many. While we wonder what to do with all the leftover food from our Christmas bounty, let us remember a tougher time during the Civil War when folks would give anything for a portion of the bountiful blessings we enjoy.

Surely, we live in the land of plenty. Let's pause to thank God for all the blessings we have enjoyed this Christmas season. May we be reminded of the multitudes in third world countries who have so little. And let us pray for Christian missionaries all over the world who minister to those who cannot enjoy the blessings we take for granted.

> "Yet he has not left himself without testimony: He has shown kindness by giving you rain from heaven and crops in their seasons; he provides you with plenty of food and fills your hearts with joy."
> —ACTS 14:17

Never Too Old to Fight

JOHN BURNS came to Gettysburg, driven by a passion and love for the Union. He had not been drafted neither had he formerly volunteered as a regular soldier. Yet, like Caleb, something in his heart drove him to dare great things for a worthy cause.

> John L. Burns, the "Old Man of Gettysburg," was a cobbler by trade when the battle of Gettysburg began. He took his old musket and walked towards the scene of the action. Once there, he fought valiantly alongside Union veteran troops and was wounded three times. After the war, President Lincoln came to visit Burns and the veteran became a national folk hero. A statue today is erected of Burns at Gettysburg.[378]

The Israelites were at the border of the Promised Land looking into "the land of milk and honey." Caleb was well up in age; nevertheless, he was ready to step out in faith for God and claim the land of promise. Age did not affect Caleb's vision or determination. He believed that God would give him the strength and ability to meet any situation.

The cause of Christ is even greater. The Spirit of Christ lives within us, giving us the ability to accomplish great things for the kingdom of God. He gives us an "I can" attitude. Paul said, "I can do everything through him who gives me strength" (Phil. 4:13). Like Caleb and Burns, may we have the determination to serve in the cause that is bigger than ourselves.

> Then Caleb silenced the people before Moses and said, "We should go up and take possession of the land, for we can certainly do it."
> —NUMBERS 13:30

Lincoln's Source
of Enlightenment

GENERAL ULYSSES S. GRANT was recorded as saying this on the subject of Abraham Lincoln:

> *Continuing to speak of Mr. Lincoln, he [Grant] said that he never knew a man in a high position who had the faculty to manage other men so easily and without giving offense in such a high degree as he. While he was gentle and humane, he was nevertheless decisive in his opinions. He was very careful of the feelings of others and approachable to all classes of persons. He was morally and intellectually great without assuming to be great, and had the gift of easily comprehending any situation with which he had to deal. He was always governed by the best of motives, and was thoroughly unselfish. The country was fortunate in having him as President during the most trying period in its history. No man could have done better, if as well. He will be more thought of as time passes. He will go down into history as one of the greatest men America has ever produced.*[379]

The king recognized that Daniel had something unique about him. His intelligence, wisdom, and insight led the king to believe there was some higher power at work in Daniel's life.

The same could be said of Abraham Lincoln. His letters and thoughts make one believe that he had more than just a nominal faith in God. Something about him exuded divine light that could only come from a heart transformed by the Holy Spirit.

When we have the light of the Lord dwelling within, others will know that we have been with Jesus.

> I have even heard of thee, that the spirit of the gods is in thee, and that light and understanding and excellent wisdom is found in thee.
> —DANIEL 5:14

Grant's Views of
Divine Providence

AT THE TIME of Lincoln's assassination, Grant felt led to go with his family to Philadelphia at the close of the war; or else, he believed he would meet the same fate as Secretary of State William Seward, who was severely wounded. Grant said of this redirection in his life:

> I am . . . a profound believer in a special and general providence that shapes the destiny of individuals and nations.[380]

Grant had always recognized the moral evil of slavery:

> Slavery was doomed and must go . . . Grant came to look upon war as a divine punishment for the sin of slavery; and God used human beings to carry out his purposes. "Thus," he said, "we see a special providence that shapes the calling and destiny of individuals, and we see a general providence that governs nations, yet all in such a way as not to destroy man's free agency." Grant was communicative to me on religious and Church matters whenever I broached these subjects. Few Christians were more conscientious and just than he was.[381]

Grant had a profound sense of God's presence in the affairs of men. Like Lincoln, Grant also believed that the Civil War was a form of chastisement on the United States for tolerating slavery. We must remember that God disciplines those whom he loves. Out of the bloody Civil War came a nation that would be stronger and more united than it had ever been in its history.

Through discipline, God makes us stronger and more resilient so we are not easily swayed by satanic opposition.

> Our fathers disciplined us for a little while as they thought best; but God disciplines us for our good, that we may share in his holiness.
> —HEBREWS 12:10

The Angel of Marye's Heights

ON DECEMBER 13, 1862, after the battle of Fredericksburg, Sergeant Richard Kirkland earned the name "The Angel of Marye's Heights." The following is a recounting of that story:

At the end of the day, when all fourteen brigades had been repulsed, and the dead and dying lay on the frozen fields in front of the stonewall, Sergeant Richard Kirkland of the 2nd South Carolina approached his commander General Kershaw. Sergeant Kirkland asked General Kershaw if he could hear the cries of the wounded on the other side of the stone wall and then he added, "I can't stand this! All day and all night I have heard those poor people crying for water, and I can stand it no longer. I . . . ask permission . . . to give them water."

General Kershaw looked at the young sergeant with his neatly mended uniform and his trimmed moustache. "You're likely enough to get a bullet through the head when you step over that wall."

The sergeant looked down at his muddied boots. "I know that," he said, as he looked the general in the eye, he added, "but if you'll permit me, sir, I am willing to try."

When Sergeant Kirkland stepped over the wall, Union sharpshooters lowered their barrels in his direction. Funny he wasn't carrying a weapon and if he was a scavenger why was he carrying all those canteens. Then Sergeant Kirkland knelt at the first wounded Union soldier and gave him water, then another, and another. Both sides watched in disbelief as what became known as the Angel of Marye's Heights ministered aid and water to the hundreds of wounded union soldiers lying in those fields.[382]

> In all their distress he too was distressed, and the angel of his presence saved them. In his love and mercy he redeemed them; he lifted them up and carried them all the days of old.
> —ISAIAH 63:8, 9

Our Lord hears the distressful cries of his children. He not only saved but also he continues to help us in time of need. He lifts us up and carries us when we get weary.

General Lee's Final Order

ONE DAY after General Lee met with General Grant at Appomattox Courthouse and signed a document of surrender, Lee issued the following statement to his armies: "After four years of arduous service marked by unsurpassed courage and fortitude, the Army of Northern Virginia has been compelled to yield to overwhelming numbers and resources." He continued:

I need not tell the brave survivors of some many hard fought battles who have remained steadfast to the last that I have consented to this result from no distrust of them.

But feeling that valor and devotion could accomplish nothing that could compensate for the loss that must have attended the continuance of the contest, I determined to avoid the useless sacrifice of those whose past services have endeared them to their countrymen.

By the terms of the agreement, officers and men can return to their homes and remain until exchanged. You will take with you the satisfaction that proceeds from a consciousness of duty faithfully performed; and I earnestly pray that a Merciful God will extend to you His blessings and protection.

With an unceasing admiration of your constancy and devotion to your Country, and a grateful remembrance of your kind and generous consideration for myself, I bid you all an affectionate farewell.[383]

> "But if serving the LORD seems undesirable to you, then choose for yourselves this day whom you will serve, whether the gods your forefathers served beyond the River, or the gods of the Amorites, in whose land you are living. But as for me and my household, we will serve the LORD."
>
> —JOSHUA 24:15

Joshua stood before the Israelites ready to give his last orders before he died. What were his orders? He urged them to continue to serve the Lord, but they had to make a conscious choice. Then once they made up their minds, they must do their best to serve God with all their hearts.

With the beginning of a New Year, make a renewed resolve to serve God with new zeal.

NOTES

1. Robert E. Lee, Captain, *The Recollections and Letters of General Robert E. Lee, by his Son Captain Robert E. Lee, 1843–1914, The Making of America*, University of Michigan, www.hti.umich.edu., 99.

2. Mary Jeffreys Bethell, University of North Carolina, Chapel Hill, NC, www.Docsouth.unc.edu.,

3. Emma Florence LeConte, University of North Carolina, Chapel Hill, NC, www. Docsouth.unc.edu.

4. Norton, Herman, *Rebel Religion*, The Story of Confederate Chaplains (St. Louis, MO: Bethany Press, 1961), 39.

5. Mary Jeffreys Bethell, University of North Carolina, Chapel Hill, NC, www.Docsouth.unc.edu.

6. Nancy Emerson, Jefferson.village.virginia.edu, University of Virginia Digital Library.

7. Peter Houck, *A Prototype of A Confederate Hospital Center in Lynchburg*, Virginia, Warwick House Pub., 720.

8. Hannah Ropes, *Civil War Nurse: The Diary and Letters of Hannah Ropes*, ed. John R. Brumgardt (Knoxville: University of Tennessee Press, 1980, 1993), 101–102.

9. Bryan Weaver and Lee Fenner, *Sacrifice at Chickamauga* (Palos Verdes, CA: Moyweave Books), 35.

10. William N. Meserve, *Meserve Civil War Record* (Oak Park, MI: Rah Publishers, 1988).

11. http://www.angelfire.com/pa5/civilwarchaplain/, 1.

12. http://www.sermonillustrations.com/a-z/d/death.htm.

13. http://civilwar.bluegrass.net/index.html.

14. Meserve, *Meserve Civil War Record*, 33.

15. George F. Robertson, *A Small Boy's Recollection of the War between the States* (Clover, SC: n.p., 1932), 102–103.

16. www.Jefferdon.village.virginia.edu/vshadow2/.

17. William Chambers, *Blood and Sacrifice: The Civil War Journal of a Confederate Soldier*, ed. Richard A. Baumgartner (Huntington, WV: Blue Acorn Press, 1994, 2006), 97.

18. Isaac Watts, "Am I a Soldier of the Cross?" (Chicago: Hope Publishing, 1942).

19. Walter Sullivan, ed., *The War the Women Lived: Female Voices from the Confederate South* (Nashville: J. S. Sanders, 1996), 30.

20. Ibid., 25.

21. Ibid., 28.

22. Ibid., 75–77.

23. Ibid., 19, 37.

24. Urban Grammar Owen, *Letters to Laura: A Confederate Surgeon's Impressions of Four Years of War* (Nashville: Tunstede Press, 1996), 19, 37.

25. Charles F. Pitts, *Chaplains in Gray: The Confederate Chaplains' Story* (Nashville: Broadman, 1957), 10–13.

26. http://clarke.cmich.edu/civilwar/cwpublished/personalna.htm.

27. Herman Norton, *Rebel Religion*, 26–27.

28. http://docsouth.unc.edu/imls/bethell/bethell.html.

29. George Squire, *The Wilderness of War*, ed. Julia A. Doyle, John D. Smit, and Richard McMurray, Voices of the Civil War Series (Knoxville: University of Tennessee Press, 1998).

30. http://docsouth.unc.edu/imls/agnew/agnew.html.

31. Lee, *Recollections and Letters.* (http://www.hti.umich.edu/cgi/t/text/pageviewer-idx?c=moa&cc=moa&idno=acp4919.0001.001&frm=frameset&view=image&seq=101)

32. Junius Henri Browne, "Four Years in Secessia": Adventures within and beyond the Union Lines, embracing a great variety of facts, incidents, and romance of the war (*National Tribune;* O. D. Case, n.d.).

33. Ibid.

34. Ibid.

35. Ibid.

36. Ibid.

37. Ibid.

38. Herman Norton, *Rebel Religion.* From Docsouth, "The Diary of Elizabeth Stouffer" (http://etext.lib.virginia.edu/etcbin/civwarlett-browse?id=F6501), 1.

39. Elias Moore, *114ᵗʰ Volunteer Regiment*, www.fortunecity.com/westwood/makeover/347/index.htm.

40. http://valley.vedh.virginia.edu/personalpapersranklin/p2stoufferletters.html.

41. http://www.fortunecity.com/westwood/makeover/347/index.htm.

42. H. C. Clarke, *Diary of the War for Separation, Vicksburg, Mississippi,* University of North Carolina, Chapel Hill, http://docsouth.unc.edu/imls/clarke/clarke.html, 108.

43. Katherine D. Moore, "The Diary of Katherine D. Moore," Unpublished, McClung Historical Library, Knoxville, TN, 1984.

44. Ibid.

45. William W. Bennett, *The Great Revival in the Southern Armies* (Harrisburg, VA: Sprinkle Publications, 1989; Hess Publications, 1998), 125.

46. http://docsouth.unc.edu/imls/bethell/bethell.html.

47. Mary Anna Jackson, *The Life and Letters of General Thomas J. Jackson (Stonewall Jackson)* (Harrisonburg, VA: Sprinkle Publications, 1998).

48. Ibid.

49. http://www.rootsweb.com~imsjasper/grays.htm.

50. Houck, *Confederate Hospital*, 87–88.

51. H. W. Crocker III, *Robert E. Lee on Leadership: Executive Lessons in Character, Courage, and Vision* (Roseville, CA: Prima Publishers, 1999; Three Rivers Press, 2000), 174.

52. Ibid., 16.

53. http://www.americancivilwar.com/women/cb.html.

54. William H. Bradbury, *While Father Is Away: The Civil War Letters of William H. Bradbury*, ed. Kassandra R. Chaney and Jennifer Bohrnstedt (Lexington, KY: University Press of Kentucky, 1863–64), 128.

55. http://members.aol.com/Gainf9reg/index20.html.

56. Michael John Cramer, *Ulysses S. Grant: Conversations and Unpublished Letters* (New York: Eaton and Maines Publishers, 1897; University of Michigan Library, 2001), 85–86.

57. Jackson, *Life and Letters of General Jackson*, 192–93.

58. http://lstholistic.com/Spl_prayers/prayers_civilwar.htm.

59. William C. Harris, *Prison Life in the Tobacco Warehouse in Richmond by a Ball's Bluff Prisoner* (n.p., BookCrafters, 1994), 111.

60. http://docsouth.unc.edu/imls/bethell/bethell.html.

61. http://valley.vcdh.virginia.edu/cwpotterlist.html.

62. Squire, *Wilderness of War*, 3.

63. Bennett, *Great Revival*, 57.

64. B. A. Botkin, ed., *A Civil War Treasury of Tales, Legends, and Folklore* (New York: Promontory Press, 1960; Lincoln: University of Nebraska Press, 2000), 77–80.

65. Garland A. Haas, *To the Mountain of Fire and Beyond: The Fifty-third Indiana Regiment from Corinth to Glory* (Carmel, IN: Guild Press, 1997, 1999), 26.

66. http://docsouth.unc.edu/imls/bethell/bethell.html.

67. Albert Goodloe, *Confederate Echoes: A Soldier's Personal Story of Life in the Confederate Army from the Mississippi to the Carolinas* (Washington, DC: Zenger Publishing, 1983), http://www.civilwarancestor.comgoodloe.htm, 244–45.

68. Crocker, *Robert E. Lee on Leadership*, 173–74.

69. http://docsouth.unc.edu/imls/agnew/agnew.html.

70. Goodloe, *Confederate Echoes*, 363.

71. http://docsouth.unc.edu/leon/leon.html, 35–37.

72. http://docsouth.unc.edu/browne/browne.html.

73. Moore, *Anecdotes, Poetry, and Incidents,* 95–96.

74. Mary Bethell, University of North Carolina digital library, docsouth.unc.edu.

75. Ibid., 130.

76. Ibid.

77. Frank Moore, ed. 1828–1904, *Anecdotes, poetry, and incidents of the war: North and South*, www.hti.umich.edu, by permission from the University of Michigan, 132.

78. Goodloe, *Confederate Echoes*, 363.

79. http://docsouth.unc.edu/neh/anderson/anderson.html, 222.

80. Herman Norton, *Rebel Religion, The Story of Confederate Chaplains* (St. Louis, MO: Bethany Press, 1961), 61.

81. Abell and Gecik, Sojourns of a Patriot, The Fields and Prison Papers of an Unreconstructed Confederate, Southern Heritage Press, Murfreesboro, TN, 1998, 236.

82. http://www.Irishvolunteers.tripod.com.

83. Ibid.

84. Edward Boots, http://home.att.net~edboots/edwardnboots-htm#overview, Previously published in the North Carolina Historical Review, 1959.

85. Robertson, James, *Soldiers, Blue and Gray,* University of South Carolina Press, 1998, 173.

86. Eliza Stouffer, *To Polly,* University of Virginia, http://wwwetext.lib.virginia.edu.

87. Norton, Herman, *Rebel Religion, The Story of Confederate Chaplains* (St. Louis, MO: Bethany Press, 1961), 44.

88. Ibid.

89. Leidner Gordon, 2003/4, by Great American History, http://members.tripod .com/~~greatamericanhistory/gr02000htm.

90. John Dyer, *From Shiloh to San Juan,* (Baton Rouge, LA: Louisiana State University Press, 1961), 3–4.

91. *Son of the South,* http://www.sonofthesouth.net/leefoundation/Notable%20 Lee%20Quotes.htm.

92. Charles Stanley, *In Touch Ministries,* Atlanta, GA.

93. B. M. Zettler, *War Stories, Company "B", Eight GA Regiment,* Neale Pub. Co., New York, www.docsouth.unc.edu, Chapel Hill, NC, 71.

94. Moore, *Anecdotes, Poetry, and Incidents,* 13.

95. Ibid., 101.

96. Ibid., 115–116.

97. http://docsouth.unc.edu/imls/bakergw/bakergw.html.

98. http://docsouth.unc.edu/imls/bethell/bethell.html.

99. http://www.iwaynet.net/~lsci/junkin/.

100. The Library of Congress, Abraham Lincoln to Lydia Bixby, Monday, November 21, 1864 (Printed copy).

101. Bennett, *Great Revival,* 20.

102. Ray Mathis, *In the Land of the Living: Wartime Letters by Confederates from the Chattahoochee Valley of Alabama and Georgia* (Troy, AL: Troy State University Press, 1982), 53.

103. Henry Woodhead, *Chickamauga,* Voices of the Civil War Series (Alexandria, VA: Time Life Books, 1997), 143–44.

104. John B. Gordon, *Reminiscences of the Civil War* (Atlanta: Charles Scribner's Sons, 1904; Baton Rouge: Louisiana State University Press, 1993), 198–199.

105. Ibid., 387.

106. Ibid., 416.

107. Ibid., 432–33.

108. Ibid., 445.

109. http://valley.vcdh.virginia.edu/KHS/creigh.html.

110. http://home.att.net/~rjnorton/Lincoln80.html.

111. Gordon, *Reminiscences of the Civil War,* 198–99.

112. http://www.pbs.org/wgbh/amex/lincolns/slavery/qt_aasouth.html.

113. http://docsouth.unc.edu/imls/giver/menu.html.

114. Moore, *Anecdotes, Poetry, and Incidents,* 62.

115. Jackson, *Life and Letters of General Jackson,* 140–41.

116. http://docsouth.unc.edu/aughey/aughey.html, 50–54.

117. Dr. Phineas Gurley, *The Making of America,* University of Michigan, www .hti.umich.edu.

118. http://www.franklin-stfb.org/letter05.htm.

119. Jackson, *Life and Letters of General Jackson,* 145–46.

120. James Robertson, *Soldiers, Blue and Gray,* 176.

121. E. P. Powell, *Sermon of E.P. Powell, Plymouth Church, The Making of America,* University of Michigan, Ann Arbor, MI. http://www.hti.umich.edu.

122. http://docsouth.unc.edu/imls/bethell/bethell.html.

123. Jackson, *Life and Letters of General Jackson,* 101.

124. Cramer, *Ulysses Grant,* 43.

125. www.worldpolicy.org/globalrights/religion/Lincoln-religion.html.

126. Ibid.

127. http://www.docsouth.unc.edu/ashby/menu.html, 224.

128. Mathis, *In the Land of the Living,* 55.

129. Ibid.

130. http://docsouth.unc.edu/grimball/menu.html, 92.

131. http://members.tripod.com/~greatamericanhistory/gr02000.htm, 2003/4.

132. Ibid.

133. Ropes, *Civil War Nurse,* n.d.

134. http://docsouth.unc.edu/imls/bethell/bethell.html.

135. H. W. Crocker, *Lee on Leadership,* 16–19.

136. Ibid., 19.

137. Phil Mellar, *Lee's Opinion,* www.sermoncentral.com/illustration.

138. James B. Macabe, *The Life and Campaigns of General Robert E. Lee,* University of Michigan, www.hti.umich.edu, 325–27.

139. http://spec.lib.vt.edu/voltz/voltz7.htm.

140. http://www.hal-pc.org/~jsb/page11.html.

141. http://docsouth.unc.edu/imls/bethell/bethell.html.

142. www.extlab1entnem.ufl.edu/olustee/letters/Ostephens.html.

143. Ibid.

144. http://www.nps.gov/vick/eduguide/chp_3/ballou.htm.

145. http://docsouth.unc.edu/imls/bethell/bethell.html.

146. Ibid.

147. Moore, *Anecdotes, Poetry, and Incidents,* 15.

148. Jackson, *Life and Letters of General Jackson,* n.d.

149. Ibid.

150. http://www.bible.org/illus.asp?topic_id=855, original source unknown.

151. http://docsouth.unc.edu/browne/browne.html, 21–22.

152. Virginia Military Institute.

153. http://my.oh.voyager.net/C8/D7/lstevens/burt/burt1ta.html.

154. Moore, *Anecdotes, Poetry, and Incidents*, 141.

155. Harry Stout, *Upon the Altar of the Nation* (New York: Penguin Group Inc, 2006), 84.

156. Harry S. Stout, *Upon the Altar of the Nation: A Moral History of the Civil War* (New York: Penguin Group, Viking Adult, 2006), 84.

157. http://www.civilwarhome.com/letter2.htm.

158. Alansa Sterett Rounds, *Diary 1860–1913*, Virginia Center for Digital History, Charlottesville, VA.

159. Robert E. Lee, http://www.sonofthesouth.net.

160. Frank Moore, ed., *Women of the War: Their Heroism and Self-Sacrifice* (n.p.: Kessinger Publishing, 2004), http://www.biblio.com/ltd/book/12532617.html.

161. Albert Bushnell Hart, *The Romance of the Civil War*, Source Readers in American History, No. 4 (New York: Macmillan, 1921), http://etext.virginia.edu.

162. http://spec.lib.vt.edu/mss/white/white.htm.

163. http://docsouth.unc.edu/imls/bethell/bethell.html.

164. Herman Norton, *Rebel Religion*.

165. McCabe Jr., Life and Campaigns of General Robert E. Lee. Crocker, H. W., *Robert E. Lee On Leadership*, Prima Pub., 3000 Lava Ridge Court, Roseville, California.

166. Moore, *Anecdotes, Poetry, and Incidents*, 266.

167. Heyser Diary, June 11, http://valley.vcdh.virginia.edu/personal/wmheyser.html. Between pages 55–88.

168. William Heyser, www.docsouth.unc.edu.

169. http://wehaveneatstuff.com/streetpapers.htm.

170. Wendell Barrett, 1855–1921, *A Literary History of America*, University Press, John Wilson & Son, Cambridge, USA, 489–90.

171. Albert Bushnell, 1854–1943, *The Romance of the Civil War*, University of Virginia, http://etext.virginia.edu, 232.

172. Henry Bleby, *Josiah: The Maimed Fugitive. A True Tale. 1809–1882*, University of North Carolina, Chapel Hill, www.docsouth.edu., 32–34.

173. Garland Haas, *"To the Mountain of Fire and Beyond, The Fifty-third Indiana Regiment, From Corinth to Glory,"* (Carmel, IN: Guild Press of Indiana, 1997), 11.

174. Phillip Hugh Wallace, www.docsouth.unc.edu.

175. Rachel Cormany, University of Virginia, http://etext.lib.virginia.edu.

176. Jackson, *Life and Letters of General Jackson*, 167.

177. http://www.docsouth.unc.edu/imls/burrows/burrows.html.

178. Rachel Cormany, University of Virginia, http://etext.lib.virginia.edu.

179. Ridley Wills, *Old Enough to Die* (Franklin, TN: Hillsboro Press, 1996), 3, 19, 59–60.

180. http://docsouth.unc.edu/imls/bethell/bethell.html.

181. Jackson, *Life and Letters of General Jackson*, 67.

182. http://docsouth.unc.edu/imls/baptist/baptist.html.

183. Ibid.

184. http://docsouth.unc.edu/imls/dabney/menu.html.

185. http://clarke.cmich.edu/civilwar/cwpublished/poetry.htm, 29.

186. http://jefferson.village.virginia.edu/vshadow2/.

187. http://docsouth.unc.edu/imls/lenoir/menu.html.

188. George Eggleston, *A Rebel's Recollections*, (Chapel Hill, NC: Riverside Press, 1865), www.docsouth.edu, 150.

189. http://docsouth.unc.edu/imls/kimberly/kimberly.html.

190. http://etext.lib.virginia.edu/toc/civilwar/publicFD1011.html.

191. http://spec.lib.vt.edu/civwar/Harris/AnnieStory1893.html#familysilver.

192. William J. Switala, *Underground Railroad in Pennsylvania* (Mechanicsburg, PA: Stockpole Books, 2001), 1–2.

193. Burton Harrison, *Recollections Grave and Gray* (New York: Charles Scribner's Sons, 1911), http://docsouth.unc.edu/harrison/summary.html, 62–63.

194. http://members.tripod.com/~greatamericanhistory/gr02000.htm.

195. http://docsouth.unc.edu/leewilliam/lee.html.

196. http://clarke.cmich.edu/civilwar/cwpublished/poetry.htm.

197. Ibid., 51.

198. Ibid.

199. Ibid., 154.

200. http://members.tripod.com/~greatamericanhistory/gr02000.htm.

201. Linus Pierpont Brockett, www.hti.unc.edu, 295.

202. http://docsouth.unc.edu/fpn/texts.html.

203. Ibid.

204. Haas, *To the Mountain of Fire and Beyond*.

205. http://valley.vcdh.virginia.edu/HIUS403/letters/dcgdiarymain.html.

206. http://valley.vcdh.virginia.edu/cwpotterlist.html.

207. Mary Anna Jackson, *The Life and Letters of Stonewall Jackson*, (Harrisonburg, VA: Sprinkle Pub., 1995) 178–79.

208. Ibid., 179.

209. http://clarke.cmich.edu/civilwar/cwpublished/poetry.htm, 543.

210. http://users.ids.net/~tandem/joshua.htm.

211. Ibid., 179.

212. http://clarke.cmich.edu/civilwar/cwpublished/poetry.htm, 543.

213. www.civilwarphotos.net/files/csos.htm.

214. Owen, *Letters to Laura*, 82–83.

215. http://docsouth.unc.edu/avary/avary.html, 248–249.

216. http://docsouth.unc.edu/bokum/bokum.html, 5.

217. Ibid., 9.

218. Belle Boyd, *Belle Boyd in Camp and Prison*, vol. 1 (Baton Rouge: Louisiana State University Press, 1998).

219. Sarah Morgan Dawson, *A Confederate Girl's Diary* (Westport, CT: Greenwood Publishing Group, 1972).

220. George E. Pickett, *The Heart of a Soldier: Intimate Wartime Letters from General George E. Pickett, C.S.A. to His Wife* (n.p.: Stan Clark Military Books, 1996).

221. C. T. Quintard, Doctor Quintard, Chaplain C.S.A. and Second Bishop of Tennessee, *The Memoir and Civil War Diary of Charles Todd Quintard* (Baton Rouge: Louisiana State University Press, 2003).

222. http://docsouth.unc.edu/imls/renfroe/renfroe.html.

223. http://docsouth.unc.edu/morgan/menu.html.

224. Cramer, *Ulysses Grant*, 152.

225. http://clarke.cmich.edu/civilwar/cwpublished/poetry.htm, 50.

226. Ibid., 52.

227. James Robertson, *Soldiers, Blue and Gray*, 178.

228. Sarah Emma Edmonds, *Memoirs of a Soldier, Nurse and Spy in the Union Army: A Woman's Adventures in the Union Army* (n.p.: Diggory Press, 2006), 228.

229. Herman Norton, *Rebel Religion*, 34.

230. Jackson, *Life and Letters of General Jackson*, 103.

231. Robertson, James, *Soldiers, Blue and Gray*, 180.

232. Ibid., 180.

233. Jackson, *Life and Letters of General Jackson*, 102.

234. Bruce Catton, *Reflections on the Civil War* (New York: Doubleday, 1981; Promontory Press, 2004), 120–121.

235. Richard Moe, *The Last Full Measure: The Life and Death of the First Minnesota Volunteers* (New York: Avon Books, 1993; Minnesota Historical Society Press, 2001), 98.

236. http://spec.lib.vt.edu/mss/huffhylton.htm.

237. Owen, *Letters to Laura*, 19.

238. http://www.marshall.edu/speccold/blake/P2-B1B.html.

239. http://spec.lib.vt.edu/mss/white/white/htm.

240. Ibid.

241. Owen, *Letters to Laura*, 29.

242. Carl Zebrowski, ed., *Walking to Cold Mountain: A Journey through Civil War America* (New York: Smithmark Publishers, 1999), 10.

243. Wiley Sword, *Mountains Touched with Fire: Chattanooga Besieged, 1863* (New York: St. Martin's Press, 1993; St. Martin's Griffin, 1997), 152.

244. http://docsouth.unc.edu/worsham/worsham.html.

245. Ibid.

246. http://etext.lib.virginia.edu/etcbin/civwarlett-browsemod?id=A0584.

247. Lincoln, http://chaucer.library.emory.edu.

248. Moore, *Anecdotes, Poetry, and Incidents*, 544.

249. http://clarke.cmich.edu/civilwar/cwpublished/poetry.htm, 546.

250. Ibid., 544.

251. Ibid., 541–42.

252. http://docsouth.unc.edu/neh/andersonw/menu.html.

253. http://docsouth.unc.edu/imls/prayers1/menu.html.

254. http://docsouth.unc.edu/ramsey/ramsey.html.

255. http://docsouth.unc.edu/wyeth/wyeth.html.

256. http://clarke.cmich.edu/civilwar/cwpublished/poetry.htm.

257. Dorothy A. Volo and James M. Volo, *Daily Life in Civil War America* (Westport, CN: Greenwood Press, 1949, 1998), 277.

258. Ibid., 296–97.

259. http://clarke.cmich.edu/civilwar/cwpublished/poetry.htm.

260. Phoebe Pember Yates, *A Southern Woman's Story: Life in Confederate Richmond* (Wilmington, NC: Broadfoot Publishing; University of South Carolina Press, 2002).

261. http://docsouth.unc.edu/imls/bethell/bethell.html.

262. http://home.att.net~edboots/edwardnboots-htm#overview.

263. David Jackson Logan, *A Rising Star of Promise: The Civil War Odyssey of David Jackson Logan,* ed. Jason H. Silverman and Samuel N. Thomas (Campbell, CA: Savas Publishing; Da Capo Press, 1998), 5.

264. Thomas J. Goree, *Longstreet's Aide: The Civil War Letters of Major Thomas J. Goree,* ed. Thomas W. Cutrer (University Press of Virginia, 1995), 53.

265. http://docsouth.unc.edu/imls/crumly/crumly.html.

266. Ibid.

267. http://docsouth.unc.edu/imls/bethell/bethell.html.

268. http://valley.vcdh.virginia.edu/cwpotterlist.html.

269. http://docsouth.unc.edu/imls/kimberly/kimberly.html.

270. http://docsouth.unc.edu/imls/wadley/wadley.html.

271. http://docsouth.unc.edu/imls/kimberly/kimberly.html.

272. http://www.civilwarhome.com/gordonchickamauga.htm, from "Reminiscences of the Civil War" (Chapter 14), By John B. Gordon, Maj. Gen., CSA, 1.

273. John B. Gordon, *Reminiscences of the Civil War,* 529–30.

274. Ibid., 204–16.

275. Ibid., 179.

276. Digby Gordon Seymour, *Divided Loyalties: Fort Sanders and the Civil War in East Tennessee* (Nashville: Williams Printing, 1963; Knoxville: University of Tennessee Press, 2002), 85.

277. http://clarke.cmich.edu/civilwar/cwpublished/poetry.htm.

278. http://docsouth.unc.edu/imls/lenoir/lenoir.html.

279. Lenoir Family Papers, *Personal Correspondence, 1861–1865,* University of North Carolina, Chapel Hill.

280. Ibid.

281. http://docsouth.unc.edu/imls/potter/potter.html.

282. Woodhead, *Chickamauga,* 59.

283. http://docsouth.unc.edu/imls/jester/jester.html, 71.

284. http://docsouth.unc.edu/imls/ford/ford.html, 33.

285. http://docsouth.unc.edu/imls/hughes/hughes.html.

286. http://valley.vcdh.virginia.edu/personal/hanger.html.

287. Woodhead, *Chickamauga,* 54.

288. http://docsouth.unc.edu/fpn/texts.html#A.

289. Brockett, www.hti.unc.edu.

290. http://members.tripod.com/~greatamericanhistory/gr02000htm.

291. http://spec.lib.vt.edu/mss/white/white.htm.

292. http://docsouth.unc.edu/imls/kimberly/kimberly.html.

293. http://clarke.cmich.edu/civilwar/cwpublished/poetry.htm.

294. Ibid., 56.

295. Ibid., 155.

296. http://members.tripod.com/greatamericanhistory/gr02012htm.

297. http://www.franklin-stfb.org/letter02.htm.

298. http://docsouth.unc.edu/fpn/texts.html#A.

299. http://www.fsu.edu/~ewoodwar/hall.html.

300. Ibid, 172.

301. http://www.fsu.edu/~ewoodwar/hall.html.

302. http://www.vmi.edu/archives/manuscripts/ms363009html.

303. Herman Norton, *Rebel Religion*, 52–53.

304. Stout, *Upon the Altar of the Nation*, 459.

305. James Robertson, *Soldiers Blue and Gray*, 172.

306. Woodhead, *Chickamauga*, 73–74.

307. *Son of the South*, http://www.sonofthesouth.net/leefoundation/Notable%20 Lee%20Quotes.htm.

308. http://www.pbs.org/wgbh/amex/lincolns/filmmore/ps_jacobs.html.

309. http://chaucer.library.emory.edu.

310. http://www.fsu.edu/~ewoodwar/hall.htm.

311. Walt Whitman, *Memoranda During the War and Death of Abraham Lincoln* (Westport, CT: Greenwood Publishing, 1972).

312. P. A. Hanaford, *Abraham Lincoln: His Life and Public Services,* Michigan Historical Reprint Series (Ann Arbor, MI: Scholarly Publishing Office, University of Michigan Library, 2005).

313. Ibid., 166.

314. http://docsouth.unc.edu/zettler/zettler.html.

315. Ibid., 73–74.

316. http://members.tripod.com/~greatamericanhistory/gr02000.htm.

317. Charles Tindley, "Nothing Between," www.cyberhymnal.org/htm/n/b/nbetween .htm.

318. http://clarke.cmich.edu/civilwar/cwpublished/poetry.htm, 123.

319. Ibid., 204.

320. Virginia Miller, www.mileslehane.com/diary.html.

321. http://valley.vcdh.virginia.edu/personal/jwaddell.html.

322. Ibid.

323. William Cowper (Nashville: Benson Publishing).

324. http://etext.lib.virginia.edu/toc/civilwar/public/FD1011.html.

325. http://valley.vedh.virginia.edu/personalpapersranklin/p2stoufferletters.html.

326. Grimsley, Miller, eds., *The Union Must Stand: The Civil War Diary of John Quincy Adams Campbell, Fifth Iowa Volunteer Infantry* (Knoxville: University of Tennessee Press, 2000), 131.

327. http://jefferson.village.virginia.edu/vshadow2/.

328. Woodhead, *Chickamauga*, 46.

329. Rev. T. V. Moore, http://docsouth.unc.edu:400.

330. James Robertson, *Soldiers Blue and Gray*, 175.

331. Jackson, *Life and Letters of General Jackson*, 100–102.

332. Robert Tisdale, *diary*, http://www.civilwardiary.net/.

333. http://valley.vcdh.virginia.edu/personal/jwaddell.html.

334. Nancy Emerson, University of Virginia Library, Charlottesville, VA.

335. Julia Ward Howe, *Reminiscences 1819–1899* (Boston and New York: Houghton, Mifflin and Co., 1899), 276–77.

336. www.cyberhymnal.org.htm/b/h/bhymnotr.htm.

337. Ropes, *Civil War Nurse*, 101–102.

338. http://clarke.cmich.edu/civilwar/cwpublished/poetry.htm, 208.

339. http://valley.vcdh.virginia.edu/personalpapersranklin/p2stoufferletters.html.

340. http://docsouth.unc.edu/imls/bethell/bethell.html.

341. http://valley.vcdh.virginia.edu/cwpotterlist.html.

342. http://clarke.cmich.edu/civilwar/cwpublished/poetry.htm, 180.

343. http://valley.vcdh.virginia.edu/cwpotterlist.html.

344. http://www.spec.lib.vit.edu/mss/hccarptr.htm.

345. http://www.fortunecity.com/westwood/makeover/347/id271.htm.

346. http://docsouth.unc.edu/zettler/zettler.html, 62–63.

347. Ibid., 158–62.

348. Jackson, *Life and Letters of General Jackson*.

349. Ibid., 158–62.

350. http://www.civilwarstudies.org/articles.Vol_4/xmas2001.htm.

351. Bennett, *Great Revival*, 67–68.

352. Ibid.

353. Elisha Coffman, "Christmas Carols and the Civil War," www.Magazine, avascript:hideAd.

354. http://www.cyberhymnal.org.

355. Richard B. Abell and Fay A. Gecik, *Sojourns of a Patriot: The Field and Prison Papers of an Unreconstructed Patriot* (Murfreesboro, TN: Southern Heritage Press, 1998), 244.

356. Cynthia Pitcock and Bill J. Gurley, *I Acted from Principle: The Civil War Diary of Dr. William M. McPheeters, Confederate Surgeon in the Trans-Mississippi* (Fayetteville, AR: University of Arkansas Press, 2002), 92–93.

357. http://www.ioweb.com/civilwar/goodwin_diary/index.html.

358. Bryan Weaver, *Sacrifice at Chickamauga* (Palos Verdes, CA: Moyweave Books, 2003), 250.

359. http://www.thewildgeese.com/pages/civwar.html.

360. Pitcock and Gurley, *I Acted from Principle*, 93.

361. Herman Norton, *Rebel Religion*, 46–47.

362. John M. King and Claire E. Swedberg, *Three Years with the 92nd Illinois: The Civil War Diary of John M. King* (Mechanicsburg, PA: Stackpole Books, 1999), 108.

363. http://goinside.com/98/5/wsc6.html.

364. http://www.docsouth.unc.edu/fisherjulia/menu/html.

365. http://oha.ci.alexandria.va.us/fortward/special-sections/christmas/ *Harpers Weekly Newspaper*, Christmas 1863.

366. Ibid.

367. http://www.oha.clalexandria.va.us/fortward/special-sections/christmas/.

368. http://www.brotherswar.com/Brotherswar.

369. Bruce Howell, *Illustration of Stonewall Jackson*, www.Sermoncentral.com.

370. http://archiver.rootsweb.com/th/read/civil-war-irish/2002-12/1040575399.

371. http://www.iwaynetnet/~lsci/DCletters.htm.

372. http://www.awod.com/gallery/probono/cwchas/fredxmas.html.

373. www.docsouth.unc.edu/burge/lunt.html.

374. http://www.thewildgeese.com/pages/civwar.html.

375. http://www.whatsaiththescripture.com/Fellowship/Edit_I.Heard.the.Bells.html.

376. Ibid.

377. Josiah Gorgas, General, *Christmas during the Civil War*, http://dburgin.tripod.com/cw_xmas/cwarxmas2html.

378. http://dburgin.tripod.com/cw_xmas/cwarxmas2.html.

379. Cramer, *Ulysses Grant*, 94.

380. Ibid., 102–103.

381. Ibid.

382. http://www.austinuu.org/sermons/2005/2005-12-25-ChristmasDay2005.html.

383. http://www.wildwestweb.net/cwphotos.html.